W9-AXT-569

Sources of
THE MAKING OF THE WEST

PEOPLES AND CULTURES

A CONCISE HISTORY

Volume II: Since 1340

Sources of
THE MAKING OF THE WEST

PEOPLES AND CULTURES

A CONCISE HISTORY

Volume II: Since 1340

Katharine J. Lualdi

University of Southern Maine

BEDFORD / ST. MARTIN'S   Boston   ◆   New York

For Bedford/St. Martin's

Publisher for History: Patricia A. Rossi
Executive Editor for History: Elizabeth M. Welch
Production Editor: Lori Chong Roncka
Production Supervisor: Maria R. Gonzalez
Marketing Manager: Jenna Bookin Barry
Editorial Assistant: Brianna Germain
Production Assistants: Thomas P. Crehan, Courtney Jossart, Kendra LeFleur
Copyeditor: Patricia Herbst
Text Design: Wanda Kossak
Cover Design: Donna Dennison
Cover Art: Charles J. Staniland, *The Emigrant Ship*, c. 1880. Bradford Art Galleries and
    Museums, West Yorkshire, UK/The Bridgeman Art Library International Ltd.
Composition: TechBooks
Printing and Binding: R.R. Donnelley & Sons Company

President: Joan E. Feinberg
Director of Marketing: Karen Melton
Director of Editing, Design, and Production: Marcia Cohen
Managing Editor: Elizabeth M. Schaaf

Copyright © 2003 by Bedford/St. Martin's

All rights reserved. No part of this book may be reproduced, stored in a retrieval system, or transmitted in any form or by any means, electronic, mechanical, photocopying, recording, or otherwise, except as may be expressly permitted by the applicable copyright statutes or in writing by the Publisher.

Manufactured in the United States of America.

7   6   5   4   3   2
f   e   d   c   b   a

For information, write: Bedford/St. Martin's, 75 Arlington Street, Boston, MA 02116
(617-399-4000)

ISBN: 0–312–40718–1 (Vol. I)
       0–312–40719–X (Vol. II)

Acknowledgments

Chapter 11
   The Black Death (14th Century). Translated and edited by Rosemary Horrox. Copyright © 1994. Reprinted with the permission of Manchester University Press.
   Christine de Pisan. *Laments on the Evils of the Civil War* (1410). From *The Epistle of the Prison of Human Life with an Epistle to the Queen of France and Lament on the Evils of the Civil War,* edited and translated by Josette A. Wisman. Copyright © 1984. Reprinted with the permission of Garland Publishing.

Acknowledgments and copyrights are continued at the back of the book on pages 134–36, which constitute an extension of the copyright page. It is a violation of the law to reproduce these selections by any means whatsoever without the written permission of the copyright holder.

Preface for Instructors

Sources of The Making of the West: A Concise History is a collection of firsthand accounts intended to provide depth and breadth to the discussion of important events, ideas, and experiences discussed in *The Making of the West: Peoples and Cultures, A Concise History,* the text for which it was specifically compiled. Organized chapter by chapter to parallel the textbook, these sources offer teachers varied opportunities to ignite a dialogue in the classroom between the past and present.

Together, these documents yield a rich array for such a dialogue within the strong, succinct framework of *The Making of the West: A Concise History.* For example, when the textbook discusses the European slave trade, students can experience it for themselves in the source collection through the eyes of Olaudah Equiano, the African slave who survived to tell his story (Document 44). Information and ideas thus come alive with the emotions, opinions, and observations of contemporaries, revealing to students the relationship between narrative history and original sources and showing them that history is not a fixed set of immutable facts but rather an ongoing process of evaluation and interpretation. *Sources of* The Making of the West: A Concise History provides the raw materials for this process.

Inspired by and tailored to *The Making of the West,* the criteria governing the selection of documents naturally reflect historians' changing understanding of Western civilization. Although traditional political sources are included, these views are broadened by less conventional documents illuminating not only social and cultural life but also Europe's increasing interconnectedness with the larger world. Women's voices received special attention in the selection process because of their crucial and often underappreciated role in shaping the course of Western history from both within and outside the corridors of power. The documents were also selected based on their accessibility and appeal to students. For this reason, I edited each primary source to speak to specific themes without impairing its overall sense and tone.

To assist students with their journey into the past, I prepared with equal care the wide range of learning aids that appear in the sourcebook. Each chapter opens with a short introduction that situates the documents within the broader historical context and addresses their relationship to one another. An explanatory headnote accompanies each document to provide fundamental background information on the author and the source while highlighting its significance. Discussion questions are also included to help students examine the key points and issues in greater depth and to suggest topics for discussion or writing assignment. Although these editorial features intentionally strengthen the coherency of each chapter as a unit, they also allow instructors to choose documents and questions that best suit their specific teaching goals and methods.

Acknowledgments

I owe many people thanks for helping to bring this project to fruition. First among them are the authors of *The Making of the West: A Concise History*, Lynn Hunt, Thomas R. Martin, Barbara H. Rosenwein, R. Po-chia Hsia, and Bonnie G. Smith, who provided invaluable suggestions, advice, and insight. I would also like to thank Larissa Juliet Taylor, Julia O'Brien, Megan Armstrong, and David K. Smith for their help and encouragement, as well as my development editor, Molly Kalkstein, for her careful eye and enthusiasm. Those at Bedford/St. Martin's also helped make this book possible: in particular, my thanks to Joan E. Feinberg, President; Charles H. Christensen, former President; Patricia A. Rossi, Publisher for History; Elizabeth M. Welch, Executive Editor for History; John Amburg, Assistant Managing Editor; Maria R. Gonzalez, Production Supervisor; and Lori Chong Roncka, Production Editor.

I also owe a debt of gratitude to the staff of the University of Maine library system who patiently endured my seemingly endless requests for books and articles. Without them, compiling this collection would not have been possible.

Last and above all, I thank my husband, John, for his sense of humor and understanding as I lost myself in books and Post-it notes.

Introduction for Students

Your textbook, *The Making of the West: Peoples and Cultures, A Concise History,* provides an essential chronological and thematic framework for understanding the development of the West as a cultural and geographic entity. Yet the process of historical inquiry extends beyond the text into the thoughts, words, and experiences of people living at the time. Firsthand accounts—that is, primary sources—expose the world that their writers inhabited, revealing the ideas, emotions, and beliefs of contemporary historical actors. Primary-source collections like this one allow you to observe, analyze, and interpret the past as it unfolds before you; unlike other sourcebooks, however, this reader's thorough integration with your textbook reveals the relationship between historical narrative and the original sources that inform it.

As the main title of your textbook, *The Making of the West,* suggests, history is not a static collection of names, facts, and dates. Rather, it is an ongoing attempt to make sense of the past and its relationship to the present, usually through the lens of primary sources. *Sources of THE MAKING OF THE WEST: A CONCISE HISTORY* provides this lens for you, with firsthand accounts representing a wide range of the documents historians use—from Egyptian chronicles and Greek poems to English feminist tracts and German political memoirs. When combined, the documents reflect historians' appreciation of the need to examine Western civilization from a variety of conceptual angles (political, social, cultural, economic) and geographic viewpoints. The composite picture that emerges as a result reveals a variety of historical experiences shaping each era from both within and outside Europe. Furthermore, the documents demonstrate that the most historically significant of these experiences are not always those of people in formal positions of power. Women, minorities, and everyday folk likewise influenced profoundly the course of Western history.

The sources in this reader were selected with an eye to their ability not only to capture the multifaceted dimensions of the past but also to ignite your historical imagination. Each document is a unique product of human endeavor and as such is often colored by the author's personal concerns, biases, and objectives. Among the most exciting challenges facing you is to sift through such nuances for what they reveal about the source and its links to the broader historical context.

Understanding how each document is connected to its author and to larger historical issues is key to the study of history. To this end, as you read each document, you should keep a series of questions at the front of your mind, just like a reporter investigating a breaking news story: Who wrote the document, when, for whom, why, and where? Each of these questions represents a crucial piece of the puzzle of the past and is an essential means of meeting every historian's basic goal, to chart change and continuity over time.

A Nazi propaganda pamphlet written in 1930 (Document 67) offers an instructive example. The author of the pamphlet, Joseph Goebbels, was the propaganda chief of Adolf Hitler, the leader of the Nazi party. Similar political goals and beliefs bound both men, including virulent anti-Semitism. At the time Goebbels wrote the document, Germany was mired in economic recession. Capitalizing on the downhearted mood of the day with promises of a better life, he successfully used pamphlets such as this one to broaden the Nazis' popular support on the eve of Hitler's rise to power. All of these factors—Goebbels's position within the Nazi party, what he was writing, for whom, when, and why—shaped the document's content, and thus should inform your interpretation of what it suggests about the Nazis and Germany in this period. By contrast, the recollections of Jews who were the victims of this propaganda (Document 69) offer a far different view of the Nazis and the human impact of their regime. This difference can be attributed not only to the nature of the sources themselves but also to the opposing perspectives they represent.

Mining documents for their multiple layers of meaning thus requires a careful balancing act, first between fact and interpretation, and second between the content of the document and the larger historical backdrop. To aid you with this process, *Sources of THE MAKING OF THE WEST: A CONCISE HISTORY* was compiled to use directly alongside your textbook. Each chapter in the collection contains three or four documents illustrative of the central ideas, issues, and events discussed in the corresponding textbook chapter, where cross-references link the narrative to the readings. In addition, *Sources of THE MAKING OF THE WEST: A CONCISE HISTORY* includes a variety of useful learning aids that supplement the materials offered in the textbook. An introduction linking the documents to the historical period in which they were written opens each chapter, and each document has an explanatory headnote that provides essential information about the author and the source and why the document is historically significant. Finally, three or four questions conclude each document to help you probe beneath the surface to understand what each document communicates and to see the similarities and differences among them.

The documents included in *Sources of THE MAKING OF THE WEST: A CONCISE HISTORY* invite you to become an active participant in discovering how history was actually lived over time by an array of different people in an array of different places. They are meant to offer snapshots of the past that, when viewed and interpreted together within the broader historical context found in the textbook, will help you paint a colorful and interconnected picture of the historical development of Western civilization—while learning that history, unlike a picture, is never finished.

Contents

Sources of
THE MAKING OF THE WEST

PEOPLES AND CULTURES

A CONCISE HISTORY

Volume II: Since 1340

CHAPTER 11
Crisis and Renaissance, 1340–1500

Pestilence, warfare, a church in crisis, rebellions, pogroms, famines, and floods—to people living in the fourteenth century, it must have appeared that the end of the world was at hand. Fourteenth-century men and women came up with explanations, yet with the historian's luxury of retrospect, we can see the interconnectedness of events—what French historians call a conjuncture. Overpopulation, soil depletion, and warfare had reduced the average life span even before plague struck. During the Black Death, scapegoats were often sought, even though many saw the plague as divine punishment. The documents in this chapter evince both a grim side to the Renaissance, particularly the horror of war and danger of politics, and man's potential to overcome his condition.

33. *The Black Death* (Fourteenth Century)

Few events have had such a shattering impact on every aspect of society as the plague, which reached Europe in 1347. The Black Death decimated a society already weakened by a demographic crisis, famines, and climatic disasters. It is estimated that one-third of Europe's population died in the first wave of plague, which was followed by repeated outbreaks. Some cities may have lost over half their people in 1347–1348 alone. The devastation was social, psychological, economic, political, and even artistic, yet many historians believe that it led to significant changes and even improvements in Western life. This set of documents describes the arrival of the plague in various places and responses to it, including searches for its cause and for people on whom to fix blame.

From Gabriele de' Mussis (d. 1356), a Lawyer in Piacenza

In 1346, in the countries of the East, countless numbers of Tartars and Saracens were struck down by a mysterious illness which brought sudden death. . . . An eastern settlement under the rule of the Tartars called Tana, which lay to the north of Constantinople and was much frequented by Italian merchants, was totally abandoned after an incident there which led to its being besieged and attacked by hordes of Tartars who gathered in a short space of time. The Christian merchants, who had been driven out by force, were so terrified of the power of the Tartars that, to save themselves and their belongings, they fled in an armed ship to Caffa, a settlement in the same part of the world which had been founded long ago by the Genoese.

Oh God! See how the heathen Tartar races, pouring together from all sides, suddenly invested the city of Caffa and besieged the trapped Christians there for almost three years. There, hemmed in by an immense army, they could hardly draw breath, although food could be shipped

From *The Black Death*, ed. and trans. Rosemary Horrox (Manchester: Manchester University Press, 1994), 16–21, 23, 207, 208, 219–22.

in, which offered them some hope. But behold, the whole army was affected by a disease which overran the Tartars and killed thousands upon thousands every day. It was as though arrows were raining down from heaven to strike and crush the Tartars' arrogance. All medical advice and attention was useless; the Tartars died as soon as the signs of disease appeared on their bodies: swellings in the armpit or groin caused by coagulating humours, followed by a putrid fever.

The dying Tartars, stunned and stupefied by the immensity of the disaster brought about by the disease, and realising that they had no hope of escape, lost interest in the siege. But they ordered corpses to be placed in catapults and lobbed into the city in the hope that the intolerable stench would kill everyone inside. What seemed like mountains of dead were thrown into the city, and the Christians could not hide or flee or escape from them, although they dumped as many of the bodies as they could in the sea. And soon the rotting corpses tainted the air and poisoned the water supply, and the stench was so overwhelming that hardly one in several thousand was in a position to flee the remains of the Tartar army. Moreover, one infected man could carry the poison to others, and infect people and places with the disease by look alone. No one knew, or could discover, a means of defence.

Thus almost everyone who had been in the East, or in the regions to the south and north, fell victim to sudden death after contracting this pestilential disease, as if struck by a lethal arrow which raised a tumour on their bodies. The scale of the mortality and the form which it took persuaded those who lived, weeping and lamenting, through the bitter events of 1346 to 1348— the Chinese, Indians, Persians, Medes, Kurds, Armenians, Cilicians, Georgians, Mesopotamians, Nubians, Ethiopians, Turks, Egyptians, Arabs, Saracens, and Greeks (for almost all the East has been affected) that the last judgement had come. . . .

As it happened, among those who escaped from Caffa by boat were a few sailors who had been infected with the poisonous disease. Some boats were bound for Genoa, others went to Venice and to other Christian areas. When the sailors reached these places and mixed with the people there, it was as if they had brought evil spirits with them: every city, every settlement, every place was poisoned by the contagious pestilence. . . .

Scarcely one in seven of the Genoese survived. In Venice, where an inquiry was held into the mortality, it was found that more than 70 percent of the people had died, and that within a short period 20 out of 24 excellent physicians had died. The rest of Italy, Sicily, and Apulia and the neighbouring regions maintain that they have been virtually emptied of inhabitants. The people of Florence, Pisa, and Lucca, finding themselves bereft of their fellow residents, emphasize their losses. The Roman Curia at Avignon, the provinces on both sides of the Rhône, Spain, France, and the Empire cry up their griefs and disasters—all of which makes it extraordinarily difficult for me to give an accurate picture.

By contrast, what befell the Saracens can be established from trustworthy accounts. In the city of Babylon alone (the heart of the Sultan's power), 480,000 of his subjects are said to have been carried off by the disease in less than three months in 1348—and this is known from the Sultan's register which records the names of the dead, because he receives a gold bezant for each person buried. . . .

I am overwhelmed, I can't go on. Everywhere one turns there is death and bitterness to be described. The hand of the Almighty strikes repeatedly, to greater and greater effect. The terrible judgement gains power as time goes by.

FROM HERMAN GIGAS, A FRANCISCAN FRIAR IN GERMANY, WHOSE ACCOUNT GOES UNTIL 1349

In 1347 there was such a great pestilence and mortality throughout almost the whole world that in the opinion of well-informed men scarcely a tenth of mankind survived. The victims did not linger long, but died on the second or third day. . . . Some say that it was brought about by the corruption of the air; others that the Jews planned to wipe out all the Christians with poison and had poisoned wells and springs everywhere. And many Jews confessed as much under torture: that they had bred spiders and toads in pots and pans, and had obtained poison from overseas; and that not every Jew knew about this, only the more powerful ones, so that it would not be betrayed. . . . [M]en say that bags full of poison were found in many wells and springs.

FROM HEINRICH TRUCHESS, A FORMER PAPAL CHAPLAIN AND CANON OF CONSTANCE

The persecution of the Jews began in November 1348, and the first outbreak in Germany was at Sölden, where all the Jews were burnt on the strength of a rumour that they had poisoned wells and rivers, as was afterwards confirmed by their own confessions and also by the confessions of Christians whom they had corrupted. . . . Within the revolution of one year, that is from All Saints [1 November] 1348 until Michaelmas [29 September] 1349 all the Jews between Cologne and Austria were burnt and killed for this crime, young men and maidens and the old along with the rest. And blessed be God who confounded the ungodly who were plotting the extinction of his church.

FROM THE COUNCILLORS OF COLOGNE TO CONRAD VON WINTERTHUR TO THE BÜRGERMEISTER AND COUNCILLORS OF STRASSBURG ON 12 JANUARY 1349

Very dear friends, all sorts of rumours are now flying about against Judaism and the Jews prompted by this unexpected and unparalleled mortality of Christians, which, alas, has raged in various parts of the world and is still woefully active in several places. Throughout our city, as in yours, many-winged Fame clamours that this mortality was initially caused, and is still being spread, by the poisonings of springs and wells, and that the Jews must have dropped poisonous substances into them. When it came to our knowledge that serious charges had been made against the Jews in several small towns and villages on the basis of this mortality, we sent numerous letters to you and to other cities and towns to uncover the truth behind these rumours, and set a thorough investigation in train. . . .

If a massacre of the Jews were to be allowed in the major cities (something which we are determined to prevent in our city, if we can, as long as the Jews are found to be innocent of these or similar actions) it could lead to the sort of outrages and disturbances which would whip up a popular revolt among the common people—and such revolts have in the past brought cities to misery and desolation. In any case we are still of the opinion that this mortality and its attendant circumstances are caused by divine vengeance and nothing else. Accordingly we intend to forbid any harassment of the Jews in our city because of these flying rumours, but to defend them faithfully and keep them safe, as our predecessors did—and we are convinced that you ought to do the same.

PAPAL BULL SICUT JUDEIS OF CLEMENT VI ISSUED IN JULY 1348

Recently, however, it has been brought to our attention by public fame—or more accurately, infamy—that numerous Christians are blaming the plague with which God, provoked by their sins, has afflicted the Christian people, on poisonings carried out by the Jews at the instigation of the devil, and that out of their own hot-headedness they have impiously slain many Jews, making no exception for age or sex; and that the Jews have been falsely accused of such outrageous behaviour. . . . [I]t cannot be true that the Jews, by such a heinous crime, are the cause or occasion of the plague, because throughout many parts of the world the same plague, by the hidden judgment of God, has afflicted and afflicts the Jews themselves and many other races who have never lived alongside them.

We order you by apostolic writing that each of you upon whom this charge has been laid, should straitly command those subject to you, both clerical and lay . . . not to dare (on their own authority or out of hot-headedness) to capture, strike, wound or kill any Jews or expel them from their service on these grounds; and you should demand obedience under pain of excommunication.

■ Discussion Questions

1. Examine the documents and try to determine their historical accuracy from internal evidence alone. What gives you clues about an author's objectivity (or lack thereof)?
2. What explanations are offered for the onset of plague? What (if any) is the understanding of the disease process?
3. Look at the account by Mussis and the bull of Pope Clement VI. What do they have in common? How did different groups of people react to the plague?
4. Why would some Christian authorities (the city councillors or the pope mentioned in these documents) attempt to protect the Jews? Why was such protection of no avail in many places? Why did some Jews confess? Discuss the attempt of societies (in some cases) to find scapegoats.

34. Christine de Pisan, *Lament on the Evils of the Civil War* (1410)

Christine de Pisan (1364–c. 1430) is considered by some to be the first feminist. Born in Italy, she was raised in Paris after her father, a scholar and physician who gave her a superb education, was called to the court of Charles V. After his death, and then that of her husband in 1389, Christine turned to writing to support her children. She became the first professional female writer in Europe. Patronized by kings, queens, and dukes, Christine wrote numerous works of prose and poetry, in-cluding The Book of the City of Ladies, *a defense of women. The epistle quoted here was written in 1410, when France was at a low point in the Hundred Years' War. In this letter she urges the lead-ers of society to look at what their disunity has done to France and its people, and she urges them to come together instead of fighting one another.*

Alone, and suppressing with great difficulty the tears which blur my sight and pour down my face like a fountain, so much that I am surprised to have the time to write this weary lament, whose writing the pity for the coming disaster makes me erase with bitter tears, and I say in pain: Oh, how can it be that the human heart, as strange as Fortune is, can make man revert to the nature of a voracious and cruel beast? Where is the reason that gives him the name of a rational animal? How can Fortune have the power to transform a man so much, that he is changed into a serpent, the enemy of mankind? Oh, alas, here is the reason why, noble French princes. With deference to you, where is now the sweet natural blood among you which has been for a long time the true summit of kindness in the world? . . .

For God's sake! For God's sake! High Princes, let these facts open your eyes and may you see as already accomplished what the preparations for taking arms will do in their end; thus you will see ruined cities, towns and castles destroyed, and fortresses razed to the ground. And where?

From Christine de Pisan, *The Epistle of the Prison of Human Life with an Epistle to the Queen of France and Lament on the Evils of the Civil War,* ed. and trans. Josette A. Wisman (New York: Garland Publishing, 1984), 85, 87, 89, 91, 93, 95.

In the very heart of France! The noble knights and youth of France, all of one nature, one single soul and body, which used to defend the crown and the public good, are now gathered in a shameful battle one against another, father against son, brother against brother, relatives against one another, with deadly swords, covering the pitiful fields with blood, dead bodies, and limbs. Oh, dishonorable victory may be to the one who has it! What glory will Fame give to it? . . .

Oh you, knight who comes from such a battle, tell me, I pray you, what honor did you win there? . . . And what will follow, in God's name? Famine, because of the wasting and ruining of things that will ensue, and the lack of cultivation, from which will spring revolts by the people who have been too often robbed, deprived and oppressed, their food taken away and stolen here and there by soldiers, subversion in the towns because of outrageous taxes. . . . So cry, cry, beat your hands and cry—as once the sad Argia did in such a case, along with the ladies of Argos— you ladies, damsels, and women of the kingdom of France! Because the swords that will make you widows and deprive you of your children and kin have already been sharpened! . . .

Oh, crowned Queen of France, are you still sleeping? Who prevents you from restraining now this side of your kin and putting an end to this deadly enterprise? Do you not see the heritage of your noble children at stake? . . .

Come, all you wise men of this realm, come with your queen! What use are you if not for the royal council? Everyone should offer his hand. You used to concern yourselves even with small matters. How shall France be proud of so many wise men, if now they cannot see to her safety, and the fount of the clergy keep her from perishing? Where then are your plans and wise thoughts? . . . For you resemble Nineveh, which God condemned to perish, and which received his wrath because of the great sins which were many there, and because of this, the situation is very doubtful, unless the sentence is not revoked by the intercession of devout prayers.

People, be firm! And you, pious woman, cry mercy for this grievous storm! Ah, France, France, once a glorious kingdom! . . .

Oh, Duke of Berry, Noble Prince, excellent father and scion of royal children, son of a King of France, brother and uncle, father of all the antiquity of the lily! How is it possible that your tender heart can bear to see you, on a given day, assembled in deadly battle array to bear painful arms against your nephews? . . .

So, come, come, Noble Duke of Berry, Prince of High Excellence, and follow the divine law which orders peace! Take a strong hold of the bridle, and stop this dishonorable army, at least until you have talked to the parties. So come to Paris, to your father's city where you were born and which cries to you with tears and sighs, asking and begging for you to come. Come quickly to comfort this suffering city. . . . [A]lthough it is now discussed in various tongues on each side that hopes for victory in the battle and they all say: "We will win and work for it"—they are bragging foolishly. For it must not be ignored that the outcome of all battles is strange and unknown. For although man proposed it, Fortune disposes it. . . . Was the victory of the King of Athens, mortally wounded in battle, of any worth to him? Is a multitude of men an advantage in such a case? Was Xerxes not defeated, although he had so many men that all vales and hills were covered with them? Are a good reason and a just quarrel of any value? If it were so, the king Saint Louis, who obtained so many beautiful victories, would not have been defeated at Tunis by the infidels. . . . And above all, although war and battles are in all cases very dangerous and difficult to avoid, no doubt that among such close kin, tied by nature in one bond of love, they are perverse. . . . I believe the cost would be less, and that this army, by a common will and true unity, should be directed against those who are our natural enemies, and that the good and faithful French should take care of these people, and not kill one another. . . . Ah, Very Reverend Prince, Noble Duke of Berry, do hear this. . . . May the Blessed Holy Spirit, Author of all peace, give you the heart and the courage to achieve such a thing! Amen. And may he greet me, a poor voice crying in this kingdom, wanting peace and welfare for all, your servant Christine, moved by a very fair mind, the gift to see that day!

■ Discussion Questions

1. What, in Christine's view, are the costs of war, in human and dynastic terms?
2. How important is it that Christine refers in several instances to "the French" and "France"? To whom does Christine direct her admonitions? Why?
3. What kind of allusions does Christine use to convince her readers that they should not continue a civil war that is keeping them from fighting the "common enemy"? What does this tell you about her education?
4. Do you think this "poor voice crying in the kingdom" can be seen as a precursor to Joan of Arc? Why or why not?

35. Giovanni Pico della Mirandola, *Oration on the Dignity of Man* (1496)

The work of Giovanni Pico della Mirandola (1463–1494), a Neo-platonic thinker and Dominican friar, celebrates man's potential. The Oration on the Dignity of Man *was the preface to nine hundred theses written by Pico in his early twenties, for a public disputation that never in fact took place. Steeped in the Aristotelian and Platonic traditions, Pico knew Latin, Arabic, Greek, Hebrew, and Aramaic. He was deeply interested in Hebrew mysticism, pre-Socratic thought, and occult knowledge attributed at the time to Hermes Trismegistus. Not surprisingly, some of Pico's ideas were deemed heretical by a papal commission. Thereafter, he lived under the protection of Lorenzo de' Medici until he died at the age of thirty-one. The* Oration *explores the concept of free will—the human ability to choose, for good or ill.*

I have read in the ancient annals of the Arabians, most reverend Fathers, that when asked what on the world's stage could be considered most admirable, Abdala the Saracen answered that there is nothing more admirable to be seen than man. In agreement with this opinion is the saying of Hermes Trismegistus: "What a great miracle, O Asclepius, is man!"

When I had thought over the meaning of these maxims, the many reasons for the excellence of man advanced by many men failed to satisfy me. . . .

At last, it seems to me that I have understood why man is the most fortunate living thing worthy of all admiration and precisely what rank is his lot in the universal chain of being, a rank to be envied not only by the brutes but even by the stars and by minds beyond this world. It is a matter past faith and extraordinary! . . .

God the Father, the supreme Architect, had already built this cosmic home which we behold, this most majestic temple of divinity, in accordance with the laws of a mysterious wisdom. He had adorned the region above the heavens with intelligences, had quickened the celestial spheres with eternal souls and had filled the vile and filthy parts of the lower world with a multitude of animals of every kind. But when the work was completed, the Maker kept wishing that there were someone who could examine the plan of so great an enterprise, who could love its beauty, who could admire its vastness. On that account, when everything was completed, as Moses and Timaeus both testify, He finally took thought of creating man. However, not a single archetype remained from which he might fashion this new creature, not a single treasure remained which he might bestow upon this new son, and not a single seat remained in the whole world in

From *The Italian Renaissance Reader,* ed. Julia Conaway Bondanella and Mark Musa (New York: Meridian, 1987), 180–83.

which the contemplator of the universe might sit. All now was complete; all things had been assigned to the highest, the middle, and the lowest orders. But it was not in the nature of the Father's power to fail in this final creative effort, as though exhausted; nor was it in the nature of His wisdom to waver in such a crucial matter through lack of counsel; and it was not in the nature of His Beneficent Love that he who was destined to praise God's divine generosity in regard to others should be forced to condemn it in regard to himself. At last, the Supreme Artisan ordained that the creature to whom He could give nothing properly his own should share in whatever He had assigned individually to the other creatures. He therefore accepted man as a work of indeterminate nature, and placing him in the center of the world, addressed him thus:

"O Adam, we have given you neither a place nor a form nor any ability exclusively your own, so that according to your wishes and your judgment, you may have and possess whatever place, form, or abilities you desire. The nature of all other beings is limited and constrained in accordance with the laws prescribed by us. Constrained by no limits, in accordance with your own free will, in whose hands we have placed you, you shall independently determine the bounds of your own nature. We have placed you at the world's center, from where you may more easily observe whatever is in the world. We have made you neither celestial nor terrestrial, neither mortal nor immortal, so that with honor and freedom of choice, as though the maker and molder of yourself, you may fashion yourself in whatever form you prefer. You shall have the power to degenerate into the inferior forms of life which are brutish; you shall have the power, through your soul's judgment, to rise to the superior orders which are divine." . . .

In man alone, at the moment of his creation, the Father placed the seeds of all kinds and the germs of every way of life. Whatever seeds each man cultivates will mature and bear their own fruit in him; if vegetative, he will be like a plant; if sensitive, he will become a brute; if rational, he will become a celestial being; if intellectual, he will be an angel and the son of God. . . .

Who would not admire this our chameleon? Or who could admire any other being more greatly than man? Asclepius the Athenian justly says that man was symbolized in the mysteries by the figure of Proteus because of his ability to change his character and transform his nature. This is the origin of those metamorphoses or transformations celebrated among the Hebrews and the Pythagoreans. For the occult theology of the Hebrews sometimes transforms the holy Enoch into an angel of divinity and sometimes transforms other people into other divinities. The Pythagoreans transform impious men into beasts and, if Empedocles is to be believed, even into plants. Echoing this, Mohammed often had this saying on his lips: "He who deviates from divine law becomes a beast," and he was right in saying so. For it is not the bark that makes the beast of burden but its irrational and sensitive soul; neither is it the spherical form which makes the heavens, but their undeviating order; nor is it the freedom from a body which makes the angel but its spiritual intelligence. . . .

Are there any who will not admire man? In the sacred Mosaic and Christian writings, man, not without reason, is sometimes described by the name of "all flesh" and sometimes by that of "every creature," since man molds, fashions, and transforms himself according to the form of all flesh and the character of every creature. For this reason, the Persian Evantes, in describing Chaldean theology, writes that man does not have an inborn and fixed image of himself but many which are external and foreign to him; whence comes the Chaldean saying: "Man is a being of varied, manifold, and inconstant nature."

But why do we reiterate all these things? To the end that from the moment we are born we are born into the condition of being able to become whatever we choose.

■ Discussion Questions

1. Examine the words Pico uses to describe God and how God went about the process of creation. Why might these ideas have been considered dangerous?

2. What, according to Pico, are man's abilities? Why were these abilities and possibilities given to human beings?

3. What kinds of sources does Pico use to support his ideas? What is their importance as part of his philosophy?

4. What makes this document a "statement" of Renaissance thought?

36. Alessandra Strozzi, *Letters from a Widow and Matriarch of a Great Family*   (1450–1465)

Women in medieval and Renaissance Europe were usually under legal guardianship—typically that of a father or husband. Women of the lower classes may have enjoyed a semblance of freedom in work and marriage early in their lives. In contrast, their upper-class counterparts gained their greatest prestige and power through widowhood. Alessandra (1407–1471) married Matteo Strozzi, a wealthy merchant whose business had branches throughout Europe. When Matteo died of the effects of the plague while exiled for being in opposition to Cosimo de' Medici (1389–1464), Alessandra's financial situation became difficult, for she had sons and daughters to marry and a great household to maintain. She engaged in lengthy correspondence with her sons about political, marital, and economic conditions that affected the family. In these excerpts from letters to her son Filippo, we can glimpse the "other" side of the Renaissance—exile; political danger if one did not agree with the ruling faction; marriages that were contracted solely for reasons of politics, honor, and clientage; and slavery.

TO FILIPPO, 1450

Really, as long as there are young girls in the house, you do nothing but work for them, so when she leaves I will have no one to attend to but you three. And when I get the house in a little better shape I would love it if you would think about coming home. You would have no cause to be ashamed with what there is now, and you could do honor to any friend who dropped in to see you at home. But two or three years from now it will all be much better. And I would love to get you a wife; you're of an age now to know how to manage the help and to give me some comfort and consolation. I have none. . . .

You know that some time ago I bought Cateruccia, our slave, and for several years now, though I haven't laid a hand on her, she has behaved so badly toward me and the children that you wouldn't believe it if you hadn't seen it. Our Lorenzo could tell you all about it. . . . I've always suffered it because I can't chastise her, and besides I thought you would come once a month so that we could come to a decision together or she could be brought to better obedience. For several months now she has been saying and is still saying that she doesn't want to stay here, and she is so moody that no one can do a thing with her. If it weren't for love of Lesandra, I would have told you to sell her, but because of her malicious tongue, I want to see Lesandra safely out of the house first. But I don't know if I can hold out that long: mark my words, I'm going to get her out of my sight because I don't want this constant battle. She pays no more attention to me than if I were the slave and she were the mistress, and she threatens us all so that Lesandra and I are both afraid of her.

From *University of Chicago Readings in Western Civilization, 5: The Renaissance,* ed. Eric Cochrane and Julius Kirshner (Chicago: University of Chicago Press, 1986), 109, 113–17.

TO FILIPPO, 1459

It grieves me, my son, that I'm not near you to take some of these troublesome things off your hands. You should have told me the first day Matteo fell sick so I could have jumped on a horse and been there in just a few days. But I know that you didn't do it for fear I would get sick or would be put to trouble. . . . I have been told that in the honors you arranged for the burial of my son you did honor to yourself as well as to him. You did all the better to pay him such honor there, since here they don't usually do anything for those who are in your condition [that is, in exile]. Thus I am pleased that you did so. Here these two girls, who are unconsolable over the death of their brother, and I have gone into mourning, and because I had not yet gotten the woolen cloth to make a mantle for myself, I have gotten it now and I will pay for it.

TO FILIPPO, 1465

I told you in my other [letter] what happened about 60 [the daughter of Francesco Tanagli], and there's nothing new there. And you have been advised that there is no talk of 59 [a woman who belonged to the Adimari family] until we have placed the older girl. 13 [Marco Parenti] believes we should do nothing further until we can see our way clearly concerning these two and see what way they will go. Considering their age, this shouldn't take too long. It's true that my wish would be to see both of you with a companion, as I have told you many times before. That way when I die I would think you ready to take the step all mothers want—seeing their sons married—so your children could enjoy what you have acquired with enormous effort and stress over the long years. To that end, I have done my very best to keep up the little I have had, foregoing the things that I might have done for my soul's sake and for that of our ancestors. But for the hope I have that you will take a wife (in the aim of having children), I am happy to have done so. So what I would like would be what I told you. Since then I have heard what Lorenzo's wants are and how he was willing to take her to keep me happy, but that he would be just as glad to wait two years before binding himself to the lady. I have thought a good deal about the matter, and it seems to me that since nothing really advantageous to us is available, and since we have time to wait these two years, it would be a good idea to leave it at that unless something unexpected turns up. Otherwise, it doesn't seem to me something that requires immediate thought, particularly considering the stormy times we live in these days, when so many young men on this earth are happy to inhabit it without taking a wife. The world is in a sorry state, and never has so much expense been loaded on the backs of women as now. No dowry is so big that when the girl goes out she doesn't have the whole of it on her back, between silks and jewels. . . . If 60 works out well, we could sound out the possibility of the other girl for him. There's good forage there if they were to give her, and at any [other] time it would have been a commendable move. As things are going now, it seems to me better to wait and see a while for him. . . . This way something may come of it, and they will not offer a wife without money, as people are doing now, since it seems superfluous to those who are giving 50 to give her a dowry. 13 wrote you that 60's father touched on the matter with him in the way I wrote you about. He says that you should leave it to us to see to it and work it out. For my part, I've done my diligent best, and I can't think what more I could have done—for your consolation than my own. . . .

Niccolò has gone out of office, and although he did some good things, they weren't the ones I would have wanted. Little honor has been paid to him or to the other outgoing magistrates, either when they were in office, or now that they have stepped down. Our scrutineer was quite upset about it, as were we, but I feel that what was done will collapse, and it is thought they will start fresh. This Signoria has spent days in deliberation, and no one can find out anything about them. They have threatened to denounce whoever reveals anything as a rebel, so things are being done in total secrecy. I have heard that 58 [the Medici] is everything and 54 [the Pitti] doesn't stand a chance. For the moment, it looks to me as if they will get back to 56 [the Pucci] in the runoffs, if things continue to go as now. May God, who can do all, set this city right, for it is in a bad way. Niccolò went in proudly and then lost heart—as 14's [Soderini] brother said, "He went in a lion and he will go out a lamb," and that's just what happened to him. When he saw the votes were going against him, he began to humble himself. Now, since he left office, he goes about accompanied by five or six armed men for fear. . . . It would have been better for him if [he had never been elected], for he would never have made so many enemies. . . .

[T]hink about having Niccolò Strozzi touch on the matter with Giovanfrancesco for 45 [Lorenzo], if you think it appropriate. Although I doubt that she would deign [to marry] so low, still, it sometimes happens that you look in places that in other times you wouldn't have dreamed of, by the force of events—deaths or other misfortunes. So think about it.

■ Discussion Questions

1. What is Alessandra's role as matriarch of her family? What else can you tell about women during the Renaissance?
2. What is Alessandra's view of the politics of the city in her day? Why would Alessandra use numbers to designate people?
3. What is Alessandra's relation to her slave? How does the existence of slavery affect your view of Florence's vaunted "liberty for all"?
4. How were marriages formed among the middle and upper classes? What was required before one could marry?

CHAPTER 12

Struggles over Beliefs, 1500–1648

For kings, nobles, and ordinary folk alike, the sixteenth through mid-seventeenth centuries was a time of turmoil and change, as the following documents illustrate. These conflicts began with the Protestant Reformation, which shattered the Christian humanist ideal of peace and unity, and came to a head in the Thirty Years' War (1618–1648), which devastated central Europe and left many rulers bankrupt. The religious wars that galvanized much of Europe in this period were fueled by both ecclesiastical and lay leaders' attempts to maintain the commonly held idea that political and social stability depended on religious conformity. With the escalation of violence, however, some people argued successfully that peace would come only if state interests took precedence over religious ones. Europeans' views of the earth and the heavens also expanded because of the rise of new scientific methods and overseas exploration.

37. Argula von Grumbach and John Hooker, *Women's Actions in the Reformation* (1520s–1530s)

Throughout the Middle Ages, laywomen were actively involved in their religion, through attendance at Mass, sermons, and pilgrimages, and their "greater piety" (than that of men) was remarked on by many churchmen. This trend continued in the early decades of the Reformation but assumed new forms, providing a particular window of opportunity for women to defend their faith when challenged through speech, print, or action. The first document is from the writings of Argula von Grumbach (1492–c. 1554), a Bavarian noblewoman who was by 1522 a follower of Martin Luther (1483–1546), whose challenges and writings initiated the Protestant Reformation. Called a silly bag, a shameless whore, and a female desperado, among other epithets, von Grumbach wrote prose and poetry beginning in 1523 in defense of Luther and Philipp Melanchthon (1497–1560), Luther's coworker and follower, and against the arrest of a Lutheran student at Ingolstadt. She also responded in kind to the sarcasm of another student. Tens of thousands of copies of her writings were in circulation within a few years. The second document is by the Englishman John Hooker, who was Exeter's city chamberlain during the dissolution of the monasteries, when the city's Catholic women took matters into their own hands on the arrival of Thomas Cromwell's visitors in 1535 or 1536.

From *http://home.infi.net/`ddisse/grumbach.html*; Argula von Grumbach, ". . . A Hundred Women Would Emerge to Write"; and Joyce Youings, *The Dissolution of the Monasteries* (London: Allen & Unwin; New York: Barnes & Noble, 1971), 164–65.

11

ARGULA VON GRUMBACH

To the Scholars of Ingolstadt

I find there is a text in Matthew 10 which runs: "Whosoever confesses me before another I too will confess before my heavenly Father." . . . Words like these, coming from the very mouth of God, are always before my eyes. For they exclude neither woman or man.

And this is why I am compelled as a Christian to write to you.

To Bavarian Princes

My heart goes out to our princes, whom you have seduced and betrayed so deplorably. For I realize that they are ill informed about divine Scripture. If they could spare the time from other business, I believe they, too, would discover the truth that no one has a right to exercise sovereignty over the word of God. . . . My heart goes out to them; for they have no one with enough integrity to tell them what is going on. And I realize very well that it is for their wealth, torn from them every day, that they are loved rather than for themselves. I am prepared to write to them in this vein, since, because of other business, they have no leisure to sit down and read for themselves.

To the Ingolstadt Scholars

I beseech you for the sake of God, and exhort you by God's judgment and righteousness, to tell me in writing which of the articles written by Martin or Melanchthon you consider heretical. In German not a single one seem heretical to me. And the fact is that a great deal has been published in German, and I've read it all. . . . I beseech and request a reply from you if you consider I am in error, though I am not aware of it. For Jerome was not ashamed of writing a great deal to women, to Blessilla, for example, to Paula, Eustochium, and so on. Yes, and Christ himself, he who is the only teacher of us all, was not ashamed to preach to Mary Magdalene, and to the young woman at the well.

I do not flinch from appearing before you, from listening to you, from discussing with you. For by the grace of God I, too, can ask questions, hear answers, and read in German. . . . I have no Latin, but you have German, being born and brought up in this tongue. What I have written to you is no woman's chit-chat, but the word of God, and as a member of the Christian Church, against which the gates of Hell cannot prevail.

In Response to a Verse Attack by an Ingolstadt Student

Now Judith when this she heard,
To the priests went straight away,
Gave them instruction manifold
How God their fathers led of old,
When, as now, in tribulation;
Gave ample scriptural demonstration.
She also took the rulers on:
Boldly said: "What have you done
To leave the people in such pain?"
Soon caused their hearts to lift again.

. . .

God therefore made her hand so strong
That Holofernes was undone.
She then lopped off his very head.
Who'd ever have believed this deed?
That him they called a mighty god
Should thus become a laughing stock.

. . .

More of the same in Judges is found,
You can read of there [*sic*], if you care.
There was a seer, Deborah by name,
Who was sent by God, much the same,
To lead the people of Israel
To judge and govern them as well.
Had you been living at that time,
Wise man, no doubt you'd have tried
To stop God carrying out his plan
By acting through a poor woman.
You'd surely could never have endured
God's victory through woman assured.

                    . . .

If you argue I'm too ignorant
Then share with me your wisdom grand!
But a spindle is all you offer,
In every teaching it's what you proffer.
But this fine Master of the Sentence
Would teach me my domestic duties!
These duties I carry out day by day
How could I ever forget them, pray?
Though Christ tells me—I hear his voice—
To hear his words is the very best choice.

JOHN HOOKER: POPULAR REACTIONS AT EXETER

The commissioners came to this city in the summertime to execute their commission, and beginning first with the priory of St. Nicholas, after that they [had] viewed the same they went thence to dinner and commanded [a man] in the time of their absence to pull down the rood loft in the church. In the meanwhile, and before they did return, certain women and wives in the city, namely Joan Reeve, Elizabeth Glandfield, Agnes Collaton, Alice Miller, Joan Reed and others, minding to stop the suppressing of that house, came in all haste to the said church, some with spikes, some with shovels, some with pikes, and some with such tools as they could get and, the church door being fast, they broke it open. And finding there the man pulling down the rood loft they all sought, [by] all the means they could, to take him and hurled stones unto him, in so much that for his safety he was driven to take to the tower for his refuge. And yet they pursued him so eagerly that he was enforced to leap out at a window and so to save himself, and very hardly he escaped the breaking of his neck, but yet he broke one of his ribs. John Blakealler, one of the aldermen of the city, being advertised thereof, he with all speed got him to the said monastery, he thinking what with fair words and what with foul words to have stayed and pacified the women. But how so ever he talked with them they were plain with him and the aforesaid Elizabeth Glandfield gave him a blow and set him packing. The Mayor [William Hurst], having understanding hereof and being very loathe the visitors should be advertised of any such disorders and troubles, he came down with his officers, before whose coming they [the women] had made fast the church doors and had bestowed themselves in places meet as they thought to stand to their defences. Notwithstanding, the Mayor broke in upon them and with much ado he apprehended and took them all and sent them to ward. The visitors being then made acquainted herewith, they gave thanks to the Mayor for his care and diligence . . . and so they proceeded to the suppressing of the house, and before their departure they intreated the Mayor for releasing of the women.

■ **Discussion Questions**

1. What can you tell of Argula von Grumbach's background and learning from her writings alone?
2. What main points does Argula von Grumbach make against the princes and, primarily, the Ingolstadt scholars?
3. Why did the Catholic women of Exeter attack the commissioners sent out to dissolve the monastery? Are you surprised by their behavior?
4. Despite their many differences, do you see anything in common between Argula von Grumbach and the women of Exeter?

38. Henry IV, *Edict of Nantes* (1598)

Henry IV's promulgation of the Edict of Nantes in 1598 marked the end of the French Wars of Religion by recognizing French Protestants as a legally protected religious minority. Drawing largely on earlier edicts of pacification, the Edict of Nantes comprised ninety-two general articles, fifty-six secret articles, and two royal warrants. The two series of articles represented the edict proper and were registered by the highest courts of law in the realm (parlements). The following excerpts from the general articles reveal the triumph of political concerns over religious conformity on the one hand, and the limitations of religious tolerance in early modern France on the other.

Henry, By the Grace of God, King of *France,* and *Navarre,* To all Present, and to Come, greeteth. Among the infinite Mercies that God hath pleased to bestow upon us, that most Signal and Remarkable is, his having given us Power and Strength not to yield to the dreadful Troubles, Confusions, and Disorders, which were found at our coming to this Kingdom, divided into so many Parties and Factions, that the most Legitimate was almost the least, enabling us with Constancy in such manner to oppose the Storm, as in the end to surmount it, reducing this Estate to Peace and Rest. . . . For the general difference among our good Subjects, and the particular evils of the soundest parts of the State, we judged might be easily cured, after the Principal cause (the continuation of the Civil Wars) was taken away, in which we have, by the blessing of God, well and happily succeeded, all Hostility and Wars through the Kingdom being now ceased, and we hope he will also prosper us in our other affairs, which remain to be composed, and that by this means we shall arrive at the establishment of a good Peace, with tranquility and rest. . . . Amongst our said affairs . . . one of the principal hath been, the many complaints we received from divers of our Provinces and Catholick Cities, for that the exercise of the Catholick Religion was not universally re-established, as is provided by Edicts or Statutes heretofore made for the Pacification of the Troubles arising from Religion; as also the Supplications and Remonstrances which have been made to us by our Subjects of the reformed Religion, as well upon the execution of what hath been granted by the said former Laws, as that they desire to have some addition for the exercise of their Religion, the liberty of their Consciences and the security of their Persons and Fortunes; presuming to have just reasons for desiring some enlargement of Articles, as not being without great apprehensions, because their Ruine hath been the principal pretext and original foundation of the late Wars, Troubles, and Commotions. Now not to burden us with too much

English text of "The Edict" as in Edmund Everard, *The Great Pressures and Grievances of the Protestants in France,* London, 1681. Appendix 4 in Roland Mousnier, *The Assassination of Henry IV,* trans. Joan Spencer (London: Faber and Faber, 1973), 316–47.

business at once, as also that the fury of War was not compatible with the establishment of Laws, how good soever they might be, we have hitherto deferred from time to time giving remedy herein. But now that it hath pleased God to give us a beginning of enjoying some Rest, we think we cannot imploy our self better, than to apply to that which may tend to the glory and service of his holy name, and to provide that he may be adored and prayed unto by all our Subjects: and if it hath not yet pleased him to permit it to be in one and the same form of Religion, that it may at the least be with one and the same intention, and with such rules that may prevent amongst them all troubles and tumults. . . . For this cause, we have upon the whole judged it necessary to give to all our said Subjects one general Law, Clear, Pure, and Absolute, by which they shall be regulated in all differences which have heretofore risen among them, or may hereafter rise, wherewith the one and other may be contented, being framed according as the time requires: and having had no other regard in this deliberation than solely the Zeal we have to the service of God, praying that he would henceforward render to all our subjects a durable and Established peace. . . . We have by this Edict or Statute perpetuall and irrevocable said, declared, and ordained, saying, declaring, and ordaining;

That the memory of all things passed on the one part and the other, since the beginning of the month of *March*, 1585. untill our coming to the Crown, and also during the other precedent troubles, and the occasion of the same, shall remain extinguished and suppressed, as things that had never been. . . .

We prohibit to all our Subjects of what State and Condition soever they be, to renew the memory thereof, to attaque, resent, injure, or provoke one the other by reproaches for what is past, under any pretext or cause whatsoever, by disputing, contesting, quarrelling, reviling, or offending by factious words; but to contain themselves, and live peaceably together as Brethren, Friends, and fellow-Citizens, upon penalty for acting to the contrary, to be punished for breakers of Peace, and disturbers of the publick quiet.

We ordain, that the Catholick Religion shall be restored and re-established in all places, and quarters of this Kingdom and Countrey under our obedience, and where the exercise of the same hath been intermitted, to be there again, peaceably and freely exercised without any trouble or impediment. . . .

And not to leave any occasion of trouble and difference among our Subjects, we have permitted and do permit to those of the Reformed Religion, to live and dwell in all the Cities and places of this our Kingdom and Countreys under our obedience, without being inquired after, vexed, molested, or compelled to do any thing in Religion, contrary to their Conscience. . . .

We permit also to those of the said Religion to hold, and continue the Exercise of the same in all the Cities and Places under our obedience, where it hath by them been Established and made publick by many and divers times, in the Year 1586, and in 1597, until the end of the Month of *August*. . . .

In like manner the said Exercise may be Established, and re-established in all the Cities and Places where it hath been established, or ought to be by the Statute of Pacification, made in the Year 1577. . . .

As also not to exercise the said Religion in our Court, nor in our Territories and Countries beyond the Mountains, nor in our City of *Paris*, nor within five Leagues of the said City. . . .

We prohibit all Preachers, Readers, and others who speak in public, to use any words, discourse, or propositions tending to excite the People to Sedition; and we enjoin them to contain and comport themselves modestly, and to say nothing which shall not be for the instruction and edification of the Auditors, and maintaining the peace and tranquillity established by us in our said Kingdom. . . .

They shall also be obliged to keep and observe the Festivals of the Catholick Church, and shall not on the same dayes work, sell, or keep open shop, nor likewise the Artisans shall not work out of their shops, in their chambers or houses privately on the said Festivals, and other dayes forbidden, of any trade, the noise whereof may be heard without by those that pass by, or by the Neighbours. . . .

We ordain, that there shall not be made any difference or distinction upon the account of the said Religion, in receiving Scholars to be instructed in the Universities, Colledges, or Schools, nor of the sick or poor into Hospitals, sick houses or publick Almshouses. . . .

We Will and Ordain, that all those of the Reformed Religion, and others who have followed their party, of what State, Quality or Condition soever they be, shall be obliged and constrained by all due and reasonable wayes, and under the penalties contained in the said Edict or Statute relating thereunto, to pay tythes to the Curates, and other Ecclesiasticks, and to all others to whom they shall appertain. . . .

To the end to re-unite so much the better the minds and good will of our Subjects, as is our intention, and to take away all complaints for the future; We declare all those who make or shall make profession of the said Reformed Religion, to be capable of holding and exercising all Estates, Dignities, Offices, and publick charges whatsoever. . . .

We declare all Sentences, Judgments, Procedures, Seisures, Sales, and Decrees made and given against those of the Reformed Religion, as well living as dead, from the death of the deceased King *Henry* the Second our most honoured Lord and Father in Law, upon the occasion of the said Religion, Tumults and Troubles since happening, as also the execution of the same Judgments and Decrees, from henceforward cancelled, revoked, and annulled. . . .

Those also of the said Religion shall depart and desist henceforward from all Practices, Negotiations, and Intelligences, as well within as without our Kingdom; and the said Assemblies and Councels established within the Provinces, shall readily separate, and also all the Leagues and Associations made or to be made under what pretext soever, to the prejudice of our present Edict, shall be cancelled and annulled, . . . prohibiting most expresly to all our Subjects to make henceforwards any Assesments or Leavy's of Money, Fortifications, Enrolments of men, Congregations and Assemblies of other than such as are permitted by our present Edict, and without Arms. . . .

We give in command to the People of our said Courts of Parliaments, Chambers of our Courts, and Courts of our Aids, Bayliffs, Chief-Justices, Provosts and other our Justices and Officers to whom it appertains, and to their Leivetenants, that they cause to be read, published, and Registred this present Edict and Ordinance in their Courts and Jurisdictions, and the same keep punctually, and the contents of the same to cause to be injoyned and used fully and peaceably to all those to whom it shall belong, ceasing and making to cease all troubles and obstructions to the contrary, for such is our pleasure: and in witness hereof we have signed these presents with our own hand; and to the end to make it a thing firm and stable for ever, we have caused to put and indorse our Seal to the same. Given at *Nantes* in the Month of *April* in the year of Grace 1598. and of our Reign the ninth.

Signed

HENRY

■ Discussion Questions

1. What are the edict's principal objectives?
2. In what ways does the edict balance the demands of French Catholics and Protestants?
3. What limits does the edict place on Protestants' religious rights?
4. Did Henry IV regard this edict as a permanent solution to the religious divisions in the realm?

39. Saint Ignatius of Loyola, *A New Kind of Catholicism*   (1546, 1549, 1553)

The interests of Ignatius of Loyola (1491–1556), born of a Spanish noble family, centered more on chivalry and national glory than religion before his serious injury in battle. While recovering, he experienced a conversion when he began reading the only books available to him, The Golden Legend *(about saints' lives) and the* Life of Christ. *Entering a monastery, he started work on* The Spiritual Exercises, *a manual of discernment for the pilgrim journeying to God. After studying at the University of Paris, Ignatius, Francis Xavier (1506–1552), and other friends made vows of chastity and poverty, determining to travel to Jerusalem. When this became impossible, they went to Italy. The Society of Jesus (the Jesuits), founded by Ignatius and his early companions, was officially recognized by Pope Paul III in 1540 as a new order directly under the papacy. Its spirituality would be expressed most prominently in teaching and missionary work. The letters of Ignatius evince a new form of Catholic spiritual expression that was active and apostolic in its orientation. It was less a "response" to Protestantism than a model for Catholic life and work. Along with the works of other early Jesuits, it embodied a new spirit that so many had sought but not found in the late medieval church.*

CONDUCT AT TRENT: ON HELPING OTHERS, 1546

Our main aim [to God's greater glory] during this undertaking at Trent is to put into practice (as a group that lives together in one appropriate place) preaching, confessions and readings, teaching children, giving good example, visiting the poor in the hospitals, exhorting those around us, each of us according to the different talents he may happen to have, urging on as many as possible to greater piety and prayer. . . .

In their preaching they should not refer to points of conflict between Protestants and Catholics, but simply exhort all to upright conduct and to ecclesiastical practice, urging everyone to full self-knowledge and to greater knowledge and love of their Creator and Lord, with frequent allusions to the Council. At the end of each session, they should (as has been mentioned) lead prayers for the Council.

They should do the same with readings as with sermons, trying their best to influence people with greater love of their Creator and Lord as they explain the meaning of what is read; similarly, they should lead their hearers to pray for the Council. . . .

They should spend some time, as convenient, in the elementary teaching of youngsters, depending on the means and disposition of all involved, and with more or less explanation according to the capacity of the pupils. . . . Let them visit the almshouses once or twice a day, at times that are convenient for the patients' health, hearing confessions and consoling the poor, if possible taking them something, and urging them to the sort of prayers mentioned above for confession. If there are three of ours in Trent, each should visit the poor at least once every four days.

When they are urging people in their dealings with them to go to confession and communion, to say mass frequently, to undertake the Spiritual Exercises and other good works, they should also be urging them to pray for the Council.

From *Saint Ignatius of Loyola, Personal Writings: Reminiscences, Spiritual Diary, Select Letters, Including the Text of The Spiritual Exercises,* ed. and trans. Joseph A. Munitiz and Philip Endean (New York: Penguin Books, 1996), 165, 166, 230, 233–34, 257, 259, 262–63.

It was said that there are advantages in being slow to speak and measured in one's state-ments when doctrinal definitions are involved. The opposite is true when one is urging people to look to their spiritual progress. Then one should be eloquent and ready to talk, full of sym-pathy and affection.

SPREADING GOD'S WORD IN A GERMAN UNIVERSITY, 1549

The aim that they should have above all before their eyes is that intended by the Supreme Pon-tiff who has sent them: to help the University of Ingolstadt, and as far as is possible the whole of Germany, in all that concerns purity of faith, obedience to the Church, and firmness and sound-ness of doctrine and upright living. . . .

They must be very competent in them, and teach solid doctrine without many technical terms (which are unpopular), especially if these are hard to understand. The lectures should be learned yet clear, sustained in argument yet not long-winded, and delivered with attention to style. . . . Besides these academic lectures, it seems opportune on feast days to hold sermons on Bible readings, more calculated to move hearts and form consciences than to produce learned minds. . . . They should make efforts to attract their students into a friendship of spiritual qual-ity, and if possible towards confession and making the Spiritual Exercises, even in the full form, if they seem suitable to join the Society. . . .

On occasion they should give time to works of mercy of a more visible character, such as in hospitals and prisons and helping other kinds of poor; such works arouse a "sweet fragrance" in the Lord. Opportunity may also arise to act as peacemakers in quarrels and to teach basic Chris-tian doctrine to the uneducated. Taking account of local conditions and the persons concerned, prudence will dictate whether they should act themselves or through others.

They should make efforts to make friends with the leaders of their opponents, as also with those who are most influential among the heretics or those who are suspected of it yet seem not absolutely immovable. They must try to bring them back from their error by sensitive skill and signs of love. . . . All must try to have at their finger-tips the main points concerning dogmas of faith that are subjects of controversy with heretics, especially at the time and place when they are present, and with those persons with whom they are dealing. Thus they will be able, whenever opportunity arises, to put forward and defend the Catholic truth, to refute errors and to strengthen the doubtful and wavering, whether by lectures and sermons or in the confessional and in con-versations. . . .

It will be helpful to lead people, as far as possible, to open themselves to God's grace, ex-horting them to a desire for salvation, to prayer, to alms, and to everything that conduces to re-ceiving grace or increasing it. . . .

Let [the duke] understand also what glory it will mean for him if he is the first to introduce into Germany seminaries in the form of such colleges, to foster sound doctrine and religion.

THE FINAL WORD ON OBEDIENCE, 1553, TO THE BROTHERS IN PORTUGAL

To form an idea of the exceptional intrinsic value of this obedience in the eyes of God Our Lord, one should weigh both the worth of the noble sacrifice offered, involving the highest human power, and the completeness of the self-offering undertaken, as one strips oneself of self, be-coming a "living victim" pleasing to the Divine Majesty. Another indication is the intensity of the difficulty experienced as one conquers self for love of God, opposing the natural human incli-nation felt by us all to follow our own opinions. . . .

Let us be unpretentious and let us be gentle! God Our Lord will grant the grace to enable you, gently and lovingly, to maintain constantly the offering you have made to Him. . . .

All that has been said does not exclude your bringing before your superiors a contrary opinion that may have occurred to you, once you have prayed about the matter and you feel that it would be proper and in accord with your respect for God to do so. . . . Such is the model on which divine Providence "gently disposes all things," so that the lower via the middle, and the middle via the higher, are led to their final ends. . . . The same can be seen upon the earth with respect to all secular constitutions that are duly established, and with respect to the ecclesiastical hierarchy, which is subordinated to you in virtue of holy obedience to select among the many routes open to you that which will bring you back to Portugal as soon and as safely as possible. So I order you in the name of Christ Our Lord to do this, even if it will be so as to return soon to India. . . . Firstly, you are well aware how important for the upkeep and advancement of Christianity in those lands, as also in Guinea and Brazil, is the good order that the King of Portugal can grant from his kingdom. When a prince of such Christian desires and holy intentions as is the King of Portugal receives information from someone of your experience about the state of affairs in those parts, you can imagine what influence this will have on him to do much more in the service of God Our Lord and for the good of those countries that you will describe to him. . . .

You are also aware how important it is for the good of the Indies that the persons sent there should be suitable for the aim that one is pursuing in those and in other lands. . . . Quite apart from all these reasons, which apply to furthering the good of India, it seems to me that you would fire the King's enthusiasm for the Ethiopian project, which has been planned for so many years without anything effective having been seen. Similarly, with regard to the Congo and Brazil, you could give no small help from Portugal, which you cannot do from India as there are not the same commercial relations. If people in India consider that your presence is important given your post, you can continue to act as superior no less from Portugal than from Japan or China, and probably much better. Just as you have gone away on other occasions for longer periods, do the same now.

▪ Discussion Questions

1. What does the Catholic life mean to Ignatius? What is innovative in his program for Catholic reform?
2. What advice does Ignatius give about dealing with the problem of heresy?
3. What role does Ignatius envision Jesuits playing throughout Europe and the rest of the world?
4. How does Ignatius think political leaders can be enlisted to support the aims of the reform movement?

40. Galileo Galilei, *Letter to the Grand Duchess Christina* (1615)

Italian-born and educated, Galileo Galilei (1564–1642) was among the most illustrious proponents of the new science in the seventeenth century. Early in his studies, he embraced Copernicus's theory that the sun, not the Earth, was at the center of the universe. Having improved on the newly invented telescope in 1609, he was able to substantiate the heliocentric view through his observations of the moon and other planets. Because Galileo's work challenged traditional scientific views, it sparked considerable controversy. In the letter excerpted here, written in 1615 to the Grand Duchess Christina of Tuscany, an important Catholic patron of learning, Galileo defends the validity of his findings while striving to separate matters of religious faith from the study of natural phenomena.

Stillman Drake, trans., *Discoveries and Opinions of Galileo* (New York: Doubleday, 1957), 175–86.

GALILEO GALILEI TO THE MOST SERENE GRAND DUCHESS MOTHER

Some years ago, as Your Serene Highness well knows, I discovered in the heavens many things that had not been seen before our own age. The novelty of these things, as well as some consequences which followed from them in contradiction to the physical notions commonly held among academic philosophers, stirred up against me no small number of professors—as if I had placed these things in the sky with my own hands in order to upset nature and overturn the sciences. . . .

Well, the passage of time has revealed to everyone the truths that I previously set forth. . . . But some, besides allegiance to their original error, possess I know not what fanciful interest in remaining hostile not so much toward the things in question as toward their discoverer. No longer being able to deny them, these men now take refuge in obstinate silence, but being more than ever exasperated by that which has pacified and quieted other men, they divert their thoughts to other fancies and seek new ways to damage me. . . .

Persisting in their original resolve to destroy me and everything mine by any means they can think of, these men are aware of my views in astronomy and philosophy. They know that as to the arrangement of the parts of the universe, I hold the sun to be situated motionless in the center of the revolution of the celestial orbs while the earth rotates on its axis and revolves about the sun. . . .

Now as to the false aspersions which they so unjustly seek to cast upon me, I have thought it necessary to justify myself in the eyes of all men, whose judgment in matters of religion and of reputation I must hold in great esteem. I shall therefore discourse of the particulars which these men produce to make this opinion detested and to have it condemned not merely as false but as heretical. To this end they make a shield of their hypocritical zeal for religion. They go about invoking the Bible, which they would have minister to their deceitful purposes. Contrary to the sense of the Bible and the intention of the holy Fathers, if I am not mistaken, they would extend such authorities until even in purely physical matters—where faith is not involved—they would have us altogether abandon reason and the evidence of our senses in favor of some biblical passage, though under the surface meaning of its words this passage may contain a different sense. . . .

The reason produced for condemning the opinion that the earth moves and the sun stands still is that in many places in the Bible one may read that the sun moves and the earth stands still. Since the Bible cannot err, it follows as a necessary consequence that anyone takes an erroneous and heretical position who maintains that the sun is inherently motionless and the earth movable.

With regard to this argument, I think in the first place that it is very pious to say and prudent to affirm that the holy Bible can never speak untruth—whenever its true meaning is understood. But I believe nobody will deny that it is often very abstruse, and may say things which are quite different from what its bare words signify. Hence in expounding the Bible if one were always to confine oneself to the unadorned grammatical meaning, one might fall into error. Not only contradictions and propositions far from true might thus be made to appear in the Bible, but even grave heresies and follies. Thus it would be necessary to assign to God feet, hands, and eyes, as well as corporeal and human affections, such as anger, repentance, hatred, and sometimes even the forgetting of things past and ignorance of those to come. These propositions uttered by the Holy Ghost were set down in that manner by the sacred scribes in order to accommodate them to the capacities of the common people, who are rude and unlearned. For the sake of those who deserve to be separated from the herd, it is necessary that wise expositors should produce the true senses of such passages, together with the special reasons for which they were set down in these words. This doctrine is so widespread and so definite with all theologians that it would be superfluous to adduce evidence for it.

Hence I think that I may reasonably conclude that whenever the Bible has occasion to speak of any physical conclusion (especially those which are very abstruse and hard to understand), the rule has been observed of avoiding confusion in the minds of the common people which would render them contumacious toward the higher mysteries. Now the Bible, merely to condescend to popular capacity, has not hesitated to obscure some very important pronouncements, attributing to God himself some qualities extremely remote from (and even contrary to) His essence. Who, then, would positively declare that this principle has been set aside, and the Bible has confined itself rigorously to the bare and restricted sense of its words, when speaking but casually of the earth, of water, of the sun, or of any other created thing? Especially in view of the fact that these things in no way concern the primary purpose of the sacred writings, which is the service of God and the salvation of souls—matters infinitely beyond the comprehension of the common people.

This being granted, I think that in discussions of physical problems we ought to begin not from the authority of scriptural passages, but from sense-experiences and necessary demonstrations; for the holy Bible and the phenomena of nature proceed alike from the divine Word, the former as the dictate of the Holy Ghost and the latter as the observant executrix of God's commands. It is necessary for the Bible, in order to be accommodated to the understanding of every man, to speak many things which appear to differ from the absolute truth so far as the bare meaning of the words is concerned. But Nature, on the other hand, is inexorable and immutable; she never transgresses the laws imposed upon her, or cares a whit whether her abstruse reasons and methods of operations are understandable to men. For that reason it appears that nothing physical which sense-experience sets before our eyes, or which necessary demonstrations prove to us, ought to be called in question (much less condemned) upon the testimony of biblical passages which may have some different meaning beneath their words. For the Bible is not chained in every expression to conditions as strict as those which govern all physical effects; nor is God any less excellently revealed in Nature's actions than in the sacred statements of the Bible. . . .

From this I do not mean to infer that we need not have an extraordinary esteem for the passages of holy Scripture. On the contrary, having arrived at any certainties in physics, we ought to utilize these as the most appropriate aids in the true exposition of the Bible and in the investigation of those meanings which are necessarily contained therein, for these must be concordant with demonstrated truths. I should judge that the authority of the Bible was designed to persuade men of those articles and propositions which, surpassing all human reasoning, could not be made credible by science, or by any other means than through the very mouth of the Holy Spirit.

Yet even in those propositions which are not matters of faith, this authority ought to be preferred over that of all human writings which are supported only by bare assertions or probable arguments, and not set forth in a demonstrative way. This I hold to be necessary and proper to the same extent that divine wisdom surpasses all human judgment and conjecture.

But I do not feel obliged to believe that that same God who has endowed us with senses, reason, and intellect has intended to forgo their use and by some other means to give us knowledge which we can attain by them. He would not require us to deny sense and reason in physical matters which are set before our eyes and minds by direct experience or necessary demonstrations. This must be especially true in those sciences of which but the faintest trace (and that consisting of conclusions) is to be found in the Bible. Of astronomy, for instance, so little is found that none of the planets except Venus are so much as mentioned, and this only once or twice under the name of "Lucifer." If the sacred scribes had had any intention of teaching people certain arrangements and motions of the heavenly bodies, or had they wished us to derive such knowledge from the Bible, then in my opinion they would not have spoken of these matters so sparingly in comparison with the infinite number of admirable conclusions which are demonstrated in that science. . . .

From these things it follows as a necessary consequence that, since the Holy Ghost did not intend to teach us whether heaven moves or stands still, whether its shape is spherical or like a discus or extended in a plane, nor whether the earth is located at its center or off to one side, then so much the less was it intended to settle for us any other conclusion of the same kind. And the motion or rest of the earth and the sun is so closely linked with the things just named, that without a determination of the one, neither side can be taken in the other matters. Now if the Holy Spirit has purposely neglected to teach us propositions of this sort as irrelevant to the highest goal (that is, to our salvation), how can anyone affirm that it is obligatory to take sides on them, and that one belief is required by faith, while the other side is erroneous? Can an opinion be heretical and yet have no concern with the salvation of souls? Can the Holy Ghost be asserted not to have intended teaching us something that does concern our salvation? I would say here something that was heard from an ecclesiastic of the most eminent degree: "That the intention of the Holy Ghost is to teach us how one goes to heaven, not how heaven goes." . . .

From this it is seen that the interpretation which we impose upon passages of Scripture would be false whenever it disagreed with demonstrated truths. And therefore we should seek the incontrovertible sense of the Bible with the assistance of demonstrated truth, and not in any way try to force the hand of Nature or deny experiences and rigorous proofs in accordance with the mere sound of words that may appeal to our frailty. . . .

To that end they would forbid him the use of reason, divine gift of Providence, and would abuse the just authority of holy Scripture—which, in the general opinion of theologians, can never oppose manifest experiences and necessary demonstrations when rightly understood and applied. If I am correct, it will stand them in no stead to go running to the Bible to cover up their inability to understand (let alone resolve) their opponents' arguments.

■ Discussion Questions

1. What is Galileo's goal in writing this letter to the Grand Duchess?
2. What is the basis of the attacks by Galileo's critics?
3. According to Galileo, what role should the Bible play in scientific inquiry?
4. Historians have credited Galileo for helping to popularize the principles and methods of the new science. How does this document support this view?

CHAPTER 13

State Building and the Search for Order, 1648–1690

The wars over religion not only left bitter memories in late-seventeenth-century Europe but also ruined economies and weakened governments. Politically, the quest for order fueled the development of two rival systems of state building: absolutism and constitutionalism, with France (first document) and England (third document), respectively, taking the lead. Despite their differences, rulers in both systems centralized their power and expanded their bureaucracies, casting an increasingly wide net over their subjects' lives. The second document indicates that not everyone submitted willingly to the expansion of state power, but such resistance was typically fruitless.

41. Louis de Rouvroy, Duke of Saint-Simon, *Memoirs*   (1694–1723)

A nobleman and godson of Louis XIV, Louis de Rouvroy, duke of Saint-Simon (1675–1755), was raised at the royal palace of Versailles. He began recording his life and impressions of the court at the age of nineteen and continued for almost three decades. The result was his multivolume Memoirs, *which paint an intimate portrait of the Sun King and the workings of the absolutist state. Saint-Simon was not an entirely objective observer. Never achieving great success within the court, he often viewed it through the lens of his own resentment. This excerpt provides insight into the reasons behind Louis XIV's move to Versailles and his method of rule there.*

Let me touch now upon some other incidents in his career, and upon some points in his character.

He early showed a disinclination for Paris. The troubles that had taken place there during the minority made him regard the place as dangerous; he wished, too, to render himself venerable by hiding himself from the eyes of the multitude; all these considerations fixed him at St. Germains soon after the death of the Queen, his mother. It was to that place he began to attract the world by fêtes and gallantries, and by making it felt that he wished to be often seen.

His love for Madame de la Vallière, which was at first kept secret, occasioned frequent excursions to Versailles, then a little card castle, which had been built by Louis XIII.—annoyed, and his suite still more so, at being frequently obliged to sleep in a wretched inn there, after he had been out hunting in the forest of Saint Leger. That monarch rarely slept at Versailles more than one night, and then from necessity; the King, his son, slept there, so that he might be more in

Bayle St. John, trans., *The Memoirs of the Duke of Saint Simon*, vol. II (Philadelphia: Gebbie and Co., 1890), 363–69.

private with his mistress; pleasures unknown to the hero and just man, worthy son of Saint Louis, who built the little château.

These excursions of Louis XIV. by degrees gave birth to those immense buildings he erected at Versailles; and their convenience for a numerous court, so different from the apartments at St. Germains, led him to take up his abode there entirely shortly after the death of the Queen. He built an infinite number of apartments, which were asked for by those who wished to pay their court to him; whereas at St. Germains nearly everybody was obliged to lodge in the town, and the few who found accommodation at the château were strangely inconvenienced.

The frequent fêtes, the private promenades at Versailles, the journeys, were means on which the King seized in order to distinguish or mortify the courtiers, and thus render them more assiduous in pleasing him. He felt that of real favours he had not enough to bestow; in order to keep up the spirit of devotion, he therefore unceasingly invented all sorts of ideal ones, little preferences and petty distinctions, which answered his purpose as well.

He was exceedingly jealous of the attention paid him. Not only did he notice the presence of the most distinguished courtiers, but those of inferior degree also. He looked to the right and to the left, not only upon rising but upon going to bed, at his meals, in passing through his apartments, or his gardens of Versailles, where alone the courtiers were allowed to follow him; he saw and noticed everybody; not one escaped him, not even those who hoped to remain unnoticed. He marked well all absentees from the court, found out the reason of their absence, and never lost an opportunity of acting towards them as the occasion might seem to justify. With some of the courtiers (the most distinguished), it was a demerit not to make the court their ordinary abode; with others 'twas a fault to come but rarely; for those who never or scarcely ever came it was certain disgrace. When their names were in any way mentioned, "I do not know them," the King would reply haughtily. Those who presented themselves but seldom were thus characterised: "They are people I never see"; these decrees were irrevocable. He could not bear people who liked Paris.

Louis XIV. took great pains to be well informed of all that passed everywhere; in the public places, in the private houses, in society and familiar intercourse. His spies and telltales were infinite. He had them of all species; many who were ignorant that their information reached him; others who knew it; others who wrote to him direct, sending their letters through channels he indicated; and all these letters were seen by him alone, and always before everything else; others who sometimes spoke to him secretly in his cabinet, entering by the back stairs. These unknown means ruined an infinite number of people of all classes who never could discover the cause; often ruined them very unjustly; for the King, once prejudiced, never altered his opinion, or so rarely, that nothing was more rare. He had, too, another fault, very dangerous for others and often for himself, since it deprived him of good subjects. He had an excellent memory; in this way, that if he saw a man who, twenty years before, perhaps, had in some manner offended him, he did not forget the man, though he might forget the offence. This was enough, however, to exclude the person from all favour. The representations of a minister, of a general, of his confessor even, could not move the King. He would not yield.

The most cruel means by which the King was informed of what was passing—for many years before anybody knew it—was that of opening letters. The promptitude and dexterity with which they were opened passes understanding. He saw extracts from all the letters in which there were passages that the chiefs of the post-office, and then the minister who governed it, thought ought to go before him; entire letters, too, were sent to him, when their contents seemed to justify the sending. Thus the chiefs of the post, nay, the principal clerks were in a position to suppose what they pleased and against whom they pleased. A word of contempt against the King or the government, a joke, a detached phrase, was enough. It is incredible how many people, justly or unjustly, were more or less ruined, always without resource, without trial, and without knowing why. The secret was impenetrable; for nothing ever cost the King less than profound silence and dissimulation. . . .

He liked splendour, magnificence, and profusion in everything: you pleased him if you shone through the brilliancy of your houses, your clothes, your table, your equipages. Thus a taste for extravagance and luxury was disseminated through all classes of society; causing infinite harm, and leading to general confusion of rank and to ruin.

■ Discussion Questions

1. How did Louis XIV use court etiquette as a form of power?
2. Why did nobles reside at Versailles? What benefits did they gain?
3. What is Saint-Simon's attitude toward Louis XIV's style of governing?
4. In what ways did court life embody the principles of absolutism?

42. Ludwig Fabritius, *The Revolt of Stenka Razin* (1670)

Despite its geographical and cultural isolation from the rest of Europe, Russia followed France's lead down the path of absolutism. In the process, Tsar Alexei (r. 1645–1676) legally combined millions of slaves and free peasants into a single serf class bound to the land and to their aristocratic masters. Not everyone passively accepted this fate, however. In 1667, a Cossack named Stenka Razin led a re-volt against serfdom that gained considerable support among people whose social and economic sta-tus was threatened by the tsar's policies, including soldiers of peasant stock. Razin's ultimate defeat at the hands of the tsar elucidates the close ties between the Russian government's enhanced power and the enforcement of serfdom. Ludwig Fabritius, a Dutch soldier who lived in Russia from 1660 to 1677 while employed as a military expert in the Russian army, wrote this account of one stage of the revolt.

Then Stenka with his company started off upstream, rowing as far as Tsaritsyn, whence it took him only one day's journey to Panshin, a small town situated on the Don. Here he began straight-away quietly gathering the common people around him, giving them money, and promises of great riches if they would be loyal to him and help to exterminate the treacherous boyars.[1]

This lasted the whole winter, until by about spring he had assembled 4,000 to 5,000 men. With these he came to Tsaritsyn and demanded the immediate surrender of the fortress; the rabble soon achieved their purpose, and although the governor tried to take refuge in a tower, he soon had to give himself up as he was deserted by one and all. Stenka immediately had the wretched governor hanged; and all the goods they found belonging to the Tsar and his officers as well as to the merchants were confiscated and distributed among the rabble.

Stenka now began once more to make preparations. Since the plains are not cultivated, the people have to bring their corn from Nizhniy-Novgorod and Kazan down the Volga in big boats known as *nasady*, and everything destined for Astrakhan has first to pass Tsaritsyn. Stenka Razin duly noted this, and occupied the whole of the Volga, so that nothing could get through to As-trakhan. Here he captured a few hundred merchants with their valuable goods, taking possession of all kinds of fine linen, silks, striped silk material, sables, soft leather, ducats, talers, and many thousands of rubles in Russian money and merchandise of every description. . . .

---

[1] **boyars:** Noblemen.

Anthony Glenn Cross, ed. *Russia under Western Eyes, 1517–1825* (London: Elek Books, 1971), 120–23.

In the meantime four regiments of *streltsy*[2] were dispatched from Moscow to subdue these brigands. They arrived with their big boats and as they were not used to the water, were easily beaten. Here Stenka Razin gained possession of a large amount of ammunition and artillery-pieces and everything else he required. While the above-mentioned *streltsy* were sent from Moscow, about 5,000 men were ordered up from Astrakhan by water and by land to capture Stenka Razin. As soon as he had finished with the former, he took up a good position, and, being in possession of reliable information regarding our forces, he left Tsaritsyn and came to meet us half way at Chernyy Yar, confronting us before we had suspected his presence or received any information about him. We stopped at Chernyy Yar for a few days and sent out scouts by water and by land, but were unable to obtain any definite information. On 10 July [*sic*: June] a council of war was held at which it was decided to advance and seek out Stenka. The next morning, at 8 o'clock, our look-outs on the water came hurriedly and raised the alarm as the Cossacks were following at their heels. We got out of our boats and took up battle positions. General Knyaz Semen Ivanovich Lvov went through the ranks and reminded all the men to do their duty and to remember the oath they had taken to His Majesty the Tsar, to fight like honest soldiers against these irresponsible rebels, whereupon they all unanimously shouted: "Yes, we will give our lives for His Majesty the Tsar, and will fight to the last drop of our blood."

In the meantime Stenka prepared for battle and deployed on a wide front; to all those who had no rifle he gave a long pole, burnt a little at one end, and with a rag or small hook attached. They presented a strange sight on the plain from afar, and the common soldiers imagined that, since there were so many flags and standards, there must be a host of people. They [the common soldiers] held a consultation and at once decided that this was the chance for which they had been waiting so long, and with all their flags and drums they ran over to the enemy. They began kissing and embracing one another and swore with life and limb to stand together and to exterminate the treacherous boyars, to throw off the yoke of slavery, and to become free men.

The general looked at the officers and the officers at the general, and no one knew what to do; one said this, and another that, until finally it was decided that they and the general should get into the boats and withdraw to Astrakhan. But the rascally *streltsy* of Chernyy Yar stood on the walls and towers, turning their weapons on us and opened fire; some of them ran out of the fortress and cut us off from the boats, so that we had no means of escape. In the meantime those curs of ours who had gone over to the Cossacks came up from behind. We numbered about eighty men, officers, noblemen, and clerks. Murder at once began. Then, however, Stenka Razin ordered that no more officers were to be killed, saying that there must be a few good men among them who should be pardoned, whilst those others who had not lived in amity with their men should be condemned to well-deserved punishment by the Ataman and his *Krug*. [A *Krug* is a meeting convened by the order of the Ataman, at which the Cossacks stand in a circle with the standard in the centre; the Ataman then takes his place beside his best officers, to whom he divulges his wishes, ordering them to make these known to the common brothers and to hear their opinion on the matter.] . . .

A *Krug* was accordingly called and Stenka asked through his chiefs how the general and his officers had treated the soldiers under their command. Thereupon the unscrupulous curs, *streltsy* as well as soldiers, unanimously called out that there was not one of them who deserved to remain alive, and they all asked that their father Stepan Timofeyevich Razin should order them to be cut down. This was granted with the exception of General Knyaz Semen Ivanovich Lvov, whose life was specially spared by Stenka himself. The officers were now brought in order of rank out of the tower, into which they had been thrown bound hand and foot the previous day, their ropes were cut and they were led outside the gate. When all the bloodthirsty curs had lined up, each

---

[2] ***streltsy:*** Sharpshooters.

was eager to deal his former superior the first blow, one with the sword, another with the lance, another with the scimitar, and others again with martels, so that as soon as an officer was pushed into the ring, the curs immediately killed him with their many wounds; indeed, some were cut to pieces and straightaway thrown into the Volga. My stepfather, Paul Rudolf Beem, and Lt. Col. Wundrum and many other officers, senior and junior, were cut down before my eyes.

My own time had not yet come: this I could tell by the wonderful way in which God rescued me, for as I—half-dead—now awaited the final blow, my [former] orderly, a young soldier, came and took me by my bound arms and tried to take me down the hill. As I was already half-dead, I did not move and did not know what to do, but he came back and took me by the arms and led me, bound as I was, through the throng of curs, down the hill into the boat and immediately cut my arms free, saying that I should rest in peace here and that he would be responsible for me and do his best to save my life. . . . Then my guardian angel told me not to leave the boat, and left me. He returned in the evening and brought me a piece of bread which I enjoyed since I had had nothing to eat for two days.

The following day all our possessions were looted and gathered together under the main flag, so that both our bloodthirsty curs and the Cossacks got their share.

■ Discussion Questions

1. What motivated Razin and his followers to take action?
2. Why were Razin and his forces able to defeat the tsar's soldiers?
3. What does this account suggest about the role of the military in the growth of the Russian government's authority?
4. With whom do you think Fabritius's sympathies lie, and why?

43. British Parliament, *The English Bill of Rights* (1689)

Louis XIV had many admirers in Europe, including King James II of England. Unlike Louis, however, James faced a major challenge to his power: Parliament. The king and Parliament had been at odds for decades over the nature of royal authority, and James's absolutist policies proved too much for Parliament to bear. As a result, in 1688 Parliament ousted the king and offered the throne to Prince William of Orange and his wife, Mary, the eldest of James's adult daughters. In exchange, William and Mary agreed to accept the Bill of Rights, which legally defined the role of Parliament as the monarchy's partner in government. The bill marked the victory of constitutionalism over absolutism in England and formed the cornerstone of the idea that government should ensure certain rights by law to protect citizens from the dangers of arbitrary power.

Whereas the said late King James II having abdicated the government, and the throne being thereby vacant, his Highness the prince of Orange (whom it hath pleased Almighty God to make the glorious instrument of delivering this kingdom from popery and arbitrary power) did (by the advice of the lords spiritual and temporal, and diverse principal persons of the Commons) cause letters to be written to the lords spiritual and temporal, being Protestants, and other letters to the several counties, cities, universities, boroughs, and Cinque Ports, for the choosing of such persons to represent them, as were of right to be sent to parliament, to meet and sit at Westminster upon the two and twentieth day of January, in this year 1689, in order to such an

Great Britain, *The Statutes*, rev. ed. (London: Eyre and Spottiswoode, 1871), vol. II, 10–12.

establishment as that their religion, laws, and liberties might not again be in danger of being subverted; upon which letters elections have been accordingly made.

And thereupon the said lords spiritual and temporal and Commons, pursuant to their respective letters and elections, being now assembled in a full and free representation of this nation, taking into their most serious consideration the best means for attaining the ends aforesaid, do in the first place (as their ancestors in like case have usually done), for the vindication and assertion of their ancient rights and liberties, declare:

1. That the pretended power of suspending laws, or the execution of laws, by regal authority, without consent of parliament is illegal.

2. That the pretended power of dispensing with the laws, or the execution of law by regal authority, as it hath been assumed and exercises of late, is illegal.

3. That the commission for erecting the late court of commissioners for ecclesiastical causes, and all other commissions and courts of like nature, are illegal and pernicious.

4. That levying money for or to the use of the crown by pretense of prerogative, without grant of parliament, for longer time or in other manner than the same is or shall be granted, is illegal.

5. That it is the right of the subjects to petition the king, and all commitments and prosecutions for such petitioning are illegal.

6. That the raising or keeping a standing army within the kingdom in time of peace, unless it be with consent of parliament, is against law.

7. That the subjects which are Protestants may have arms for their defense suitable to their conditions, and as allowed by law.

8. That election of members of parliament ought to be free.

9. That the freedom of speech, and debates or proceedings in parliament, ought not to be impeached or questioned in any court or place out of parliament.

10. That excessive bail ought not to be required, nor excessive fines imposed, nor cruel and unusual punishments inflicted.

11. That jurors ought to be duly impaneled and returned, and jurors which pass upon men in trials for high treason ought to be freeholders.

12. That all grants and promises of fines and forfeitures of particular persons before conviction are illegal and void.

13. And that for redress of all grievances, and for the amending, strengthening, and preserving of the laws, parliament ought to be held frequently.

And they do claim, demand, and insist upon all and singular the premises, as their undoubted rights and liberties: and that no declarations, judgments, doings, or proceedings, to the prejudice of the people in any of the said premises, ought in any wise to be drawn hereafter into consequence or example.

To which demand of their rights they are particularly encouraged by the declaration of his Highness the prince of Orange, as being the only means for obtaining a full redress and remedy therein.

Having therefore an entire confidence that his said Highness the prince of Orange will perfect the deliverance so far advanced by him, and will still preserve them from the violation of their rights, which they have here asserted, and from all other attempt upon their religion, rights, and liberties:

The said lords spiritual and temporal, and commons, assembled at Westminster, do resolve that William and Mary, prince and princess of Orange, be, and be declared, king and queen of England, France, and Ireland, the dominions thereunto belonging, to hold the crown and royal dignity of the said kingdoms and dominions to them the said prince and princess during their lives. . . .

Upon which their said Majesties did accept the crown and royal dignity of the kingdoms of England, France, and Ireland, and the dominions thereunto belonging, according to the resolution and desire of the said lords and commons contained in the said declaration.

■ Discussion Questions

1. In what ways does the Bill of Rights limit the powers of the crown?
2. What role does the Bill of Rights grant Parliament in government?
3. How does the Bill of Rights give weight to the attitude of members of Parliament who thought that they had "made" the king and queen, William and Mary?

CHAPTER 14

The Atlantic System and Its Consequences, 1690–1740

The growth of European domestic economies and overseas colonization in the eighteenth century infused Europe with money, new products, and a new sense of optimism. Yet, as the first document illustrates, the good times came at a horrible price for the millions of African slaves who formed the economic backbone of the colonial system. Changes were afoot on the political front, too, with the stabilization of the European state system. Consequently, states such as Russia shone more brightly over the political landscape while others lost their luster. The second and third documents reveal that intellectual circles were also ablaze with change as scholars and writers cast political, social, and religious issues in a new, critical light. Even women's traditional place in society was for the first time systematically called into question.

44. Olaudah Equiano, *The Interesting Narrative of the Life of Olaudah Equiano, Written by Himself* (1789)

The autobiography of Olaudah Equiano (c. 1745–1797) puts a human face on the eighteenth-century Atlantic slave trade and its tragic consequences. While historians debate whether he was born in what is now Nigeria or in the colonies, Equiano was captured by local raiders and sold into slavery in his early teens. He gained his freedom in 1766 and soon thereafter became a vocal supporter of the English abolitionist movement. Having learned English as a young man, he published his autobiography in 1789, a best-seller in its day, with numerous editions published in Britain and America. In this excerpt, Equiano recounts his experience on the slave ship that took him away from his homeland, his freedom, and his very identity. Millions of others shared this same fate.

The first object which saluted my eyes when I arrived on the coast was the sea, and a slave ship which was then riding at anchor and waiting for its cargo. These filled me with astonishment, which was soon converted into terror when I was carried on board. I was immediately handled and tossed up to see if I were sound by some of the crew, and I was now persuaded that I had gotten into a world of bad spirits and that they were going to kill me. Their complexions too differing so much from ours, their long hair and the language they spoke (which was very different from any I had ever heard) united to confirm me in this belief. Indeed such were the horrors of

---

Abridged and edited by Paul Edwards, *Equiano's Travels: His Autobiography* (London: Heinemann, 1967), 25–32.

my views and fears at the moment that, if ten thousand worlds had been my own, I would have freely parted with them all to have exchanged my condition with that of the meanest slave in my own country. When I looked round the ship too and saw a large furnace or copper boiling and a multitude of black people of every description chained together, every one of their countenances expressing dejection and sorrow, I no longer doubted of my fate; and quite overpowered with horror and anguish, I fell motionless on the deck and fainted. When I recovered a little I found some black people about me, who I believed were some of those who had brought me on board and had been receiving their pay; they talked to me in order to cheer me, but all in vain. I asked them if we were not to be eaten by those white men with horrible looks, red faces, and loose hair. They told me I was not, and one of the crew brought me a small portion of spirituous liquor in a wine glass, but being afraid of him I would not take it out of his hand. One of the blacks therefore took it from him and gave it to me, and I took a little down my palate, which instead of reviving me, as they thought it would, threw me into the greatest consternation at the strange feeling it produced, having never tasted such any liquor before. Soon after this the blacks who brought me on board went off, and left me abandoned to despair.

I now saw myself deprived of all chance of returning to my native country or even the least glimpse of hope of gaining the shore, which I now considered as friendly; and I even wished for my former slavery in preference to my present situation, which was filled with horrors of every kind, still heightened by my ignorance of what I was to undergo. I was not long suffered to indulge my grief; I was soon put down under the decks, and there I received such a salutation in my nostrils as I had never experienced in my life: so that with the loathsomeness of the stench and crying together, I became so sick and low that I was not able to eat, nor had I the least desire to taste anything. I now wished for the last friend, death, to relieve me; but soon, to my grief, two of the white men offered me eatables, and on my refusing to eat, one of them held me fast by the hands and laid me across I think the windlass, and tied my feet while the other flogged me severely. I had never experienced anything of this kind before, and although, not being used to the water, I naturally feared that element the first time I saw it, yet nevertheless could I have got over the nettings I would have jumped over the side, but I could not; and besides, the crew used to watch us very closely who were not chained down to the decks, lest we should leap into the water: and I have seen some of these poor African prisoners most severely cut for attempting to do so, and hourly whipped for not eating. This indeed was often the case with myself. In a little time after, amongst the poor chained men I found some of my own nation, which in a small degree gave ease to my mind. I inquired of these what was to be done with us; they gave me to understand we were to be carried to these white people's country to work for them. I then was a little revived, and thought if it were no worse than working, my situation was not so desperate: but still I feared I should be put to death, the white people looked and acted, as I thought, in so savage a manner; for I had never seen among my people such instances of brutal cruelty, and this not only shewn towards us blacks but also to some of the whites themselves. One white man in particular I saw, when we were permitted to be on deck, flogged so unmercifully with a large rope near the foremast that he died in consequence of it; and they tossed him over the side as they would have done a brute. This made me fear these people the more, and I expected nothing less than to be treated in the same manner. . . . At last, when the ship we were in had got in all her cargo, they made ready with many fearful noises, and we were all put under deck so that we could not see how they managed the vessel. But this disappointment was the last of my sorrow. The stench of the hold while we were on the coast was so intolerably loathsome that it was dangerous to remain there for any time, and some of us had been permitted to stay on the deck for the fresh air; but now that the whole ship's cargo were confined together it became absolutely pestilential. The closeness of the place and the heat of the climate, added to the number in the ship, which was so crowded that each had scarcely room to turn himself, almost suffocated us. This produced copious perspirations, so that the air soon became unfit for respiration from a variety of loathsome smells, and brought on a sickness among the slaves, of which many died, thus falling victims to the improvident avarice, as I may call it, of their purchasers. This wretched situation was again aggravated by the galling of the chains, now become insupportable, and the filth of the necessary tubs, into which the children often fell and were almost suffocated. The shrieks of the women and the groans of the dying rendered the whole a scene of horror almost inconceivable. Happily perhaps for myself I was soon reduced so low here that it was thought necessary to keep me almost always on deck, and from my extreme youth I was not put in fetters. In this situation I expected every hour to share the fate of my companions, some of whom were almost daily brought upon deck at the point of death, which I began to hope would soon put an end to my miseries. . . . At last we came in sight of the island of Barbados, at which the whites on board gave a great shout and made many signs of joy to us. We did not know what to think of this, but as the vessel drew nearer we plainly saw the harbour and other ships of different kinds and sizes, and we soon anchored amongst them off Bridgetown. Many merchants and planters now came on board, though it was in the evening. They put us in separate parcels and examined us attentively. They also made us jump, and pointed to the land, signifying we were to go there. . . . We were not many days in the merchant's custody before we were sold after their usual manner, which is this: On a signal given, (as the beat of a drum) the buyers rush at once into the yard where the slaves are confined, and make choice of that parcel they like best. The noise and clamour with which this is attended and the eagerness visible in the countenances of the buyers serve not a little to increase the apprehensions of the terrified Africans, who may well be supposed to consider them as the ministers of that destruction to which they think themselves devoted. In this manner, without scruple, are relations and friends separated, most of them never to see each other again. I remember in the vessel in which I was brought over, in the men's apartment there were several brothers who, in the sale, were sold in different lots; and it was very moving on this occasion to see and hear their cries at parting. O, ye nominal Christians! might not an African ask you, Learned you this from your God who says unto you, Do unto all men as you would men should do unto you?

■ Discussion Questions

1. What are Equiano's impressions of the white men on the ship and their treatment of the slaves?
2. How does this treatment reflect the slave traders' primary concerns?
3. What message do you think Equiano sought to convey to his readers?
4. To whom do you think Equiano's book especially appealed?

45. Montesquieu, *Persian Letters: Letter 37*   (1721)

As Europe's economy expanded, so did its intellectual horizons with the birth of the Enlightenment in the 1690s. Charles-Louis de Secondat, baron of Montesquieu (1689–1755), was an especially important literary figure on this front. In 1721, he published Persian Letters, *in which he uses fictional characters to explore an array of topics with the critical, reasoning spirit characteristic of the period. Letter 37 points to one of his and other Enlightenment writers' main targets: Louis XIV and his absolutist state. Along with its criticism of the king's vanity, ostentation, and life at court, the letter implicitly passes even more serious judgment on the aging ruler in noting his esteem for "oriental policies." Montesquieu condemns these same policies elsewhere in the letters as inhumane and unjust.*

Charles-Louis de Secondat, baron of Montesquieu, *Persian Letters*, vol. I, trans. John Davidson (London: Privately printed, 1892), 85–86.

USBEK TO IBBEN, AT SMYRNA

The King of France is old.[1] We have no examples in our histories of such a long reign as his. It is said that he possesses in a very high degree the faculty of making himself obeyed: he governs with equal ability his family, his court, and his kingdom: he has often been heard to say, that, of all existing governments, that of the Turks, or that of our august Sultan, pleased him best: such is his high opinion of Oriental statecraft.[2]

I have studied his character, and I have found certain contradictions which I cannot reconcile. For example, he has a minister who is only eighteen years old,[3] and a mistress who is fourscore;[4] he loves his religion, and yet he cannot abide those who assert that it ought to be strictly observed;[5] although he flies from the noise of cities, and is inclined to be reticent, from morning till night he is engaged in getting himself talked about; he is fond of trophies and victories, but he has as great a dread of seeing a good general at the head of his own troops, as at the head of an army of his enemies. It has never I believe happened to anyone but himself, to be burdened with more wealth than even a prince could hope for, and yet at the same time steeped in such poverty as a private person could ill brook.

He delights to reward those who serve him; but he pays as liberally the assiduous indolence of his courtiers, as the labours in the field of his captains; often the man who undresses him, or who hands him his serviette at table, is preferred before him who has taken cities and gained battles; he does not believe that the greatness of a monarch is compatible with restriction in the distribution of favours; and, without examining into the merit of a man, he will heap benefits upon him, believing that his selection makes the recipient worthy; accordingly, he has been known to bestow a small pension upon a man who had run off two leagues from the enemy, and a good government on another who had gone four.

Above all, he is magnificent in his buildings; there are more statues in his palace gardens[6] than there are citizens in a large town. His bodyguard is as strong as that of the prince before whom all the thrones of the earth tremble;[7] his armies are as numerous, his resources as great, and his finances as inexhaustible.

Paris, the 7th of the moon of Maharram, 1713.

■ Discussion Questions

1. What contradictions does Usbek see in Louis's character, and what do they reveal about his method of rule?
2. In what ways does this letter reflect Montesquieu's general interest in the foundation of good government?
3. Having read this letter, why do you think that scholars regard Montesquieu as a herald of the Enlightenment?

---

[1] Louis XIV. was then seventy-five years old, and had reigned for seventy. [All notes are Davidson's.]

[2] When Louis XIV. was in his sixteenth year, some courtiers discussed in his presence the absolute power of the Sultans, who dispose as they like of the goods and the lives of their subjects. "That is something like being a king," said the young monarch. Marshal d'Estrées, alarmed at the tendency revealed in that remark, rejoined, "But, sire, several of these emperors have been strangled even in my time."

[3] Barbezieux, son of Louvois, Louis's youngest minister, held office at twenty-three, not eighteen; and he was dead in 1713.

[4] Madame de Maintenon.   [5] The Jansenists.

[6] At Versailles.   [7] The shah of Persia.

46. Mary Astell, *Reflections upon Marriage*   (1706)

Like Montesquieu, English author Mary Astell (1666–1731) helped to usher in the Enlightenment by surveying society with a critical eye. First published anonymously in 1700, Reflections upon Marriage *is one of her best-known books; it shows her keen interest in the institution of marriage, education, and relations between the sexes. Only the third edition (1706) divulged her gender, but still not her name. As this excerpt reveals, Astell held a dim view of women's inequality in general and of their submissive role in marriage in particular. She argues that one should abhor the use of arbitrary power within the state, and so, too, within the family. Among the book's principal goals was to present spinsterhood as a viable alternative to marriage. Perhaps not surprisingly, Astell herself never married.*

These Reflections being made in the Country, where the Book that occasion'd them came but late to Hand, the *Reader* is desir'd to excuse their Unseasonableness as well as other Faults; and to believe that they have no other Design than to Correct some Abuses, which are not the less because Power and Prescription seem to Authorize them. If any are so needlessly curious as to enquire from what Hand they come, they may please to know, that it is not good Manners to ask, since the Title-Page does not tell them: We are all of us sufficiently Vain, and without doubt the Celebrated Name of *Author,* which most are so fond of, had not been avoided but for very good Reasons: To name but one; *Who will care to pull upon themselves an Hornet's nest?* 'Tis a very great Fault to regard rather who it is that Speaks, than what is Spoken; and either to submit to Authority, when we should only yield to Reason; or if Reason press too hard, to think to ward it off by Personal Objections and Reflections. Bold Truths may pass while the Speaker is Incognito, but are not endur'd when he is known; few Minds being strong enough to bear what Contradicts their Principles and Practices without Recriminating when they can. And tho' to tell the Truth be the most Friendly Office, yet whosoever is so hardy as to venture at it, shall be counted an Enemy for so doing.

Thus far the old Advertisement, when the Reflections first appear'd, A.D. 1700.

But the *Reflector,* who hopes *Reflector* is not bad English, now Governor is happily of the feminine Gender, had as good or better have said nothing; For People by being forbid, are only excited to a more curious Enquiry. A certain Ingenuous Gentleman (as she is inform'd) had the Good-Nature to own these Reflections, so far as to affirm that he had the Original M.S. in his Closet, a Proof she is not able to produce;[1] and so to make himself responsible for all their Faults, for which she returns him all due Acknowledgment. However, the Generality being of Opinion, that a Man would have had more Prudence and Manners than to have Publish'd such unseasonable Truths, or to have betray'd the *Arcana Imperii* of his Sex, she humbly confesses, that the Contrivance and Execution of this Design, which is unfortunately accus'd of being so destructive to the government, of the Men I mean, is entirely her own. She neither advis'd with Friends, nor turn'd over Antient or Modern Authors, nor prudently submitted to the Correction of such as are, or such as *think* they are good Judges, but with an *English* Spirit and Genius, set out upon the Forlorn Hope, meaning no hurt to any body, nor designing any thing but the Publick Good, and to retrieve, if possible, the Native Liberty, the Rights and Privileges of the Subject.

---

[1]Alas, Mary Astell never revealed the identity of this "Ingenuous Gentleman." [All notes are Hill's.]

Bridget Hill, ed., *The First English Feminist:* Reflections upon Marriage *and Other Writings by Mary Astell* (New York: St. Martin's Press, 1986), 69–76.

Far be it from her to stir up Sedition of any sort, none can abhor it more; and she heartily wishes that our Masters wou'd pay their Civil and Ecclesiastical Governors the same Submission, which they themselves extract from their Domestic Subjects. Nor can she imagine how she any way undermines the Masculine Empire, or blows the Trumpet of Rebellion to the Moiety of Mankind. Is it by exhorting Women, not to expect to have their own Will in any thing, but to be entirely Submissive, when once they have made choice of a Lord and Master, tho' he happen not to be so Wise, so Kind, or even so Just a Governor as was expected? She did not indeed advise them to think his Folly Wisdom, nor his Brutality that Love and Worship he promised in his Matrimonial Oath, for this required a Flight of Wit and Sense much above her poor Ability, and proper only to Masculine Understandings. However she did not in any manner prompt them to Resist, or to Abdicate the Perjur'd Spouse, tho' the Laws of GOD and the Land make special Provision for it, in a case wherein, as is to be fear'd, few Men can truly plead Not Guilty.

Tis true, thro' Want of Learning, and of that Superior Genius which Men as Men lay claim to, she was ignorant of the *Natural Inferiority* of our Sex, which our Masters lay down as a Self-Evident and Fundamental Truth.[2] She saw nothing in the Reason of Things, to make this either a Principle or a Conclusion, but much to the contrary; it being Sedition at least, if not Treason to assert it in this Reign. For if by the Natural Superiority of their Sex, they mean that every Man is by Nature superior to every Woman, which is the obvious meaning, and that which must be stuck to if they would speak Sense, it wou'd be a Sin in *any* Woman to have Dominion over *any* Man, and the greatest Queen ought not to command but to obey her Footman, because no Municipal Laws can supersede or change the Law of Nature; so that if the dominion of the Men be such, the *Salique Law*, as unjust as *English Men* have ever thought it, ought to take place over all the Earth, and the most glorious Reigns in the *English, Danish, Castilian*, and other Annals, were wicked Violations of the Law of Nature!

If they mean that *some* Men are superior to *some* Women, this is no great Discovery; had they turn'd the Tables they might have seen that *some* Women are Superior to *some* Men. Or had they been pleased to remember their Oaths of Allegiance and Supremacy, they might have known that *One* Woman is superior to *All* the Men in these Nations, or else they have sworn to very little purpose. And it must not be suppos'd, that their Reason and Religion wou'd suffer them to take Oaths, contrary to the Law of Nature and Reason of things.

By all which it appears, that our Reflector's Ignorance is very pitiable, it may be her Misfortune but not her Crime, especially since she is willing to be better inform'd, and hopes she shall never be so obstinate as to shut her Eyes against the Light of Truth, which is not to be charg'd with Novelty, how late soever we may be bless'd with the Discovery. Nor can Error, be it as Ancient as it may, ever plead Prescription against Truth. And since the only way to remove all Doubts, to answer all Objections, and to give the Mind entire Satisfaction, is not by *Affirming*, but by *Proving*, so that every one may see with their *own* Eyes, and Judge according to the best of their *own* Understandings, She hopes it is no Presumption to insist on this Natural Right of Judging for her self, and the rather, because by quitting it, we give up all the Means of Rational Conviction. Allow us then as many Glasses as you please to help our Sight, and as many good Arguments as you can afford to Convince our Understandings: But don't exact of us we beseech you, to affirm that we see such things as are only the Discovery of Men who have quicker Senses; or that we understand and Know what we have by Hearsay only, for to be so excessively Complaisant, is neither to see nor to understand.

---

[2]Possibly a reference to William Nichols, D.D., *The Duty of Inferiours Towards their Superiours in Five Practical Discourses*, 1701, in which he argued that man possesses "a higher state of natural perfection and dignity, and thereupon puts in a just claim of superiority, which everything which is of more worth has a right to, over that which has less" (pp. 87–88).

That the Custom of the World has put Women, generally speaking, into a State of Subjection, is not deny'd; but the Right can no more be prov'd from the Fact, than the Predominancy of Vice can justifie it. A certain great Man has endeavour'd to prove by Reasons not contemptible, that in the Original State of things the Woman was the Superior, and that her Subjection to the Man is an Effect of the Fall, and the Punishment of her Sin. And that Ingenious Theorist Mr. *Whiston*[3] asserts, That before the Fall there was a greater equality between the two Sexes. However this be 'tis certainly no Arrogance in a Woman to conclude, that she was made for the Service of GOD, and that this is her End. Because GOD made all Things for Himself, and a Rational Mind is too noble a Being to be Made for the Sake and Service of any Creature. The Service she at any time becomes oblig'd to pay to a Man, is only a Business by the Bye. Just as it may be any Man's Business and Duty to keep Hogs; he was not Made for this, but if he hires himself out to such an Employment, he ought conscientiously to perform it. Nor can anything be concluded to the contrary from St. *Paul's* Argument, *I Cor. II.* For he argues only for Decency and Order, according to the present Custom and State of things. Taking his Words strictly and literally, they prove too much, in that *Praying and Prophecying in the Church* are allow'd the Women, provided they do it with their Head Cover'd, as well as the Men; and no inequality can be inferr'd from hence, their Reverence to the Sacred Oracles who engage them in such Disputes. And therefore the blame be theirs, who have unnecessarily introduc'd them in the present Subject, and who by saying that the *Reflections* were not agreeable to Scripture, oblige the Reflector to shew that those who affirm it must either mistake her Meaning, or the Sense of Holy Scripture, or both, if they think what they say, and do not find fault merely because they resolve to do so. For had she ever writ any thing contrary to those sacred Truths, she wou'd be the first in pronouncing its Condemnation.

But what says the Holy Scripture? It speaks of Women as in a State of Subjection, and so it does of the *Jews* and *Christians* when under the Dominion of the *Chaldeans* and *Romans*, requiring of the one as well as of the other a quiet submission to them under whose Power they liv'd. But will any one say that these had a *Natural Superiority* and Right to Dominion? that they had a superior Understanding, or any Pre-eminence, except what their greater Strength acquir'd? Or that the other were subjected to their Adversaries for any other Reason but the Punishment of their sins, and in order to their Reformation? Or for the Exercise of their Vertue, and because the Order of the World and the Good of Society requir'd it?

If Mankind had never sinn'd, Reason wou'd always have been obey'd, there wou'd have been no struggle for Dominion, and Brutal Power wou'd not have prevail'd. But in the laps'd State of Mankind, and now that Men will not be guided by their Reason but by their Appetites, and do not what they *ought* but what they *can*, the Reason, or that which stands for it, the Will and Pleasure of the Governor is to be the Reason of those who will not be guided by their own, and must take place for Order's sake, altho' it shou'd not be conformable to right Reason. Nor can there be any Society great or little, from Empires down to private Families, with a last Resort, to determine the Affairs of that Society by an irresistible Sentence. Now unless this Supremacy be fix'd somewhere, there will be a perpetual Contention about it, such is the love of Dominion, and let the Reason of things be what it may, those who have least Force, or Cunning to supply it, will have the Disadvantage. So that since Women are acknowledg'd to have least Bodily strength, their being commanded to obey is in pure kindness to them and for their Quiet and Security, as well as for the Exercise of their Vertue. But does it follow that Domestic Governors have more Sense than their Subjects, any more than that other Governors have? We do not find that any Man

---

[3]William Whiston (1667–1752), divine, mathematician, and Newtonian. Author of many works including *A New Theory of the Earth* (1696). He succeeded Newton as the Lucasian Professor and did much to popularize Newton's ideas. In 1710 he was deprived of his chair for casting doubt on the doctrine of the Trinity.

thinks the worse of his own Understanding because another has superior Power; or concludes himself less capable of a Post of Honour and Authority, because he is not Prefer'd to it. How much time wou'd lie on Men's hands, how empty wou'd the Places of Concourse be, and how silent most Companies, did Men forbear to Censure their Governors, that is in effect to think themselves Wiser. Indeed Government wou'd be much more desirable than it is, did it invest the Possessor with a superior Understanding as well as Power. And if mere Power gives a Right to Rule, there can be no such thing as Usurpation; but a Highway-Man so long as he has strength to force, has also a Right to require our Obedience.

Again, if Absolute Sovereignty be not necessary in a State, how comes it to be so in a family? or if in a Family why not in a State; since no Reason can be alledg'd for the one that will not hold more strongly for the other? If the Authority of the Husband so far as it extends, is sacred and inalienable, why not of the Prince? The Domestic Sovereign is without Dispute Elected, and the Stipulations and Contract are mutual, is it not then partial in Men to the last degree, to contend for, and practise that Arbitrary Dominion in their Families, which they abhor and exclaim against in the State? For if Arbitrary Power is evil in itself, and an improper Method of Governing Rational and Free Agents, it ought not to be Practis'd any where; Nor is it less, but rather more mischievous in Families than in Kingdoms, by how much 100000 Tyrants are worse than one. What tho' a Husband can't deprive a Wife of Life without being responsible to the Law, he may however do what is much more grievous to a generous Mind, render Life miserable, for which she has no Redress, scarce Pity which is afforded to every other Complainant. It being thought a Wife's Duty to suffer everything without Complaint. *If all Men are born free,* how is it that all Women are born slaves? as they must be if the being subjected to the *inconstant, uncertain, unknown, arbitrary Will of Men,* be the *perfect Condition of Slavery?* and if the Essence of Freedom consists, as our Masters say it does, in having a *standing Rule to live by*? And why is Slavery so much condemn'd and strove against in one Case, and so highly applauded, and held so necessary and so sacred in another?

■ Discussion Questions

1. According to Mary Astell, what is women's customary status in society, and why?
2. What evidence does Astell present to challenge this status?
3. What does the language Astell uses reveal about her style of thinking and basic intellectual beliefs?
4. Why do you think scholars characterize *Reflections upon Marriage* as a "feminist" work?

CHAPTER 15

The Promise of Enlightenment, 1740–1789

In these documents, we hear some of the voices of the Enlightenment, an intellectual and cultural movement in the eighteenth century that captured the minds of middle- and upper-class people across Europe and British North America. Enlightenment writers were united by their belief that reason provided the key to humanity's advancement as the basis of truth, liberty, and justice. They cultivated and spread their ideals through letters, published works, and personal exchanges, particularly at gatherings known as *salons,* which were organized by upper-class women. By midcentury, people as diverse as a French artisan and the king of Prussia began to echo the Enlightenment principle that progress depended on the destruction of all barriers to reason, including religious intolerance.

47. Marie-Thérèse Geoffrin and Monsieur d'Alembert, *The Salon of Madame Geoffrin* (1765)

Beginning as an intellectual movement against absolutism, the Enlightenment became a formidable force of change by the mid-eighteenth century. The role of salons was crucial in this regard. By bringing innovative intellectuals, writers, and artists together in private homes on a regular basis, salons provided an arena for the discussion and dissemination of Enlightenment ideas. Madame Marie-Thérèse Geoffrin (1699–1777) presided over the most influential salon in Paris at the time, as described in the memoirs of a beneficiary of her patronage, Jean d'Alembert (1717–1783). In addition to nurturing the intellectual scene in Paris, Madame Geoffrin also cultivated it abroad by corresponding with important European leaders, including King Stanislaw of Poland, to whom she wrote the following letter in 1765. Together, these two documents elucidate the life of a woman who was actively engaged in Enlightenment thinking.

[MONSIEUR D'ALEMBERT RECALLS MADAME GEOFFRIN'S SALON]

Much has been said respecting Madame Geoffrin's goodness, to what a point it was active, restless, obstinate. But it has not been added, and which reflects the greatest honour upon her, that, as she advanced in years, this habit constantly increased. For the misfortune of society, it too often happens that age and experience produce a directly contrary effect, even in very virtuous characters, if virtue be not in them a powerful sentiment indeed, and of no common stamp. The more disposed they have been at first to feel kindness towards their fellow creatures, the more,

---

Correspondance inédite du roi Stanislaw-Auguste Poniatowski et de Madame Geoffrin, ed. Charles de Nouy (Geneva: Satine, 1970; reprint of 1875 edition); trans. by Lynn Hunt as published in *Connecting with the Past,* 164–68.

finding daily their ingratitude, do they repent of having served them, and even consider it almost as a reproach to themselves to have loved them. Madame Geoffrin had learnt, from a more reflected study of mankind, from taking a view of them more *enlightened* by reason and justice, that they are more weak and vain than wicked; that we ought to compassionate their weakness, and bear with their vanity, that they may bear with ours. . . .

The passion of *giving*, which was an absolute necessity to her, seemed born with her, and tormented her, if I may say so, even from her earliest years. While yet a child, if she saw from the window any poor creature asking alms, she would throw whatever she could lay her hands upon to them; her bread, her linen, and even her clothes. She was often scolded for this *intemperance* of charity, sometimes even punished, but nothing could alter the disposition, she would do the same the very next day. . . .

Always occupied with those whom she loved, always anxious about them, she even anticipated every thing which might interrupt their happiness. A young man,[1] for whom she interested herself very much, who had till that moment been wholly absorbed in his studies, was suddenly seized with an unfortunate passion, which rendered study, and even life itself insupportable to him. She succeeded in curing him. Some time after she observed that the same young man, mentioned to her, with great interest, an amiable woman with whom he had recently become acquainted. Madame Geoffrin, who knew the lady, went to her. "I am come," she said, "to intreat a favour of you. Do not evince too much friendship for **** or too much desire to see him, he will be soon in love with you, he will be unhappy, and I shall be no less so to see him suffer; nay, you yourself will be a sufferer, from consciousness, of the sufferings you occasion him." This woman, who was truly amiable, promised what Madame Geoffrin desired, and kept her word.

As she had always among the circle of her society persons of the highest rank and birth, as she appeared even to seek an acquaintance with them, it was supposed that this flattered her vanity. But here a very erroneous opinion was formed of her; she was in no respect the dupe of such prejudices, but she thought that by managing the humours of these people, she could render them useful to her friends. "You think," said she, to one of the latter, for whom she had a particular regard, "that it is for my own sake I frequent ministers and great people. Undeceive yourself,—it is for the sake of you, and those like you who may have occasion for them. . . ."

MADAME GEOFFRIN WRITES TO THE KING OF POLAND

I am sending to you a banker named Claudel who is returning to Warsaw. He will have with him a printed memoir on a new kind of mill. The more I have learned about it, the more I see that this machine is very well-known. Your Majesty is best advised to invite a miller to come from France; he will know how to set it up and show how to use it, and use of it can spread from there.

Prince Sulkowski [a Polish nobleman] met Mr. Hennin at my salon. Mr. Hennin had been for a long time in Warsaw, and they talked together about Poland. I see with pain that it has a very bad government [Stanislaw was elected king only in 1764]; it seems almost impossible to make it better. . . .

I sent you the catalogue of the diamonds of Madame de Pompadour [King Louis XV's mistress had died recently and her diamonds were auctioned off]. . . .

Do not forget, my dear son, to send the memoir on commerce to Mr. Riancourt when he returns. . . .

I cannot report any news yet on your project for paintings; I am very sad about the death of poor Carle Vanloo [a leading French painter who died in July 1765]. It was a horrible loss for the arts.

---

[1]This young man was Monsieur d'Alembert himself.

■ Discussion Questions

1. Given these documents, how would you describe Madame Geoffrin's personality? In what ways was she "enlightened"?
2. What impressions do the documents give of her salon and how it functioned?
3. What does Madame Geoffrin's letter to the king of Poland suggest about the range of her interests? How was this typical of Enlightenment thinkers?

48. Jacques-Louis Ménétra, *Journal of My Life* (1764–1802)

The philosophes *directed their message to the educated elite, but Jacques-Louis Ménétra's* Journal of My Life *suggests that some people from the lower classes heard it, too. Born in Paris in 1738, Ménétra learned to read and write in local parish schools. Following his father's example, he became a master glazier. He began the* Journal *in 1764 and organized it principally around his recollections of his journeyman's "tour de France" from 1757 to 1764. Here he reveals not only his quick wit and sense of adventure but also his affinity for the intellectual spirit of criticism that characterized the Enlightenment. Alongside the tales of his amusements, Ménétra commented on many of the fundamental issues of the day, including the question of religious tolerance. The excerpt is printed as it was originally written, without punctuation.*

I went to Paris to see Denongrais   Madame la Police had been interfering with business   she made up her mind to sell her property and to retire with her cuckold of a husband to her native village for she'd put by quite a bit in the course of her work   I was all for it   She said to me I see clearly from what you've just said that you never loved me   She was right   for never had a woman touched my heart except for sensual pleasure and nothing else   I promised her to come say my farewells and they've yet to be said

Since it was the good season we went to Champigny and went with some friends of mine to what are called *guinguettes* [open-air cafés with music and dancing—Trans.]   Sundays and holidays we went to dance in front of the castle and other days usually with the people from the *guinguette* we played tennis or went visiting the local festivals   One holiday in a village one league from Montigny people were playing tennis on the square when Du Tillet showed up accompanied by the lord the magistrate or sheriff and the priest   I heard somebody say   That's the Parisian over there   I wondered what this was all about   It's because they know you're good at tennis said my friend   they're going to propose a match   In fact six young men came and politely gave each of us a racket   My friend said no since he didn't know how to play but he said   But as for my friend he'll give you a good show   I declined   They insisted   the lord the sheriff and the priest joined in   I played   applause   hands were heard to clap   They took us to the castle (and) gave us refreshment

I was greatly applauded   I promised again that the fellows from Montigny and I would be waiting for them next Sunday   People came from all around   I was all over the court and we had a good time   we won and whatever else they were well entertained   My friend went all out because M Trudaine had wanted to see me play and when I passed in front of him he and the people around him said to me Courage   So I answered that that was one thing I wasn't lacking

Jacques-Louis Ménétra, *Journal of My Life*, intro. Daniel Roche, trans. Arthur Goldhammer (New York: Columbia University Press, 1986), 129–30.

One day I followed the game warden   Since I had no rifle I let him run all over the fields and went to a village where I had seen the curate pay his respects to M Trudaine   who recognized me   and said I was pretty nimble at tennis and took me to his presbytery for a drink

After some idle talk we finally got onto the subject of religion   We talked about the mysteries of the sacraments. . . . I spoke passionately about the sufferings that had been inflicted on men who worshipped the same God except for a few matters of opinion   And (I said that) the Roman religion should be tolerant if it followed the maxims of its lawgiver   that because of its mysteries it was absurd and that all mysteries were in my opinion nothing but lies   And that so long as they sold indulgences and gave remission for sins in exchange for money   fear of hell which was like purgatory just an invention of the first impostors   that Jesus had never spoken of purgatory   And that all those sacraments were nothing but pure inventions to make money and impress the vulgar   And that he himself who was a very intelligent man was not capable of making his God   chewing him and then swallowing him   That we mistreated those peoples who did not share our belief (and who) according to the Church should have been damned because all the priests went around saying   Outside the Church there is no salvation   And that we accused those who worship idols of being idolators when we prostrate ourselves before statues   We even worship a piece of dough which we eat in the firm belief that it is God   And those idolators only worship all those things to keep from being hurt by them and other things in the hope of getting some good out of them while we on the other hand we were real man-eaters   After praying to him and worshipping him in order to satisfy him we've got to eat him too

He answered me with objections as many others had answered me   His one and only response was to say to me   All these mysteries must be believed because the Church believes them   he said to me   My friend you are enlightened   It is necessary that for the sake of government nations live always in ignorance and credulity   I answered him So be it. . . .

■ Discussion Questions

1. Why is Ménétra so critical of the Catholic church?
2. How do his criticisms echo those of the great Enlightenment thinkers?
3. What does the priest mean when he describes Ménétra as enlightened?
4. How would you characterize Ménétra's style of writing?

49. Frederick II, *Political Testament* (1752)

The Enlightenment's triumph is perhaps best reflected in the politics of the second half of the eighteenth century. Rather than working to suppress the philosophes' *calls for change, rulers across continental Europe now embraced them as a means of enhancing their power and prestige. They did so at their own discretion, however, and often with an iron hand, as the case of Frederick II of Prussia (r. 1740–1786) vividly reveals. A devotee of the Enlightenment as well as an exemplary soldier and statesman, Frederick transformed Prussia into a leading European state during his reign. In his* Political Testament *of 1752, he outlines his political philosophy, which blended Enlightenment ideals with an uncompromising view of his own power.*

George L. Mosse, Rondo E. Cameron, Henry Bertram Hill, and Michael B. Petrovich, eds., *Europe in Review* (Chicago: Rand McNally and Company, 1957), 111–12.

One must attempt, above all, to know the special genius of the people which one wants to govern in order to know if one must treat them leniently or severely, if they are inclined to revolt . . . to intrigue. . . .

[The Prussian nobility] has sacrificed its life and goods for the service of the state, its loyalty and merit have earned it the protection of all its rulers, and it is one of the duties [of the ruler] to aid those [noble] families which have become impoverished in order to keep them in possession of their lands: for they are to be regarded as the pedestals and the pillars of the state. In such a state no factions or rebellions need be feared . . . it is one goal of the policy of this state to preserve the nobility.

A well conducted government must have an underlying concept so well integrated that it could be likened to a system of philosophy. All actions taken must be well reasoned, and all financial, political and military matters must flow towards one goal: which is the strengthening of the state and the furthering of its power. However, such a system can flow but from a single brain, and this must be that of the sovereign. Laziness, hedonism and imbecility, these are the causes which restrain princes in working at the noble task of bringing happiness to their subjects . . . a sovereign is not elevated to his high position, supreme power has not been confined to him in order that he may live in lazy luxury, enriching himself by the labor of the people, being happy while everyone else suffers. The sovereign is the first servant of the state. He is well paid in order that he may sustain the dignity of his office, but one demands that he work efficiently for the good of the state, and that he, at the very least, pay personal attention to the most important problems. . . .

You can see, without doubt, how important it is that the King of Prussia govern personally. Just as it would have been impossible for Newton to arrive at his system of attractions if he had worked in harness with Leibnitz and Descartes, so a system of politics cannot be arrived at and continued if it has not sprung from a single brain. . . . All parts of the government are inexorably linked with each other. Finance, politics and military affairs are inseparable; it does not suffice that one be well administered; they must all be . . . a Prince who governs personally, who has formed his [own] political system, will not be handicapped when occasions arise where he has to act swiftly: for he can guide all matters towards the end which he has set for himself. . . .

Catholics, Lutherans, Reformed, Jews and other Christian sects live in this state, and live together in peace: if the sovereign, actuated by a mistaken zeal, declares himself for one religion or another, parties will spring up, heated disputes ensue, little by little persecutions will commence and, in the end, the religion persecuted will leave the fatherland and millions of subjects will enrich our neighbors by their skill and industry.

It is of no concern in politics whether the ruler has a religion or whether he has none. All religions, if one examines them, are founded on superstitious systems, more or less absurd. It is impossible for a man of good sense, who dissects their contents, not to see their error; but these prejudices, these errors and mysteries were made for men, and one must know enough to respect the public and not to outrage its faith, whatever religion be involved.

▪ Discussion Questions

1. Given this excerpt, in what ways does the term *enlightened despot* apply to Frederick II? How is he enlightened? How is he despotic?
2. What reasons does Frederick advance in favor of religious tolerance?
3. According to Frederick, what should the one goal of government be?

CHAPTER 16

The French Revolution and Napoleon, 1789–1815

When the Estates General convened at Versailles in May 1789, no one could have fore-seen what lay ahead: ten years of upheaval that established the model of modern revo-lution and set the course of modern politics. At each stage—from the politically charged months preceding the convocation of the Estates General to the formation of a repub-lic and a government of terror designed to destroy enemies of the Revolution from both within and without—the revolutionaries remained committed to the Enlightenment principle of using reason to reshape society and government (Document 50). Nonethe-less, they were not always in control of events either in France or beyond, as peasants, working-class city folk, and even slaves from the French colony of St. Domingue (modern-day Haiti) rose up with their own demands, taking the Revolution in ever more radical directions (Document 51).

Napoleon Bonaparte (1769–1821) ended the French Revolution even while main-taining some of its most important innovations. He transformed France from a dem-ocratically elected republic to an empire with a new aristocracy based on military ser-vice. Although he tolerated no opposition at home, he prided himself on bringing French-style liberation to peoples elsewhere. At the same time, he continued the revo-lutionary policy of conquest and annexation to forge the biggest empire Europe had experienced since Roman times. The third document describes a key stage in this trans-formation, Napoleon's invasion of Egypt in 1798. Although the campaign ultimately failed, it foreshadowed Napoleon's subsequent efforts to colonize large parts of Europe along similar lines.

50. National Assembly, *The Declaration of the Rights of Man and of the Citizen* (1789)

Promulgated by the fledgling National Assembly in August 1789, the Declaration gave the Revolu-tion a clear sense of purpose and direction after the dizzying series of events of that summer. In it, the delegates set forth the guiding principles of the new government, echoing many of the ideals of influential eighteenth-century thinkers. The document also marked the definitive end of the old regime by presenting the protection of individual rights, not royal prerogative, as the cornerstone of politi-cal authority. The deputies did not regard the Declaration as an end in and of itself, however, but

James Harvey Robinson, *Readings in European History,* vol. 2 (Boston: Ginn and Company, 1906), 409–11.

rather as a preliminary step toward their primary goal: to write a constitution that would transform France into an enlightened constitutional monarchy. This goal was met with the Constitution of 1791, to which the Declaration was attached.

The representatives of the French people, organized as a National Assembly, believing that the ignorance, neglect, or contempt of the rights of man are the sole cause of public calamities and of the corruption of governments, have determined to set forth in a solemn declaration the natural, inalienable, and sacred rights of man, in order that this declaration, being constantly before all the members of the social body, shall remind them continually of their rights and duties; in order that the acts of the legislative power, as well as those of the executive power, may be compared at any moment with the objects and purposes of all political institutions and may thus be more respected; and, lastly, in order that the grievances of the citizens, based hereafter upon simple and incontestable principles, shall tend to the maintenance of the constitution and redound to the happiness of all. Therefore the National Assembly recognizes and proclaims, in the presence and under the auspices of the Supreme Being, the following rights of man and of the citizen:

Article 1. Men are born and remain free and equal in rights. Social distinctions may be founded only upon the general good.

2. The aim of all political association is the preservation of the natural and imprescriptible rights of man. These rights are liberty, property, security, and resistance to oppression.

3. The principle of all sovereignty resides essentially in the nation. No body nor individual may exercise any authority which does not proceed directly from the nation.

4. Liberty consists in the freedom to do everything which injures no one else; hence the exercise of the natural rights of each man has no limits except those which assure to the other members of the society the enjoyment of the same rights. These limits can only be determined by law.

5. Law can only prohibit such actions as are hurtful to society. Nothing may be prevented which is not forbidden by law, and no one may be forced to do anything not provided for by law.

6. Law is the expression of the general will. Every citizen has a right to participate personally, or through his representative, in its formation. It must be the same for all, whether it protects or punishes. All citizens, being equal in the eyes of the law, are equally eligible to all dignities and to all public positions and occupations, according to their abilities, and without distinction except that of their virtues and talents.

7. No person shall be accused, arrested, or imprisoned except in the cases and according to the forms prescribed by law. Any one soliciting, transmitting, executing, or causing to be executed, any arbitrary order, shall be punished. But any citizen summoned or arrested in virtue of the law shall submit without delay, as resistance constitutes an offense.

8. The law shall provide for such punishments only as are strictly and obviously necessary, and no one shall suffer punishment except it be legally inflicted in virtue of a law passed and promulgated before the commission of the offense.

9. As all persons are held innocent until they shall have been declared guilty, if arrest shall be deemed indispensable, all harshness not essential to the securing of the prisoner's person shall be severely repressed by law.

10. No one shall be disquieted on account of his opinions, including his religious views, provided their manifestation does not disturb the public order established by law.

11. The free communication of ideas and opinions is one of the most precious of the rights of man. Every citizen may, accordingly, speak, write, and print with freedom, but shall be responsible for such abuses of this freedom as shall be defined by law.

12. The security of the rights of man and of the citizen requires public military forces. These forces are, therefore, established for the good of all and not for the personal advantage of those to whom they shall be intrusted.

13. A common contribution is essential for the maintenance of the public forces and for the cost of administration. This should be equitably distributed among all the citizens in proportion to their means.

14. All the citizens have a right to decide, either personally or by their representatives, as to the necessity of the public contribution; to grant this freely; to know to what uses it is put; and to fix the proportion, the mode of assessment and of collection and the duration of the taxes.

15. Society has the right to require of every public agent an account of his administration.

16. A society in which the observance of the law is not assured, nor the separation of powers defined, has no constitution at all.

17. Since property is an inviolable and sacred right, no one shall be deprived thereof except where public necessity, legally determined, shall clearly demand it, and then only on condition that the owner shall have been previously and equitably indemnified.

■ Discussion Questions

1. In delineating the rights of the individual, how did the National Assembly respond to Enlightenment writers' calls for reforms?
2. According to the Declaration, what are the fundamental roles of government and the individual citizen?
3. How does the Declaration define political sovereignty, and how is this definition related to the deputies' collective sense of identity and purpose?

51. François-Dominique Toussaint L'Ouverture, *Revolution in the Colonies* (1794–1795)

In declaring that all men are born free and equal, the National Convention unleashed a debate with momentous consequences. Did blacks fall within the category of "all men"? This question proved explosive in the French colony of St. Domingue. News of the Revolution's progress traveled quickly to the island, prompting slaves in the north to launch an insurrection against their white masters in August 1791. Their revolt sparked more than a decade of war. The former slave François Dominique Toussaint L'Ouverture (1743–1803) became the most prominent black leader of the revolution. Allied first in 1793 with Spain, which controlled much of the island, he and his troops switched sides to join the French the following year, for reasons he explained in the letter excerpted here to the chief French commander in northern St. Domingue. The letter is followed by extracts from two proclamations made by Toussaint to local dissenters in 1795 that further illuminate his revolutionary principles and actions.

TOUSSAINT L'OUVERTURE TO GENERAL ETIENNE LAVEAUX, MAY 1794

It is very true, general, that I was led into error by the enemies of the Republic [of France] and of mankind, but who is the man who can hope to avoid all the traps of the wicked? Indeed, I fell

Gérard M. Laurent, *Toussaint L'Ouverture à travers sa correspondance (1794–1798)* (Madrid, 1953), 103–04, 169–72. Translated by Katharine J. Lualdi.

into their nets, but not without reason . . . the Spanish offered me their protection, and freedom for all those who fought for the kings' cause;[1] and having always fought to possess this same freedom, I clung to their offer, seeing myself abandoned by the French, my brothers.[2] But an experience a little later opened my eyes to these treacherous protectors; and being aware of their deceit and villainy, I saw clearly that their intentions were to make us cut each other's throats in order to reduce our numbers and oppress those remaining in chains and cause them to sink back into their former slavery. No, they never would reach their base goal! And in our turn we will avenge ourselves of these wretched beings in every respect. Thus let us unite forever and, forgetting the past, henceforth concern ourselves only with crushing our enemies. . . .

TOUSSAINT L'OUVERTURE TO THE FRENCH CITIZENS ENCAMPED IN MOTET, MARCH 1795

Frenchmen, the alarm rings, wake up, return from the deadly errors where you have been thrown; the opportunity for it is offered to you for the last time. The chains of the despot of England were not made for you; recover your dignity as French citizens, recover your national character. The heroic trumpet must have instructed you about the great feats of your country, which is cloaked in glory before the eyes of the universe. I was sent by Laveaux . . . to bring you words of peace. If, cured by time and experience, you return under the benevolent laws of the Republic, say the word, and nothing will be neglected to spare you from the deplorable fate which awaits you if you persist in your dreadful rebellion.

I exhort you to return to the nation. . . . Like all republicans, I am motivated by an ardent desire to find only brothers and friends wherever I have the troops under my command march. Humanity is one of the sacred duties that will make us surpass all other peoples. It is also among our principles to rescue our brothers from their error and to hold out a helping hand to them. . . .

After this outpouring of my heart for you, I can call upon you, in the name of the Republic, to join me within an hour. Once this hour is up, I will deploy force against you and I will conquer you.

TOUSSAINT L'OUVERTURE TO THE PEOPLE OF VERRETTES, MARCH 1795

Brothers and sisters,

The moment has arrived when the thick veil that was blocking the light must fall. One must no longer forget the decrees of the National Convention. Its principles, its love of liberty, are unchanging, and henceforth, there can be no hope of this sacred edifice crumbling. . . .

I have learned with infinite joy about the return of some citizens of Verrettes to the bosom of the Republic; they will find the happiness that eluded them at the instigation of the soldiers of tyranny and royalty.

---

[1]The royalist governments of both Britain and Spain participated in the war. Spain already controlled the eastern half of the island of Hispaniola, and jumped at the opportunity to expand its holdings once the slave revolts had begun. To this end, they joined forces with Britain, which had been at war with France since February 1793, to destroy France's hold on St. Domingue.

[2]In 1793, Toussaint wrote to Laveaux, offering to join the French in exchange for a full amnesty for black rebels and freedom for all slaves. Laveaux rejected the offer, and Toussaint continued fighting for royalist Spain. By spring 1794, the situation had changed radically. Not only had British and Spanish forces gained control of most of the island, making Laveaux desperate for Toussaint's support, but the National Convention had also sanctioned the abolition of slavery.

. . . To give them help, console them regarding past faults and prompt them to abjure the errors in which they were insidiously nourished, is an absolute duty and the sacred maxim of the French for all republicans.

This is why not only by virtue of the powers entrusted by General Laveaux, but also animated by the feelings of humanity and brotherhood with which I am filled, I must remind the citizens of Verrettes of their errors; but as much as they are detrimental to the interests of the Republic, as much I feel that their return, if sincere, can be advantageous to the growth of our success. . . .

The French are brothers; the English, the Spanish, and royalists are ferocious beasts who caress them only in order to suck their blood, that of their wives, and of their children at leisure, until satiation.

Citizens, I am not searching here to make a show of your faults. . . . You have returned to the bosom of the Republic, and well! Since then the past is forgotten; your duty is now to unite all of your physical and moral means to revive your parish and let the principles of sacred liberty germinate.

■ Discussion Questions

1. What links can you find between the ideals of the French Revolution and those of Toussaint as expressed in the preceding documents?
2. What was Toussaint's ultimate goal as a leader in the Revolution, whether fighting for the Spanish or the French?
3. What do these documents reveal about his strategies for achieving this goal?

52. Abd al-Rahman al-Jabartî, *Napoleon in Egypt* (1798)

While the Directory government that came to power in 1795 worked to establish order in France, Napoleon continued the Revolution's policy of conquest and annexation abroad, first in Italy (1796–1797) and then in Egypt (1798–1801). At the time, Egypt was France's most important trading partner outside of the Caribbean; it was also a key base for challenging British interests in Asia. Egyptian historian Abd al-Rahman al-Jabartî's (1753–c. 1826) account of the first six months of the French invasion allows us to see Napoleon from a native's perspective. In this excerpt, Jabartî views Napoleon's actions skeptically through the lens of his own culture. His skepticism proved well founded, for Napoleon failed to colonize Egypt. Even so, he retained his reputation as a great military leader, preparing the way for his mastery of France and much of Europe through a similar blend of authoritarian policies and revolutionary principles as that used in Egypt.

On Monday news arrived that the French had reached Damanhūr and Rosetta, bringing about the flight of their inhabitants to Fuwwa and its surroundings. Contained in this news was mention of the French sending notices throughout the country demanding impost for the upkeep of the military. Furthermore they printed a large proclamation in Arabic, calling on the people to obey them and to raise their "Bandiera." In this proclamation were inducements, warnings, all

Shmuel Moreh, trans. *Napoleon in Egypt: al-Jabartî's Chronicle of the French Occupation, 1798* (Princeton: Markus Wiener, 1993), 24–33.

manner of wiliness and stipulations. Some copies were sent from the provinces to Cairo and its text is:

In the name of God, the Merciful, the Compassionate. There is no god but God. He has no son, nor has He an associate in His Dominion.

On behalf of the French Republic which is based upon the foundation of liberty and equality, General Bonaparte, Commander-in-Chief of the French armies makes known to all the Egyptian people that for a long time the Sanjaqs[1] who lorded it over Egypt have treated the French community basely and contemptuously and have persecuted its merchants with all manner of extortion and violence. Therefore the hour of punishment has now come.

Unfortunately this group of Mamlūks,[2] imported from the mountains of Circassia and Georgia have acted corruptly for ages in the fairest land that is to be found upon the face of the globe. However, the Lord of the Universe, the Almighty, has decreed the end of their power.

O ye Egyptians, they may say to you that I have not made an expedition hither for any other object than that of abolishing your religion; but this is a pure falsehood and you must not give credit to it, but tell the slanderers that I have not come to you except for the purpose of restoring your rights from the hands of the oppressors and that I more than the Mamlūks, serve God. . . .

And tell them also that all people are equal in the eyes of God and the only circumstances which distinguish one from the other are reason, virtue, and knowledge. But amongst the Mamlūks, what is there of reason, virtue, and knowledge, which would distinguish them from others and qualify them alone to possess everything which sweetens life in this world? Wherever fertile land is found it is appropriated to the Mamlūks; and the handsomest female slaves, and the best horses, and the most desirable dwelling-places, all these belong to them exclusively. If the land of Egypt is a fief of the Mamlūks, let them then produce the title-deed, which God conferred upon them. But the Lord of the Universe is compassionate and equitable toward mankind, and with the help of the Exalted, from this day forward no Egyptian shall be excluded from admission to eminent positions nor from acquiring high ranks, therefore the intelligent and virtuous and learned ('ulamā') amongst them, will regulate their affairs, and thus the state of the whole population will be rightly adjusted. . . .

Blessing on blessing to the Egyptians who will act in concert with us, without any delay, for their condition shall be rightly adjusted, and their rank raised. Blessing also, upon those who will abide in their habitations, not siding with either of the two hostile parties, yet when they know us better, they will hasten to us with all their hearts. But woe upon woe to those who will unite with the Mamlūks and assist them in the war against us, for they will not find the way of escape, and no trace of them shall remain. . . .

Here is an explanation of the incoherent words and vulgar constructions which he put into this miserable letter.

His statement "In the name of God, the Merciful, the Compassionate. There is no god but God. He has no son, nor has He an associate in His Dominion." In mentioning these three sentences there is an indication that the French agree with the three religions, but at the same time they do not agree with them, not with any religion. They are consistent with the Muslims in stating the formula "In the name of God," in denying that He has a son or an associate. They dis-

---

[1]**Sanjaqs:** Provincial governors in the Ottoman Empire.
[2]**Mamlūks:** Descendants of medieval slave-soldiers who enjoyed considerable political power until the French invasion.

agree with the Muslims in not mentioning the two Articles of Faith, in rejecting the mission of Muhammad, and the legal words and deeds which are necessarily recognized by religion. They agree with the Christians in most of their words and deeds, but disagree with them by not mentioning the Trinity, and denying the mission and furthermore in rejecting their beliefs, killing the priests and destroying the churches. Then, their statement "On behalf of the French Republic, etc.," that is, this proclamation is sent from their Republic, that means their body politic, because they have no chief or sultan with whom they all agree, like others, whose function is to speak on their behalf. For when they rebelled against their sultan six years ago and killed him, the people agreed unanimously that there was not to be a single ruler but that their state, territories, laws, and administration of their affairs, should be in the hands of the intelligent and wise men among them. They appointed persons chosen by them and made them heads of the army, and below them generals and commanders of thousands, two hundreds, and tens, administrators and advisers, on condition that they were all to be equal and none superior to any other in view of the equality of creation and nature. They made this the foundation and basis of their system. This is the meaning of their statement "based upon the foundation of liberty and equality." . . . They follow this rule: great and small, high and low, male and female are all equal. Sometimes they break this rule according to their whims and inclinations or reasoning. Their women do not veil themselves and have no modesty; they do not care whether they uncover their private parts. Whenever a Frenchman has to perform an act of nature he does so wherever he happens to be, even in full view of people, and he goes away as he is, without washing his private parts after defecation. If he is a man of taste and refinement he wipes himself with whatever he finds, even with a paper with writing on it, otherwise he remains as he is. They have intercourse with any woman who pleases them and vice versa. Sometimes one of their women goes into a barber's shop, and invites him to shave her pubic hair. If he wishes he can take his fee in kind. It is their custom to shave both their moustaches and beard. Some of them leave the hair of their cheeks only. . . .

His saying *qad hattama* etc. (has decreed) shows that they are appointing themselves controllers of God's secrets, but there is no disgrace worse than disbelief. . . .

His statement *wa-qūlū li 'l-muftariyīn* (but tell the slanderers) is the plural of *muftari* (slanderer) which means liar, and how worthy of this description they are. The proof of that is his saying "I have not come to you except for the purpose of restoring your rights from the hands of the oppressors," which is the first lie he uttered and a falsehood which he invented. Then he proceeds to something even worse than that, may God cast him into perdition, with his words: "I more than the Mamlūks serve God. . . ." There is no doubt that this is a derangement of his mind, and an excess of foolishness. . . .

His saying [all people] are equal in the eyes of God the Almighty, this is a lie and stupidity. How can this be when God has made some superior to others as is testified by the dwellers in the Heavens and on the Earth? . . .

May God hurry misfortune and punishment upon them, may He strike their tongues with dumbness, may He scatter their hosts, and disperse them, confound their intelligence, and cause their breath to cease. He has the power to do that, and it is up to Him to answer.

■ Discussion Questions

1. What strategy did Napoleon use in his proclamation to garner the support of the Egyptian people?
2. What does this strategy suggest about his personal ambitions and method of rule?
3. Why is Jabartî critical of Napoleon's intentions as stated in his proclamation?
4. What do Jabartî's criticisms suggest about the differences between French and Egyptian culture?

CHAPTER 17

Industrialization and Social Ferment, 1815–1850

The nineteenth century was a time of momentous economic and social change as factories sprang up across much of Europe and railroad tracks crisscrossed the landscape. Although Britain initially led the way in industrial growth, continental Europe soon began to catch up. For the middle classes, industrialization opened the door to new riches, comforts, and prestige. By contrast, for the men, women, and children who labored in the new factories, it often meant a life of urban drudgery and extreme poverty. The first document here reveals the grueling regime of factory work, while the second and third illuminate the great political ideologies that industrialization fostered: liberalism and communism. The final document shows the cultural response to the changing European landscape, romanticism, which strove to strip away artifice and expose truth as embodied in nature and daily life.

53. *Factory Rules in Berlin* (1844)

Industrialization did not simply create new social classes, new jobs, and new problems; it also created new work habits regimented by the pace of machines and the time clock. It fell upon the factory owners and managers to instill these habits in their workforce to ensure efficient and consistent levels of production. This was no easy task, as most people, whether former peasants or skilled workers, were accustomed to controlling their own time. The list of rules distributed to the employees of the Foundry and Engineering Works of the Royal Overseas Trading Company in Berlin provides a telling example of one approach to this challenge. This document also illustrates the spread of industrialization eastward across continental Europe.

In every large works, and in the co-ordination of any large number of workmen, good order and harmony must be looked upon as the fundamentals of success, and therefore the following rules shall be strictly observed.

Every man employed in the concern named below shall receive a copy of these rules, so that no one can plead ignorance. Its acceptance shall be deemed to mean consent to submit to its regulations.

(1) The normal working day begins at all seasons at 6 a.m. precisely and ends, after the usual break of half an hour for breakfast, a hour for dinner and half an hour for tea, at 7 p.m., and it shall be strictly observed.

Sidney Pollard and C. Holmes, *Documents of European Economic History,* vol. I, *The Process of Industrialization, 1750–1870* (New York: St. Martin's Press, 1968), 534–36.

Five minutes before the beginning of the stated hours of work until their actual commencement, a bell shall ring and indicate that every worker employed in the concern has to proceed to his place of work, in order to start as soon as the bell stops.

The doorkeeper shall lock the door punctually at 6 a.m., 8.30 a.m., 1 p.m. and 4.30 p.m.

Workers arriving 2 minutes late shall lose half an hour's wages; whoever is more than 2 minutes late may not start work until after the next break, or at least shall lose his wages until then. Any disputes about the correct time shall be settled by the clock mounted above the gatekeeper's lodge.

These rules are valid both for time- and for piece-workers, and in cases of breaches of these rules, workmen shall be fined in proportion to their earnings. The deductions from the wage shall be entered in the wage-book of the gatekeeper whose duty they are; they shall be unconditionally accepted as it will not be possible to enter into any discussions about them.

(2) When the bell is rung to denote the end of the working day, every workman, both on piece- and on day-wage, shall leave his workshop and the yard, but is not allowed to make preparations for his departure before the bell rings. Every breach of this rule shall lead to a fine of five silver groschen to the sick fund. Only those who have obtained special permission by the overseer may stay on in the workshop in order to work.—If a workman has worked beyond the closing bell, he must give his name to the gatekeeper on leaving, on pain of losing his payment for the overtime.

(3) No workman, whether employed by time or piece, may leave before the end of the working day, without having first received permission from the overseer and having given his name to the gatekeeper. Omission of these two actions shall lead to a fine of ten silver groschen payable to the sick fund.

(4) Repeated irregular arrival at work shall lead to dismissal. This shall also apply to those who are found idling by an official or overseer, and refuse to obey their order to resume work.

(5) Entry to the firm's property by any but the designated gateway, and exit by any prohibited route, e.g. by climbing fences or walls, or by crossing the Spree, shall be punished by a fine of fifteen silver groschen to the sick fund for the first offences, and dismissal for the second.

(6) No worker may leave his place of work otherwise than for reasons connected with his work.

(7) All conversation with fellow-workers is prohibited; if any worker requires information about his work, he must turn to the overseer, or to the particular fellow-worker designated for the purpose.

(8) Smoking in the workshops or in the yard is prohibited during working hours; anyone caught smoking shall be fined five silver groschen for the sick fund for every such offence.

(9) Every worker is responsible for cleaning up his space in the workshop, and if in doubt, he is to turn to his overseer.—All tools must always be kept in good condition, and must be cleaned after use. This applies particularly to the turner, regarding his lathe.

(10) Natural functions must be performed at the appropriate places, and whoever is found soiling walls, fences, squares, etc., and similarly, whoever is found washing his face and hands in the workshop and not in the places assigned for the purpose, shall be fined five silver groschen for the sick fund.

(11) On completion of his piece of work, every workman must hand it over at once to his foreman or superior, in order to receive a fresh piece of work. Pattern makers must on no account hand over their patterns to the foundry without express order of their supervisors. No workman may take over work from his fellow-workman without instruction to that effect by the foreman.

(12) It goes without saying that all overseers and officials of the firm shall be obeyed without question, and shall be treated with due deference. Disobedience will be punished by dismissal.

(13) Immediate dismissal shall also be the fate of anyone found drunk in any of the workshops.

(14) Untrue allegations against superiors or officials of the concern shall lead to stern reprimand, and may lead to dismissal. The same punishment shall be meted out to those who knowingly allow errors to slip through when supervising or stocktaking.

(15) Every workman is obliged to report to his superiors any acts of dishonesty or embezzlement on the part of his fellow workmen. If he omits to do so, and it is shown after subsequent discovery of a misdemeanour that he knew about it at the time, he shall be liable to be taken to court as an accessory after the fact and the wage due to him shall be retained as punishment. Conversely, anyone denouncing a theft in such a way as to allow conviction of the thief shall receive a reward of two Thaler, and, if necessary, his name shall be kept confidential.—Further, the gatekeeper and the watchman, as well as every official, are entitled to search the baskets, parcels, aprons etc. of the women and children who are taking dinners into the works, on their departure, as well as search any worker suspected of stealing any article whatever. . . .

(18) Advances shall be granted only to the older workers, and even to them only in exceptional circumstances. As long as he is working by the piece, the workman is entitled merely to his fixed weekly wage as subsistence pay; the extra earnings shall be paid out only on completion of the whole piece contract. If a workman leaves before his piece contract is completed, either of his own free will, or on being dismissed as punishment, or because of illness, the partly completed work shall be valued by the general manager with the help of two overseers, and he will be paid accordingly. There is no appeal against the decision of these experts.

(19) A free copy of these rules is handed to every workman, but whoever loses it and requires a new one, or cannot produce it on leaving, shall be fined 2½ silver groschen, payable to the sick fund.

■ **Discussion Questions**

1. As delineated here, what new modes of discipline did factory work require, and why?
2. What was the principal method used to encourage compliance to these rules?
3. Given this document, how would you describe a typical workday in this factory?

54. T. B. Macaulay, *Speech on Parliamentary Reform*   (1831)

Upon Napoleon's defeat in 1815, the allied powers worked to erase the imprint that the French Revolution and Napoleon's conquests had left on European society and politics. They faced many obstacles, however, including the new ideology of liberalism. Unlike their political rivals, liberals heralded individual rights and the need for broader political representation, two hallmarks of the French Revolution. Even so, they shared conservatives' fear of popular unrest. British politician Thomas B. Macaulay (1800–1859) sought to capitalize on this common ground in a speech he delivered to Parliament in support of a bill for electoral reform at the very moment when mass unrest gripped Europe. His words struck a chord, for the bill passed a year later, expanding the British electorate to more than 800,000. Although this represented a tiny fraction of the country's growing population, which reached more than 20 million by 1850, it marked a triumph over exclusive aristocratic politics and opened the door to yet more sweeping changes.

T. B. Macaulay, *Miscellanies*, vol. I (Boston: Houghton Mifflin, 1901), 1–19.

It is a circumstance, Sir, of happy augury for the motion before the House, that almost all those who have opposed it have declared themselves hostile on principle to parliamentary reform. . . . For what I feared was, not the opposition of those who are averse to all reform, but the disunion of reformers. I knew that, during three months, every reformer had been employed in conjecturing what the plan of the government would be. I knew that every reformer had imagined in his own mind a scheme. . . . I felt therefore great apprehension that one person would be dissatisfied with one part of the bill, that another person would be dissatisfied with another part, and that thus our whole strength would be wasted in internal dissensions. That apprehension is now at an end. I have seen with delight the perfect concord which prevails among all who deserve the name of reformers in this House. . . . I will not, Sir, at present express any opinion as to the details of the bill; but, having during the last twenty-four hours given the most diligent consideration to its general principles, I have no hesitation in pronouncing it a wise, noble, and comprehensive measure, skilfully framed for the healing of great distempers, for the securing at once of the public liberties and of the public repose, and for the reconciling and knitting together of all the orders of the state.

The honorable Baronet who has just sat down[1] has told us, that the Ministers have attempted to unite two inconsistent principles in one abortive measure. Those were his very words. He thinks, if I understand him rightly, that we ought either to leave the representative system such as it is, or to make it perfectly symmetrical. I think, Sir, that the Ministers would have acted unwisely if they had taken either course. Their principle is plain, rational, and consistent. It is this, to admit the middle class to a large and direct share in the representation, without any violent shock to the institutions of our country. . . . The government has, in my opinion, done all that was necessary for the removal of a great practical evil, and no more than was necessary.

I consider this, Sir, as a practical question. I rest my opinion on no general theory of government. I distrust all general theories of government. I will not positively say, that there is any form of polity which may not, in some conceivable circumstances, be the best possible. I believe that there are societies in which every man may safely be admitted to vote. Gentlemen may cheer, but such is my opinion. I say, Sir, that there are countries in which the condition of the laboring classes is such that they may safely be entrusted with the right of electing Members of the Legislature. If the laborers of England were in that state in which I, from my soul, wish to see them, if employment were always plentiful, wages always high, food always cheap, if a large family were considered not as an encumbrance but as a blessing, the principal objection to Universal Suffrage would, I think, be removed. Universal Suffrage exists in the United States without producing any very frightful consequences; and I do not believe that the people of those States, or of any part of the world, are in any good quality naturally superior to our own countrymen. But, unhappily, the laboring classes in England, and in all old countries, are occasionally in a state of great distress. Some of the causes of this distress are, I fear, beyond the control of the government. We know what effect distress produces, even on people more intelligent than the great body of the laboring classes can possibly be. . . . It is therefore no reflection on the poorer class of Englishmen, who are not, and who cannot in the nature of things be, highly educated, to say that distress produces on them its natural effects, those effects which it would produce on the Americans, or on any other people, that it blinds their judgment, that it inflames their passions, that it makes them prone to believe those who flatter them, and to distrust those who would serve them. For the sake, therefore, of the whole society, for the sake of the laboring classes themselves, I hold it to be clearly expedient that, in a country like this one, the right of suffrage should depend on a pecuniary qualification.

---

[1]Sir John Walsh.

But, Sir, every argument which would induce me to oppose Universal Suffrage induces me to support the plan which is now before us. I am opposed to Universal Suffrage, because I think that it would produce a destructive revolution. I support this plan, because I am sure that it is our best security against a revolution. . . . I do in my conscience believe that, unless the plan proposed, or some similar plan, be speedily adopted, great and terrible calamities will befall us. Entertaining this opinion, I think myself bound to state it, not as a threat, but as a reason. I support this bill because it will improve our institutions; but I support it also because it tends to preserve them. That we may exclude those whom it is necessary to exclude, we must admit those whom it may be safe to admit. At present we oppose the schemes of revolutionists with only one half, with only one quarter of our proper force. We say, and we say justly, that it is not by mere numbers, but by property and intelligence, that the nation ought to be governed. Yet, saying this, we exclude from all share in the government great masses of property and intelligence, great numbers of those who are most interested in preserving tranquility, and who know best how to preserve it. We do more. We drive over to the side of revolution those whom we shut out from power. Is this a time when the cause of law and order can spare one of its natural allies? . . .

If it be said that there is an evil in change as change, I answer that there is also an evil in discontent as discontent. This, indeed, is the strongest part of our case. It is said that the system works well. I deny it. I deny that a system works well, which the people regard with aversion. We may say here, that it is a good system and a perfect system. But if any man were to say so to any six hundred and fifty-eight respectable farmers or shopkeepers, chosen by lot in any part of England, he would be hooted down, and laughed to scorn. Are these the feelings with which any part of the government ought to be regarded? Above all, are these the feelings with which the popular branch of the legislature ought to be regarded? It is almost as essential to the utility of a House of Commons, that it should possess the confidence of the people, as that it should deserve that confidence. Unfortunately, that which is in theory the popular part of our government is in practice the unpopular part. Who wishes to dethrone the King? Who wishes to turn the Lords out of their House? Here and there a crazy radical, whom the boys in the street point at as he walks along. Who wishes to alter the constitution of this House? The whole people. It is natural that it should be so. . . .

Now, . . . if I were convinced that the great body of the middle class in England look with aversion on monarchy and aristocracy, I should be forced, much against my will, to come to this conclusion, that monarchical and aristocratical institutions are unsuited to my country. Monarchy and aristocracy, valuable and useful as I think them, are still valuable and useful as means, and not as ends. The end of government is the happiness of the people, and I do not conceive that, in a country like this, the happiness of the people can be promoted by a form of government in which the middle classes place no confidence, and which exists only because the middle classes have no organ by which to make their sentiments known. But, Sir, I am fully convinced that the middle classes sincerely wish to uphold the Royal prerogatives and the constitutional rights of the Peers. . . .

Now therefore while everything at home and abroad forebodes ruin to those who persist in a hopeless struggle against the spirit of the age, now, while the crash of the proudest throne of the Continent is still resounding in our ears, now, while the roof of a British palace affords an ignominious shelter to the exiled heir of forty kings, now, while we see on every side ancient institutions subverted, and great societies dissolved, now, while the heart of England is still sound, now, while old feelings and old associations retain a power and a charm which may too soon pass away, now, in this your accepted time, now, in this your day of salvation, take counsel, not of prejudice, not of party spirit, not of the ignominious pride of a fatal consistency, but of history, of reason, of the ages which are past, of the signs of this most portentous time. Pronounce in a manner worthy of the expectation with which this great debate has been anticipated, and of the long remembrance which it will leave behind. Renew the youth of the state. Save property, divided against itself. Save the multitude, endangered by its own ungovernable passions. Save the aristocracy, endangered by its own unpopular power. Save the greatest, and fairest, and most highly civilized community that ever existed, from calamities which may in a few days sweep away all the rich heritage of so many ages of wisdom and glory. The danger is terrible. The time is short. If this bill should be rejected, I pray to God that none of those who concur in rejecting it may ever remember their votes with unavailing remorse, amidst the wreck of laws, the confusion of ranks, the spoliation of property, and the dissolution of social order.

■ Discussion Questions

1. What, according to Macaulay, is the main goal of the reform bill?
2. Why is he against universal manhood suffrage?
3. What strategy does Macaulay use to sway opponents of the bill to support it?
4. In what ways does Macaulay's speech reflect liberal principles?

55. Friedrich Engels, *Draft of a Communist Confession of Faith* (1847)

When Friedrich Engels (1820–1895) composed this draft of a communist "confession of faith" in 1847, the Industrial Revolution was in full swing in Great Britain and rapidly gaining ground in continental Europe. Engels observed the impact of this process on the working class with a critical eye. Two years earlier, he had joined forces with another critic of industrialization, Karl Marx (1818–1883), and together they launched an ideological revolution with the publication of the Communist Manifesto *in 1848. There they set forth a new understanding of industrial society and its problems and proposed a new set of solutions centered on the abolition of capitalist, "private" property. Engels's "confession of faith" illuminates key landmarks on his and Marx's intellectual journey, for it was among the materials Marx used to compose the* Manifesto. *The confession was debated and approved in 1847 at the first congress of the Communist League. The first six questions reveal Engels's debt to the utopian principle of the community of property. The rest reflect his and Marx's distinct historical vision.*

DRAFT OF A COMMUNIST CONFESSION OF FAITH
JUNE 9, 1847

QUESTION 1:   *Are you a Communist?*
ANSWER: Yes.
QUESTION 2:   *What is the aim of the Communists?*
ANSWER: To organise society in such a way that every member of it can develop and use all his capabilities and powers in complete freedom and without thereby infringing the basic conditions of this society.
QUESTION 3:   *How do you wish to achieve this aim?*
ANSWER: By the elimination of private property and its replacement by community of property.
QUESTION 4:   *On what do you base your community of property?*

John E. Toews, ed., *The Communist Manifesto with Related Documents* (Boston: Bedford/St. Martin's, 1999), 99–104.

Answer: Firstly, on the mass of productive forces and means of subsistence resulting from the development of industry, agriculture, trade and colonisation, and on the possibility inherent in machinery, chemical and other resources of their infinite extension.

Secondly, on the fact that in the consciousness or feeling of every individual there exist certain irrefutable basic principles which, being the result of the whole of historical development, require no proof.

Question 5: *What are such principles?*

Answer: For example, every individual strives to be happy. The happiness of the individual is inseparable from the happiness of all, etc.

Question 6: *How do you wish to prepare the way for your community of property?*

Answer: By enlightening and uniting the proletariat.

Question 7: *What is the proletariat?*

Answer: The proletariat is that class of society which lives exclusively by its labour and not on the profit from any kind of capital; that class whose weal and woe, whose life and death, therefore, depend on the alternation of times of good and bad business; in a word, on the fluctuations of competition.

Question 8: *Then there have not always been proletarians?*

Answer: No. There have always been poor and working classes; and those who worked were almost always the poor. But there have not always been proletarians, just as competition has not always been free.

Question 9: *How did the proletariat arise?*

Answer: The proletariat came into being as a result of the introduction of the machines which have been invented since the middle of the last century and the most important of which are: the steam-engine, the spinning machine, and the power loom. These machines, which were very expensive and could therefore only be purchased by rich people, supplanted the workers of the time, because by the use of machinery it was possible to produce commodities more quickly and cheaply than could the workers with their imperfect spinning wheels and handlooms. The machines thus delivered industry entirely into the hands of the big capitalists and rendered the workers' scanty property which consisted mainly of their tools, looms, etc., quite worthless, so that the capitalist was left with everything, the worker with nothing. In this way the factory system was introduced. Once the capitalists saw how advantageous this was for them, they sought to extend it to more and more branches of labour. They divided work more and more between the workers so that workers who formerly had made a whole article now produced only a part of it. Labour simplified in this way produced goods more quickly and therefore more cheaply and only now was it found in almost every branch of labour that here also machines could be used. As soon as any branch of labour went over to factory production it ended up, just as in the case of spinning and weaving, in the hands of the big capitalists, and the workers were deprived of the last remnants of their independence. We have gradually arrived at the position where almost *all* branches of labour are run on a factory basis. This has increasingly brought about the ruin of the previously existing middle class, especially of the small master craftsmen, completely transformed the previous position of the workers, and two new classes which are gradually swallowing up all other classes have come into being, namely:

I.   The class of the big capitalists, who in all advanced countries are in almost exclusive possession of the means of subsistence and those means (machines, factories, workshops, etc.) by which these means of subsistence are produced. This is the *bourgeois* class, or the *bourgeoisie.*

II. The class of the completely propertyless, who are compelled to sell their labour to the first class, the bourgeois, simply to obtain from them in return their means of subsistence. Since the parties to this trading in labour are not *equal,* but the bourgeois have the advantage, the propertyless must submit to the bad conditions laid down by the bourgeois. This class, dependent on the bourgeois, is called the class of the *proletarians* or the *proletariat.*

QUESTION 10:   *In what way does the proletarian differ from the slave?*

ANSWER: The slave is sold once and for all, the proletarian has to sell himself by the day and by the hour. The slave is the property of one master and for that very reason has a guaranteed subsistence, however wretched it may be. The proletarian is, so to speak, the slave of the entire bourgeois *class,* not of one master, and therefore has no guaranteed subsistence, since nobody buys his labour if he does not need it. The slave is accounted a *thing* and not a member of civil society. The proletarian is recognised as a *person,* as a member of civil society. The slave *may,* therefore, have a better subsistence than the proletarian but the latter stands at a higher stage of development. The slave frees himself by *becoming a proletarian,* abolishing from the totality of property relationships *only* the relationship of *slavery.* The proletarian can free himself only by abolishing *property in general.*

QUESTION 11:   *In what way does the proletarian differ from the serf?*

ANSWER: The serf has the piece of land, that is, of an instrument of production, in return for handing over a greater or lesser portion of the yield. The proletarian works with instruments of production which belong to someone else who, in return for his labour, hands over to him a portion, determined by competition, of the products. In the case of the serf, the share of the labourer is determined by his own labour, that is, by himself. In the case of the proletarian it is determined by competition, therefore in the first place by the bourgeois. The serf has guaranteed subsistence, the proletarian has not. The serf frees himself by driving out his feudal lord and becoming a property owner himself, thus entering into competition and joining for the time being the possessing class, the privileged class. The proletarian frees himself by doing away with property, competition, and all class differences.

QUESTION 12:   *In what way does the proletarian differ from the handicraftsman?*

ANSWER: As opposed to the proletarian, the so-called handicraftsman, who still existed nearly everywhere during the last century and still exists here and there, is at most a *temporary* proletarian. His aim is to acquire capital himself and so to exploit other workers. He can often achieve this aim where the craft guilds still exist or where freedom to follow a trade has not yet led to the organisation of handwork on a factory basis and to intense competition. But as soon as the factory system is introduced into handwork and competition is in full swing, this prospect is eliminated and the handicraftsman becomes more and more a proletarian. The handicraftsman therefore frees himself *either* by becoming a bourgeois or in general passing over into the middle class, *or,* by becoming a proletarian as a result of competition (as now happens in most cases) and joining the movement of the proletariat—i.e., the more or less conscious communist movement.

QUESTION 13:   *Then you do not believe that community of property has been possible at any time?*

ANSWER: No. Communism has only arisen since machinery and other inventions made it possible to hold out the prospect of an all-sided development, a happy existence, for all members of society. Communism is the theory of a liberation which was not possible for the slaves, the serfs, or the handicraftsmen, but only for the proletarians and hence it belongs of necessity to the nineteenth century and was not possible in any earlier period.

QUESTION 14:   *Let us go back to the sixth question. As you wish to prepare for community of property by the enlightening and uniting of the proletariat, then you reject revolution?*

ANSWER: We are convinced not only of the uselessness but even of the harmfulness of all conspiracies. We are also aware that revolutions are not made deliberately and arbitrarily but that everywhere and at all times they are the necessary consequence of circumstances which are not in any way whatever dependent either on the will or on the leadership of individual parties or of whole classes. But we also see that the development of the proletariat in almost all countries of the world is forcibly repressed by the possessing classes and that thus a revolution is being forcibly worked for by the opponents of communism. If, in the end, the oppressed proletariat is thus driven into a revolution, then we will defend the cause of the proletariat just as well by our deeds as now by our words.

QUESTION 15: *Do you intend to replace the existing social order by community of property at one stroke?*

ANSWER: We have no such intention. The development of the masses cannot be ordered by decree. It is determined by the development of the conditions in which these masses live, and therefore proceeds gradually.

QUESTION 16: *How do you think the transition from the present situation to community of property is to be effected?*

ANSWER: The first, fundamental condition for the introduction of community of property is the political liberation of the proletariat through a democratic constitution.

QUESTION 17: *What will be your first measure once you have established democracy?*

ANSWER: Guaranteeing the subsistence of the proletariat.

QUESTION 18: *How will you do this?*

ANSWER: I. By limiting private property in such a way that it gradually prepares the way for its transformation into social property, e.g., by progressive taxation, limitation of the right of inheritance in favour of the state, etc., etc.

II. By employing workers in national workshops and factories and on national estates.

III. By educating all children at the expense of the state.

QUESTION 19: *How will you arrange this kind of education during the period of transition?*

ANSWER: All children will be educated in state establishments from the time when they can do without the first maternal care.

QUESTION 20: *Will not the introduction of community of property be accompanied by the proclamation of the community of women?*

ANSWER: By no means. We will only interfere in the personal relationship between men and women or with the family in general to the extent that the maintenance of the existing institution would disturb the new social order. Besides, we are well aware that the family relationship has been modified in the course of history by the property relationships and by periods of development, and that consequently the ending of private property will also have a most important influence on it.

QUESTION 21: *Will nationalities continue to exist under communism?*

ANSWER: The nationalities of the peoples who join together according to the principle of community will be just as much compelled by this union to merge with one another and thereby supersede themselves as the various differences between estates and classes disappear through the superseding of their basis—private property.

QUESTION 22: *Do Communists reject the existing religions?*

ANSWER: All religions which have existed hitherto were expressions of historical stages of development of individual peoples or groups of peoples. But communism is that stage of historical development which makes all existing religions superfluous and supersedes them.

∎ Discussion Questions

1. According to the confession, what were the central goals of the communists, and how did they aim to achieve them?
2. How does Engels define the proletariat, and what sets it apart from other types of workers?
3. How does the confession explicitly link communist ideology to industrialization? What place did revolution have in this ideology?

56. Victor Hugo, *Preface to* Cromwell   (1827)

The economic and political changes sweeping across Europe in the first half of the nineteenth cen-
tury found cultural expression in the reigning artistic movement of the period: romanticism. As a
whole, the movement shunned the rules and models of the past and embraced freedom, creative ge-
nius, and originality instead. Victor Marie, Count Hugo (1802–1885), was among the most cele-
brated Romantic French poets and novelists of his day. In this excerpt from the preface to one of his
early works, the play Cromwell, *published in 1827, he paints a colorful picture of his artistic ideals.*
His passionate vision helped shape the explosion of culture after 1830 when painters, poets, play-
wrights, and authors turned not only to nature for inspiration but also to the gritty realities of every-
day life in an increasingly industrial and urban society.

Let us then speak boldly. The time for it has come, and it would be strange if, in this age, liberty,
like the light, should penetrate everywhere except to the one place where freedom is most natural—the domain of thought. Let us take the hammer to theories and poetic systems. Let us throw
down the old plastering that conceals the façade of art. There are neither rules nor models; or,
rather, there are no other rules than the general laws of nature, which soar above the whole field
of art, and the special rules which result from the conditions appropriate to the subject of each
composition. The former are of the essence, eternal, and do not change; the latter are variable,
external, and are used but once. The former are the framework that supports the house; the latter the scaffolding which is used in building it, and which is made anew for each building. In a
word, the former are the flesh and bones, the latter the clothing, of the drama. But these rules
are not written in the treatises on poetry. Richelet has no idea of their existence. Genius, which
divines rather than learns, devises for each work the general rules from the general plan of things,
the special rules from the separate *ensemble* of the subject treated; not after the manner of the
chemist, who lights the fire under his furnace, heats his crucible, analyzes and destroys; but after
the manner of the bee, which flies on its golden wings, lights on each flower and extracts its
honey, leaving it as brilliant and fragrant as before.

The poet—let us insist on this point—should take counsel therefore only of nature, truth
and inspiration, which is itself both truth and nature. "*Quando he,*" says Lope de Vega:

Quando he de escrivir una comedia,
Encierro los preceptos con seis llaves.[1]

To secure these precepts "six keys" are none too many, in very truth. Let the poet beware especially of copying anything whatsoever—Shakespeare no more than Molière, Schiller no more
than Corneille. If genuine talent could abdicate its own nature in this matter, and thus lay aside
its original personality, to transform itself into another, it would lose everything by playing this
role of its own double. It is as if a god should turn valet. We must draw our inspiration from the
original sources. . . .

Let there be no misunderstanding: if some of our poets have succeeded in being great, even
when copying, it is because, while forming themselves on the antique model, they have often listened to the voice of nature and to their own genius—it is because they have been themselves in
some one respect. Their branches became entangled in those of the near-by tree, but their roots
were buried deep in the soil of art. They were the ivy, not the mistletoe. Then came imitators of

---

[1]When I have to write a comedy, / I enclose the precepts with six keys.
The Dramatic Works of Victor Hugo, vol. III (New York: The Athenaeum Society, 1909), 3–54.

the second rank, who, having neither roots in the earth, nor genius in their souls, had to confine themselves to imitation. As Charles Nodier says: "After the school of Athens, the school of Alexandria." Then there was a deluge of mediocrity; then there came a swarm of those treatises on poetry, so annoying to true talent, so convenient for mediocrity. We were told that everything was done, and God was forbidden to create more Molières or Corneilles. Memory was put in place of imagination. Imagination itself was subjected to hard-and-fast rules, and aphorisms were made about it: "To imagine," says La Harpe, with his naive assurance, "is in substance to remember, that is all."

But nature! Nature and truth!—And here, in order to prove that, far from demolishing art, the new ideas aim only to reconstruct it more firmly and on a better foundation, let us try to point out the impassable limit which in our opinion, separates reality according to art from reality according to nature. It is careless to confuse them as some ill-informed partisans of *romanticism* do. Truth in art cannot possibly be, as several writers have claimed, *absolute* reality. Art cannot produce the thing itself. Let us imagine, for example, one of those unreflecting promoters of absolute nature, of nature viewed apart from art, at the performance of a romantic play, say *Le Cid*. "What's that?" he will ask at the first word. "The Cid speaks in verse? It isn't *natural* to speak in verse."—"How would you have him speak, pray?"—"In prose." Very good. A moment later, "How's this!" he will continue, if he is consistent; "the Cid is speaking French!"—"Well?"— "Nature demands that he speak his own language; he can't speak anything but Spanish."

We shall fail entirely to understand but again—very good. You imagine that this is all? By no means: before the tenth sentence in Castilian, he is certain to rise and ask if the Cid who is speaking is the real Cid, in flesh and blood. By what right does the actor, whose name is Pierre or Jacques, take the name of the Cid? That is *false*. There is no reason why he should not go on to demand that the sun should be substituted for the footlights, *real* trees and *real* houses for those deceitful wings. For, once started on that road, logic has you by the collar, and you cannot stop.

We must admit therefore, or confess ourselves ridiculous, that the domains of art and of nature are entirely distinct. Nature and art are two things—were it not so, one or the other would not exist. Art, in addition to its idealistic side, has a terrestrial, material side. Let it do what it will, it is shut in between grammar and prosody, between Vaugelas and Richelet. For its most capricious creations, it has formulae, methods of execution, a complete apparatus to set in motion. For genius there are delicate instruments, for mediocrity, tools.

It seems to us that someone has already said that the drama is a mirror wherein nature is reflected. But if it be an ordinary mirror, a smooth and polished surface, it will give only a dull image of objects, with no relief—faithful, but colourless; everyone knows that colour and light are lost in a simple reflection. The drama, therefore, must be a concentrating mirror, which, instead of weakening, concentrates and condenses the coloured rays, which make a mere gleam a light, and of a light a flame. Then only is the drama acknowledged by art.

The stage is an optical point. Everything that exists in the world—in history, in life, in man— should be and can be reflected therein, but under the magic wand of art. Art turns the leaves of the ages, of nature, studies chronicles, strives to reproduce actual facts (especially in respect to manners and peculiarities, which are much less exposed to doubt and contradiction than are concrete facts), restores what the chroniclers have lopped off, harmonises what they have collected, divines and supplies their omissions, fills their gaps with imaginary scenes which have the colour of the time, groups what they have left scattered about, sets in motion anew the threads of Providence which work the human marionettes, clothes the whole with a form at once poetical and natural, and imparts to it that vitality of truth and brilliancy which gives birth to illusion, that prestige of reality which arouses the enthusiasm of the spectator, and of the poet first of all, for the poet is sincere. Thus the aim of art is almost divine: to bring to life again if it is writing history, to create if it is writing poetry. . . .

It will readily be imagined that, for a work of this kind, if the poet must *choose* (and he must), he should choose, not the *beautiful*, but the *characteristic*. Not that it is advisable to "make local colour," as they say to-day; that is, to add as an afterthought a few discordant touches here and there to a work that is at best utterly conventional and false. The local colour should not be on the surface of the drama, but in its substance, in the very heart of the work, whence it spreads of itself, naturally, evenly, and, so to speak, into every corner of the drama, as the sap ascends from the root to the tree's topmost leaf. The drama should be thoroughly impregnated with this colour of the time, which should be, in some sort, in the air, so that one detects it only on entering the theatre, and that on going forth one finds one's self in a different period and atmosphere. It requires some study, some labour, to attain this end; so much the better. It is well that the avenues of art should be obstructed by those brambles from which everybody recoils except those of powerful will. Besides, it is this very study, fostered by an ardent inspiration, which will ensure the drama against a vice that kills it—the *commonplace*. To be commonplace is the failing of short-sighted, short-breathed poets. In this tableau of the stage, each figure must be held down to its most prominent, most individual, most precisely defined characteristic. Even the vulgar and the trivial should have an accent of their own. Like God, the true poet is present in every part of his work at once. Genius resembles the die which stamps the king's effigy on copper and golden coins alike. . . .

■ Discussion Questions

1. According to Hugo, why should artists turn to nature for guidance and inspiration?
2. As described here, what is the relationship between art and reality?
3. Why does Hugo think that it is especially important for poets to include "local color" in their works?
4. What links do you see between Hugo's ideas and the broader political and social context?

CHAPTER 18

Constructing the Nation-State, c. 1850–1880

The second half of the nineteenth century marked the dawning of a new age in European politics and culture. After the failed revolutions of 1848–1849, politicians, artists, intellectuals, and the general public cast aside the promises of idealists and claimed to see society as it really was: combative, competitive, and inherently disordered. The first document elucidates how European leaders sought to master this unruly scene and strengthen state power from above. The making of the modern nation-state also assumed global proportions as governments expanded their empires abroad. The second document illuminates the human scope of such efforts by the greatest colonial power of the day, Great Britain. The biological research of Charles Darwin reflected the scientific dimensions of the new age, as the final document reveals. To some observers, his work suggested that just as in politics, only the hardiest survived in the natural world. The social applications of Darwin's theories supported industrial Europe's march toward world dominance.

57. Alexander II, *Address in the State Council* (1861)

Russia's defeat in the Crimean War (1853–1856) revealed its inability to compete in the rapidly changing industrial world. Among its greatest liabilities was the institution of serfdom, which, by binding the peasant population to the land, inhibited the growth of a modern labor force while fostering widespread discontent. To combat these problems, Alexander II chose a momentous solution: the emancipation of the serfs. After years of discussion and debate, drafts of the reform were presented at a meeting of the State Council on January 28, 1861. The tsar began the meeting with the following speech, in which he underscores the importance of emancipation to Russia's future. His audience clearly shared his sense of urgency, for the general statute on the emancipation of the serfs was approved less than a month later.

The matter of the liberation of the serfs, which has been submitted for the consideration of the State Council, I consider to be a vital question for Russia, upon which will depend the development of her strength and power. I am sure that all of you, gentlemen, are just as convinced as I am of the benefits and necessity of this measure. I have another conviction, which is that this matter cannot be postponed; therefore I demand that the State Council finish with it in the first half of February so that it can be announced before the start of work in the fields; . . . I repeat— and this is my absolute will—that this matter should be finished right away.

A Source Book for Russian History, vol. III (New Haven: University Press, Yale, 1972), 599–600.

For four years now it has dragged on and has been arousing various fears and anticipations among both the estate owners and the peasants. Any further delay could be disastrous to the state. I cannot help being surprised and happy, and I am sure all of you are happy, at the trust and calm shown by our good people in this matter. Although the apprehensions of the nobility are to a certain extent understandable, for the closest and material interests of each are involved, notwithstanding all this, I have not forgotten and shall never forget that the approach to the matter was made on the initiative of the nobility itself, and I am happy to be able to be a witness to this before posterity. In my private conversations with the guberniia marshals of the nobility, and during my travels about Russia, when receiving the nobility, I did not conceal the trend of my thoughts and opinions on the question that occupies us all and said everywhere that this transformation cannot take place without certain sacrifices on their part and that all my efforts consist in making these sacrifices as little weighty and burdensome as possible for the nobility. I hope, gentlemen, that on inspection of the drafts presented to the State Council, you will assure yourselves that all that can be done for the protection of the interests of the nobility has been done; if on the other hand you find it necessary in any way to alter or to add to the presented work, then I am ready to receive your comments; but I ask you only not to forget that the basis of the whole work must be the improvement of the life of the peasants—an improvement not in words alone or on paper but in actual fact.

Before proceeding to a detailed examination of this draft itself, I would like to trace briefly the historical background of this affair. You are acquainted with the origin of serfdom. Formerly it did not exist among us; this law was established by autocratic power and only autocratic power can abolish it, and that is my sincere will.

My predecessors felt all the evils of serfdom and continually endeavored, if not to destroy it completely, to work toward the gradual limitation of the arbitrary power of the estate owners.

. . . My late father [Nicholas I] was continuously occupied with the thought of freeing the serfs. Sympathizing completely with this thought, already in 1856, before the coronation, while in Moscow I called the attention of the leaders of the nobility of the Moscow guberniia to the necessity for them to occupy themselves with improving the life of the serfs, adding that serfdom could not continue forever and that it would therefore be better if the transformation took place from above rather than from below. . . .

The Editorial Commissions worked for a year and seven months and, notwithstanding all the reproaches, perhaps partly just, to which the commissions were exposed, they finished their work conscientiously and presented it to the Main Committee. The Main Committee, under the chairmanship of my brother [Grand Duke Konstantin Nikolaevich], toiled with indefatigable energy and zeal. I consider it my duty to thank all the members of the committee, especially my brother, for their conscientious labors in this matter.

There may be various views on the draft presented, and I am willing to listen to all the different opinions. But I have the right to demand one thing from you: that you, putting aside all personal interests, act not like estate owners but like imperial statesmen invested with my trust. Approaching this important matter I have not concealed from myself all those difficulties that awaited us and I do not conceal them now; but, firmly believing in the grace of God and being convinced of the sacredness of this matter, I trust that God will not abandon us but will bless us to finish it for the future prosperity of our beloved fatherland.

■ **Discussion Questions**

1. What were Alexander's principal goals in granting the serfs freedom?
2. How did Alexander consider emancipation to be an expression of his power as tsar?
3. In calling for emancipation, did Alexander seek to undermine the existing social hierarchy?

58. Krupa Sattianadan, *Saguna: A Story of Native Christian Life*   (1887–1888)

Along with strengthening state power at home in the late nineteenth century, European leaders expanded their empires abroad and tightened their control therein. Great Britain's decision to assume direct control of India in 1858 provides a dramatic example of this shift in colonial policy. In her autobiographical novel Saguna, *Krupa Sattianadan (1862–1894) illuminates the everyday dimensions of British imperialism. She was born to Christian parents in the Bombay Presidency, an administrative unit of the colonial administration. While in her teens, the death of her beloved brother, Bhasker, gravely affected her physical and emotional health. She was sent to a nearby mission school to recover and in the following passage describes her experiences there. As she recounts, her white teachers strove to mold her according to English tastes, morals, and behavior, thereby exposing the racist attitudes underlying British rule. Her book found a ready audience and was published both in English and in Tamil, a language widely used in southern India.*

My sister paid a visit to the city, not long after Bhasker's death. She noticed my retired ways and my peculiar moods and took me to her home. One day as I was sitting in the hall, puzzling my head over some books that I found in the study, two ladies were announced, and before I had time to run away, they were in the hall. The first grasped my sister's hand in hers and gave her a hearty kiss. Her appearance at once attracted my notice. She seemed fresh coloured, tall, as she looked with a good-humoured smile at me over sister's shoulder. There was a twinkle in her eye, as if she wished every one to be a partaker of her high spirits. She was certainly strikingly different from other ladies, I thought, and I listened with great attention to what she had to say. . . . Then she turned round toward me, and, catching hold of both of my hands, put question after question to me in such a way that I could not but answer. She had large light brown eyes, a fine, full long face, a nose rather blunt, and a broad, high forehead. I liked her. Presently she turned toward my sister and talked aside for a few minutes while her companion smiled to me and drew me toward her. But before we could talk much the other turned toward me, and said, "So that's settled; you are to come next month and stay with me. You will learn to your heart's content there, but mind you are to be very free with me and tell me everything. I mean to quarrel with you very often. Ah! you critical thing. Don't I know what you are thinking?" and with a warm, but rather rough hug and a brushing kiss she left me. My sister said I must go and stay with the two ladies for some time. I liked the idea and made up my mind to go. The first thing that I was told on going to Miss Roberts'—for that was the name of the lady who took charge of me—was that I was a little girl; that in England girls of fourteen and fifteen were considered mere chits, and that I was to lay aside all solemnity of manner and behave as a girl. When it came to the lessons I was asked what I was learning.

I said: "History, geography, etc."

"What in history?"

"I have finished *Landmarks of the History of Greece*, and am reading—"

"Greece! Greece! What have you to do with Greece?"

I had loved this little book. It was like a storybook, and I thought that she would have been pleased, but she only murmured, "Well! I will see. I must get something more suited to you. What about English? Can you read fluently?"

Susie Tharu and K. Lalita, eds., *Women Writing in India: 600 B.C. to the Present*, vol. I, *600 B.C. to the Early Twentieth Century* (New York: The Feminist Press, 1991), 277–81.

Longfellow's poems were put into my hand. The volume opened at "Pleasant it was when woods were green." I read this fast enough.

"Too fast."

"Oh I know it by heart," I exclaimed, anxious to show my cleverness. I shut the book and repeated the whole thing to her. I had once learnt it in a fit of study, and it had given me much pleasure.

"Well! I tell you what," she said, shutting the book, "you know a little too much. When a horse goes too fast, what does his master do?"

I did not know what he did, but I thought the comparison was not a good one, and I exclaimed abruptly, "I am not a horse."

"Well! Well!" she said laughing, "we won't discuss that point. I think you want occupation. You must teach in my little school this afternoon. Now we have done with our lessons for one day."

To my great surprise she shut up the books and put them by. When dinner time came I saw the other lady for the first time. She gave me a smile and pointed to my place by her side, but Miss Roberts never left me alone. She began by saying to her neighbour, "Girls in England never sit at the table with their elders, but of course we shall allow this one." In my sister's house I had learned to some extent how to use spoon and fork, but when I found the lady's eyes fixed on me my fingers trembled, and I thought I was sure to make all kinds of mistakes to her amusement. Already her eyes were twinkling with fun and laughter. I refused many a tempting thing that was offered, while she kept on remarking: "That's right, don't eat if you don't care. Girls in England don't eat these things." At last came curry and rice, of which I took a little, and enjoyed it. . . .

During the day, the school was my delight. This Miss Roberts managed. She instructed me in the art of teaching, in which I found a great delight. I was astonished at the explanations which I was able to give, and the way in which a knowledge of things seemed to spring into existence when it was required. I was in a whirl of delight with the blackboards, the large maps and the pictures, and the new dignity that all these conferred on me. Miss Roberts smiled at my eagerness, and forgot to say that I was only a child. I loved to think myself grown up and important. Miss Roberts used to quarrel with me as impetuously and passionately as if she had been of my own age, and then make it up by giving me a hearty hug and a kiss. She had very peculiar views, and we often had little fights with each other. I can hardly help thinking that she sometimes gave expression to her views for the sole purpose of teasing me. "Oh, Miss D., what made you receive the Bible woman in the drawing room?" she said one day, alluding to a very respectable person, a great friend of our family. "In England we receive them in the kitchen. She is no better than a servant, I assure you."

"In the kitchen?" I said, in amazement and indignation. I was angry, and thought of many grievances that I had heard spoken of. I had also heard that we were the real aristocrats of our country, and that the English ladies who came to India only belonged to the middle class, and I resolved to tell her that, so I boldly added: "What do you think of us? We are real aristocrats of this place." Unfortunately I pronounced the big word wrongly, and she burst out laughing and repeated it again and again, as I had done. "I don't care. Anyhow, you are middle-class people. She is a brahmin, and only takes money from the Mission because she is poor. She is no servant. In your country you are no brahmins. You are sudras." Tears fell from my eyes, and I felt as if I should choke.

"Miss D.," exclaimed the angry lady, now quite beside herself, "do girls ever talk at table like this? I protest against this. I can't have it. I tell you I can't,"—this with so much emphasis that I was quite frightened. Miss D. looked at me and shook her head. The tears that were rolling from my eyes I hastily wiped. "What can I do?" I said, while a shower of words, such as "rude," "bad," "naughty," "disrespectful," etc., fell on my head. Tiffin over, Miss Roberts went with a bounce to her room and I went to mine and began to cry. "Natives," I said to myself, "we are natives. Tomorrow she will say that my mother was a Bible woman too. Oh! I will go away from her," and I began to cry more. About five minutes afterward the door behind me opened, and Miss Roberts rushed in, took hold of me, and kissed me profusely. "Now it is all right," she said smiling and wonderfully changed. "We won't talk about it."

"And you won't send Bible women to the kitchen?" I said.

She shook her head and rushed away from me laughing.

In the evenings we generally sat together in the lobby. It was our free time, and I was told to say anything I liked. I used to sit far back on the deep seat with my hands on my lap, although there was a table in front. I liked to draw my own pictures, with the stars and shadows outside, and often my thoughts were with Bhasker; but I was always disturbed and told to talk. Generally the ladies had some fancy work in their hands; but I never brought any. One day Miss Roberts rebuked me and said: "Why did you not bring some work?"

I felt guilty, but still as I rose I said somehow, "I thought we were expected to be free at this time."

"Yes, but we must not appear so. I hate laziness."

Something in this remark caught my attention. I stood near the table and looked out. All my pictures vanished. I looked into her face and said, "It is only for appearance, is it? What is the good of that? Won't it be acting falsely?"

She flew into a passion, and when I tried to escape to my room, she forced me down. "Falsely! Sit and be lazy," she said, "and let every one of us put you to shame."

The second lady, however, calmed her, saying, "Really I don't do anything. I had better sit quietly too."

"Sit, sit," said Miss Roberts, who had by this time nearly spent her wrath and was in a little pet.

The other lady had on various occasions whispered to me, "She is Irish and means nothing," and now she looked and smiled at me.

My greatest trials always came through my tongue. I had got into the habit of thinking loudly. Bhasker had encouraged it, and the discussions carried on by my other brothers, in which I often took part, had made me quite adept in defending my views. I had had to stand up for my rights from my childhood. I had not then learnt the beauty of silence. One day I was sitting in the lobby in my usual half-sleepy, half-dreamy state, when I heard a visitor announced. As soon as Miss Roberts heard the name, she broke out abruptly, "Oh, how disgusting! What a bore she is! and she wants me, that is true enough." So saying she walked out, and an elderly lady met her near the lobby.

"Oh! I am so glad to see you. How do you do?" Miss Roberts said in a hearty tone as she brought in the visitor. Surely this is somebody else, and I am glad that it is a surprise for Miss Roberts, I said to myself. The talk evidently was cheerful and genial, but as soon as it was over, I was rather taken aback to hear Miss Roberts say, "Oh, what a bore to be sure! How glad I am she is gone! We must really not have visitors at this time."

"She! she!" I said, "was not she a surprise to you?"

"What do you mean?" said Miss Roberts, turning abruptly round on me.

"No! I thought the lady was a surprise to you. You said you were so glad to see her."

"Oh! Oh!" she said, lifting her voice and her hands.

"Miss D., I tell you I can't have this imper—"

"You said free speech was allowed here," I answered, interrupting her.

"Free speech, but not to your superiors, not to me," this with a thump on the table. "You naughty girl."

But it was a little overdone, and there was a burst from the other lady in which Miss Roberts found herself heartily joining.

Later on I came to know that they did not mean anything. It was only the custom, and they used the few set phrases that etiquette compelled them to use. But my readers will understand from this what a boor I was. I loved these two ladies and stayed with them for months, and in spite of little quarrels now and then, I lived very happily with them. Not long after I was attacked with fever, and my sister was compelled to take me away.

■ Discussion Questions

1. How would you describe the attitudes of Sattianadan's teachers toward her, and vice versa?
2. As described by Sattianadan, in what ways did the mission school further advance the goals of British colonial policy?
3. What does this passage suggest about both the benefits and drawbacks of this policy?

59. Charles Darwin, *The Descent of Man* (1871)

As Bismarck and other Realpolitikers *were transforming European political views in the mid- to late nineteenth century, the English naturalist Charles Darwin (1809–1882) was transforming their scientific ones. In 1859, he published* On the Origin of Species, *which argued that animal species evolved over time through a process of natural selection by which the strongest, and most well adapted to any given environment, survived. The biblical story of creation had no place in Darwin's conclusions, and this incited considerable debate. The debate intensified twelve years later when Darwin applied his theory of evolution directly to humans in* The Descent of Man. *The ramifications of this work extended beyond the field of biology when some people began to use evolutionary principles to understand, justify, and perpetuate the social and political inequalities of the day.*

The main conclusion here arrived at, and now held by many naturalists who are well competent to form a sound judgment, is that man is descended from some less highly organised form. The grounds upon which this conclusion rests will never be shaken, for the close similarity between man and the lower animals in embryonic development, as well as in innumerable points of structure and constitution, both of high and of the most trifling importance,—the rudiments which he retains, and the abnormal reversions to which he is occasionally liable,—are facts which cannot be disputed. They have long been known, but until recently they told us nothing with respect to the origin of man. Now when viewed by the light of our knowledge of the whole organic world, their meaning is unmistakable. The great principle of evolution stands up clear and firm, when these groups of facts are considered in connection with others such as the mutual affinities of the members of the same group, their geographical distribution in past and present times, and their geological succession. It is incredible that all these facts should speak falsely. He who is not content to look, like a savage, at the phenomena of nature as disconnected, cannot any longer believe that man is the work of a separate act of creation. He will be forced to admit that the close resemblance of the embryo of man to that, for instance, of a dog—the construction of his skull, limbs and whole frame on the same plan with that of other mammals, independently of the uses to which the parts may be put—the occasional re-appearance of various structures, for instance of several muscles, which man does not normally possess, but which are common to the

Charles Darwin, *The Descent of Man and Selection in Relation to Sex* (New York: D. Appleton and Company, 1896), 606–19.

Quadrumana—and a crowd of analogous facts—all point in the plainest manner to the conclusion that man is the co-descendant with other mammals of a common progenitor.

We have seen that man incessantly presents individual differences in all parts of his body and in his mental faculties. These differences or variations seem to be induced by the same general causes, and to obey the same laws as with the lower animals. In both cases similar laws of inheritance prevail. Man tends to increase at a greater rate than his means of subsistence; consequently he is occasionally subjected to a severe struggle for existence, and natural selection will have effected whatever lies within its scope. A succession of strongly-marked variations of a similar nature is by no means requisite; slight fluctuating differences on the individual suffice for the work of natural selection; not that we have any reason to suppose that in the same species, all parts of the organisation tend to vary to the same degree. . . .

Through the means just specified, aided perhaps by others as yet undiscovered, man has been raised to his present state. But since he attained to the rank of manhood, he has diverged into distinct races, or as they may be more fitly called, subspecies. Some of these, such as the Negro and European, are so distinct that, if specimens had been brought to a naturalist without any further information, they would undoubtedly have been considered by him as good and true species. Nevertheless all the races agree in so many unimportant details of structure and in so many mental peculiarities, that these can be accounted for only by inheritance from a common progenitor; and a progenitor thus characterised would probably deserve to rank as man.

It must not be supposed that the divergence of each race from the other races, and of all from a common stock, can be traced back to any one pair of progenitors. On the contrary, at every stage in the process of modification, all the individuals which were in any way better fitted for their conditions of life, though in different degrees, would have survived in greater numbers than the less well-fitted. The process would have been like that followed by man, when he does not intentionally select particular individuals, but breeds from all the superior individuals, and neglects the inferior. He thus slowly but surely modifies his stock, and unconsciously forms a new strain. So with respect to modifications acquired independently of selection, and due to variations arising from the nature of the organism and the action of the surrounding conditions, or from changed habits of life, no single pair will have been modified much more than the other pairs inhabiting the same country, for all will have been continually blended through free intercrossing.

By considering the embryological structure of man,—the homologies which he presents with the lower animals,—the rudiments which he retains,—and the reversions to which he is liable, we can partly recall in imagination the former condition of our early progenitors; and can approximately place them in their proper place in the zoological series. We thus learn that man is descended from a hairy, tailed quadruped, probably arboreal in its habits, and an inhabitant of the Old World. This creature, if its whole structure had been examined by a naturalist, would have been classed amongst the Quadrumana, as surely as the still more ancient progenitor of the Old and New World monkeys. The Quadrumana and all the higher mammals are probably derived from an ancient marsupial animal, and this through a long line of diversified forms, from some amphibian-like creature, and this again from some fish-like animals. In the dim obscurity of the past we can see that the early progenitor of all the Vertebrata must have been an aquatic animal, provided with branchiae, with the two sexes united in the same individual, and with the most important organs of the body (such as the brain and heart) imperfectly or not at all developed. This animal seems to have been more like the larvae of the existing marine Ascidians than any other known form.

The high standard of our intellectual powers and moral disposition is the greatest difficulty which presents itself, after we have been driven to this conclusion on the origin of man. But everyone who admits the principle of evolution, must see that the mental powers of the higher animals, which are the same in kind with those of man, though so different in degree, are capable of advancement. Thus the interval between the mental powers of one of the higher apes and of a fish, or between those of an ant and scale-insect, is immense; yet their development does not offer any special difficulty; for with our domesticated animals, the mental faculties are certainly variable, and the variations are inherited. No one doubts that they are of the utmost importance to animals in a state of nature. Therefore the conditions are favourable for their development through natural selection. The same conclusion may be extended to man; the intellect must have been all-important to him, even at a very remote period, as enabling him to invent and use language, to make weapons, tools, traps, etc., whereby with the aid of his social habits, he long ago became the most dominant of all living creatures. . . .

The belief in God has often been advanced as not only the greatest, but the most complete of all the distinctions between man and the lower animals. It is however impossible, as we have seen, to maintain that this belief is innate or instinctive in man. On the other hand a belief in all-pervading spiritual agencies seems to be universal; and apparently follows from a considerable advance in man's reason, and from a still greater advance in his faculties of imagination, curiosity and wonder. I am aware that the assumed instinctive belief in God has been used by many persons as an argument for His existence. But this is a rash argument, as we should thus be compelled to believe in the existence of many cruel and malignant spirits, only a little more powerful than man; for the belief in them is far more general than in a beneficent Deity. The idea of a universal and beneficent Creator does not seem to arise in the mind of man, until he has been elevated by long-continued culture. . . .

I am aware that the conclusions arrived at in this work will be denounced by some as highly irreligious; but he who denounces them is bound to show why it is more irreligious to explain the origin of man as a distinct species by descent from some lower form, through the laws of variation and natural selection, than to explain the birth of the individual through the laws of ordinary reproduction. The birth both of the species and of the individual are equally parts of that grand sequence of events, which our minds refuse to accept as the result of blind chance. The understanding revolts at such a conclusion, whether or not we are able to believe that every slight variation of structure,—the union of each pair in marriage,—the dissemination of each seed,—and other such events, have all been ordained for some special purpose. . . .

The main conclusion arrived at in this work, namely that man is descended from some lowly organised form, will, I regret to think, be highly distasteful to many. But there can hardly be a doubt that we are descended from barbarians. The astonishment which I felt on first seeing a party of Fuegians on a wild and broken shore will never be forgotten by me, for the reflection at once rushed into my mind—such were our ancestors. These men were absolutely naked and bedaubed with paint, their long hair was tangled, their mouths frothed with excitement, and their expression was wild, startled, and distrustful. They possessed hardly any arts, and like wild animals lived on what they could catch; they had no government, and were merciless to everyone not of their own small tribe. He who has seen a savage in his native land will not feel much shame, if forced to acknowledge that the blood of some more humble creature flows in his veins. For my own part I would as soon be descended from that heroic little monkey, who braved his dreaded enemy in order to save the life of his keeper, or from that old baboon, who descending from the mountains, carried away in triumph his young comrade from a crowd of astonished dogs—as from a savage who delights to torture his enemies, offers up bloody sacrifices, practises infanticide without remorse, treats his wives like slaves, knows no decency, and is haunted by the grossest superstitions.

Man may be excused for feeling some pride at having risen, though not through his own exertions, to the very summit of the organic scale; and the fact of his having thus risen, instead of having been aboriginally placed there, may give him hope for a still higher destiny in the distant future. But we are not here concerned with hopes or fears, only with the truth as far as our reason permits us to discover it; and I have given the evidence to the best of my ability. We must, however, acknowledge, as it seems to me, that man with all his noble qualities, with sympathy which feels for the most debased, with benevolence which extends not only to other men but to the humblest living creature, with his god-like intellect which has penetrated into the movements and constitution of the solar system—with all these exalted powers—Man still bears in his bodily frame the indelible stamp of his lowly origin.

▪ Discussion Questions

1. What evidence does Darwin supply to support his theory of human evolution?
2. How does this evidence call into question the relationship between religion and science?
3. In what ways does Darwin voice the concern for realism and concrete facts that marked the general mood of his day?

CHAPTER 19

Empire, Modernity, and the Road to War, c. 1880–1914

The dual phenomena of industry and empire changed Europe and the world profoundly in the late nineteenth century. With domestic industries booming, European leaders looked abroad for new markets and raw materials. The widespread belief that imperial holdings were an indication of a nation's strength and racial superiority also fueled the quest for empire. Industrial growth went hand in hand with imperial expansion, and as the twentieth century dawned, Europeans had cause for both elation and fear. On the one hand, many enjoyed unprecedented prosperity. On the other, domestic and international tensions abounded. At home people struggled to navigate the hazards of modern life, while abroad nation-states faced mounting competition and dissent in their quests for imperial glory. As the following documents reveal, the road of modernity was rocky and uncertain, casting a permanent shadow over Enlightenment faith in the inevitability of progress.

60. Jules Ferry, *Speech before the French National Assembly* (1883)

French politician Jules Ferry (1832–1893) fueled his country's quest to compete in Europe's race to conquer foreign territory in the closing decades of the nineteenth century. While serving two terms as premier during the Third Republic, Ferry took the lead in France's colonial expansion in Africa and Asia. Yet not everyone embraced his imperialist policies, including his conservative and socialist colleagues within the government. In this speech, delivered before the National Assembly in July 1883, Ferry faced his opponents head-on, defending not only the political and economic necessity of French expansionism but also its moral justness. At the same time, his critics voice their views, revealing the basis of their anticolonial sentiment.

M. JULES FERRY: Gentlemen, it embarrasses me to make such a prolonged demand upon the gracious attention of the Chamber, but I believe that the duty I am fulfilling upon this platform is not a useless one. It is as strenuous for me as for you, but I believe that there is some benefit in summarizing and condensing, in the form of arguments, the principles, the motives, and the various interests by which a policy of colonial expansion may be justified; it goes without saying that I will try to remain reasonable, moderate, and never lose sight of the major continental in-

---

Ralph A. Austin, ed., *Modern Imperialism: Western Overseas Expansion and Its Aftermath, 1776–1965* (Lexington, Mass.: D. C. Heath, 1969), 69–74.

terests which are the primary concern of this country. What I wish to say, to support this proposition, is that in fact, just as in word, the policy of colonial expansion is a political and economic system; I wish to say that one can relate this system to three orders of ideas: economic ideas, ideas of civilization in its highest sense, and ideas of politics and patriotism.

In the area of economics, I will allow myself to place before you, with the support of some figures, the considerations which justify a policy of colonial expansion from the point of view of that need, felt more and more strongly by the industrial populations of Europe and particularly those of our own rich and hard working country: the need for export markets. Is this some kind of chimera? Is this a view of the future or is it not rather a pressing need, and, we could say, the cry of our industrial population? I will formulate only in a general way what each of you, in the different parts of France, is in a position to confirm. Yes, what is lacking for our great industry, drawn irrevocably on to the path of exportation by the [free trade] treaties of 1860, what it lacks more and more is export markets. Why? Because next door to us Germany is surrounded by barriers, because beyond the ocean, the United States of America has become protectionist, protectionist in the most extreme sense, because not only have these great markets, I will not say closed but shrunk, and thus become more difficult of access for our industrial products, but also these great states are beginning to pour products not seen heretofore onto our own markets. . . . It is not necessary to pursue this demonstration any farther. Yes, gentlemen, I am speaking to the economists, whose convictions and past services no one appreciates more than I do; I am speaking to the honorable M. Passy, whom I see here and who is one of the most authoritative representatives among us of the old school of economics [*smiles*]; I know very well what they will reply to me, what is at the bottom of their thoughts . . . the old school, the great school, gentlemen; one, M. Passy, which your name has embellished, which was led in France by Jean-Baptiste Say and by Adam Smith in England. I do not mean to treat you with any irony, M. Passy, believe me.

I say that I know very well the thoughts of the economists, whom I can call doctrinaires without offending M. Passy. They say to us, "The true export markets are the commercial treaties which furnish and assure them." Gentlemen, I do not look down upon commercial treaties: if we could return to the situation which existed after 1860, if the world had not been subjected to that economic revolution which is the product of the development of science and the speeding up of communications, if this great revolution had not intervened, I would gladly take up the situation which existed after 1860. It is quite true that in that epoch the competition of grain from Odessa did not ruin French agriculture, that the grain of America and of India did not yet offer us any competition; at that moment we were living under the regime of commercial treaties, not only with England, but with the other great powers, with Germany, which had not yet become an industrial power. I do not look down upon them, these treaties; I had the honor of negotiating some of less importance than those of 1860; but gentlemen, in order to make treaties, it is necessary to have two parties: one does not make treaties with the United States; this is the conviction which has grown among those who have attempted to open some sort of negotiations in this quarter, whether officially or officiously.

Gentlemen, there is a second point, a second order of ideas to which I have to give equal attention, but as quickly as possible, believe me; it is the humanitarian and civilizing side of the question. On this point the honorable M. Camille Pellatan has jeered in his own refined and clever manner; he jeers, he condemns, and he says "What is this civilization which you impose with cannonballs? What is it but another form of barbarism? Don't these populations, these inferior races, have the same rights as you? Aren't they masters of their own houses? Have they called upon you? You come to them against their will, you offer them violence, but not civilization." There, gentlemen, is the thesis; I do not hesitate to say that this is not politics, nor is it history: it is political metaphysics. ["Ah, Ah," *on far left.*]

... Gentlemen, I must speak from a higher and more truthful plane. It must be stated openly that, in effect, superior races have rights over inferior races. [*Movement on many benches on the far left.*]

M. JULES MAIGNE: Oh! You dare to say this in the country which has proclaimed the rights of man!

M. DE GUILLOUTET: This is a justification of slavery and the slave trade!

M. JULES FERRY: If M. Maigne is right, if the declaration of the rights of man was written for the blacks of equatorial Africa, then by what right do you impose regular commerce upon them? They have not called upon you.

M. RAOUL DUVAL: We do not want to impose anything upon them. It is you who wish to do so!

M. JULES MAIGNE: To propose and to impose are two different things!

M. GEORGES PERIN: In any case, you cannot bring about commerce by force.

M. JULES FERRY: I repeat that superior races have a right, because they have a duty. They have the duty to civilize inferior races. . . . [*Approbation from the left. New interruptions from the extreme left and from the right.*]

That is what I have to answer M. Pelletan in regard to the second point upon which he touched.

He then touched upon a third, more delicate, more serious, and upon which I ask your permission to express myself quite frankly. It is the political side of the question. The honorable M. Pelletan, who is a distinguished writer, always comes up with remarkably precise formulations. I will borrow from him the one which he applied the other day to this aspect of colonial policy.

"It is a system," he says, "which consists of seeking out compensations in the Orient with a circumspect and peaceful seclusion which is actually imposed upon us in Europe."

I would like to explain myself in regard to this. I do not like this word, "compensation," and, in effect, not here but elsewhere it has often been used in treacherous way. If what is being said or insinuated is that any government in this country, any Republican minister could possibly believe that there are in any part of the world compensations for the disasters which we have experienced, an injury is being inflicted . . . and an injury undeserved by that government. [*Applause at the center and left.*] I will ward off this injury with all the force of my patriotism! [*New applause and bravos from the same benches.*]

Gentlemen, there are certain considerations which merit the attention of all patriots. The conditions of naval warfare have been profoundly altered. ["Very true! Very true!"]

At this time, as you know, a warship cannot carry more than fourteen days' worth of coal, no matter how perfectly it is organized, and a ship which is out of coal is a derelict on the surface of the sea, abandoned to the first person who comes along. Thence the necessity of having on the oceans provision stations, shelters, ports for defense and revictualling. [*Applause at the center and left. Various interruptions.*] And it is for this that we needed Tunisia, for this that we needed Saigon and the Mekong Delta, for this that we need Madagascar, that we are at Diégo-Suarez and Vohemar [two Madagascar ports] and will never leave them! [*Applause from a great number of benches.*] Gentlemen, in Europe as it is today, in this competition of so many rivals which we see growing around us, some by perfecting their military or maritime forces, others by the prodigious development of an ever growing population; in a Europe, or rather in a universe of this sort, a policy of peaceful seclusion or abstention is simply the highway to decadence! Nations are great in our times only by means of the activities which they develop; it is not simply "by the peaceful shining forth of institutions" [*Interruptions on the extreme left and right*] that they are great at this hour.

As for me, I am astounded to find the monarchist parties becoming indignant over the fact that the Republic of France is following a policy which does not confine itself to that ideal of modesty, of reserve, and, if you will allow me the expression, of bread and butter [*Interruptions and laughter on the left*] which the representatives of fallen monarchies wish to impose upon France. [*Applause at the center.*]

... [The Republican Party] has shown that it is quite aware that one cannot impose upon France a political ideal conforming to that of nations like independent Belgium and the Swiss Republic; that something else is needed for France: that she cannot be merely a free country, that she must also be a great country, exercizing all of her rightful influence over the destiny of Europe, that she ought to propagate this influence throughout the world and carry everywhere that she can her language, her customs, her flag, her arms, and her genius. [*Applause at center and left.*]

■ **Discussion Questions**

1. Why does Ferry consider colonial expansion to be an economic necessity?
2. Aside from its economic benefits, why, according to Ferry, is colonial expansion justified?
3. How does Ferry appeal to nationalist sentiment to defend his imperialist stance, and why?
4. What is the basis of his critics' arguments against imperialism?

61. The I-ho-ch'uan (Boxers), *The Boxers Demand Death for All "Foreign Devils"* (1900)

Despite Europe's domination of the globe, the glow of imperial glory was starting to fade in the late nineteenth and early twentieth centuries. In many places, Europeans' hold on their colonial territories was increasingly tenuous as local resistance to foreign rule and interference mounted. The following placard exposes the beliefs driving one such uprising in China, where Western nations had recently made significant inroads. It was written and circulated by the Boxers at the height of their mass revolt against foreign powers in 1900, during which they burned churches, destroyed telegraph lines and railways, and murdered Chinese Christians and missionaries. As the document reveals, an amalgam of distinctive spiritual values and overt hostility to the trappings of modern "progress" fueled the Boxers' actions. Although brutally repressed, the Boxer rebellion strengthened Chinese nationalist sentiment, which ultimately undermined Western imperialism in China.

The Gods assist the Boxers,
The Patriotic Harmonious corps,
It is because the "Foreign Devils" disturb the "Middle Kingdom."
Urging the people to join their religion,
To turn their backs on Heaven,
Venerate not the Gods and forget the ancestors.

Men violate the human obligations,
Women commit adultery,
"Foreign Devils" are not produced by mankind,
If you do not believe,
Look at them carefully.

Louis L. Snyder, ed., *The Imperialism Reader: Documents and Readings on Modern Expansionism* (Princeton: Van Nostrand, 1962), 322–23.

The eyes of all the "Foreign Devils" are bluish,
No rain falls,
The earth is getting dry,
This is because the churches stop Heaven,
The Gods are angry;
The Genii are vexed;
Both come down from the mountain to deliver the doctrine.

This is no hearsay,
The practices of boxing will not be in vain;
Reciting incantations and pronouncing magic words,
Burn up yellow written prayers,
Light incense sticks
To invite the Gods and Genii of all the grottoes.

The Gods come out from grottoes,
The Genii come down from mountains,
Support the human bodies to practice the boxing.
When all the military accomplishments or tactics
Are fully learned,
It will not be difficult to exterminate the "Foreign Devils" then.

Push aside the railway tracks,
Pull out the telegraph poles,
Immediately after this destroy the steamers.

The great France
Will grow cold and downhearted.
The English and Russians will certainly disperse.
Let the various "Foreign Devils" all be killed.
May the whole Elegant Empire of the Great Ching [Qing] Dynasty be ever prosperous!

▪ Discussion Questions

1. Why do the Boxers describe foreigners as "devils"?
2. What forces do the Boxers believe are on their side?
3. In addition to killing foreigners, why do you think the Boxers call for an attack on railways, telegraph lines, and steamers?
4. What type of society do the Boxers desire for China?

62. Sigmund Freud, *The Interpretation of Dreams*   (1900)

The fast-paced and conflict-ridden nature of life in industrial Europe undermined many people's optimism about their own and society's future. Austrian doctor Sigmund Freud (1856–1939) developed the method of psychoanalysis to tap into and cure such anxieties. After studying medicine in Vienna,

A. A. Brill, trans. and ed., *The Basic Writings of Sigmund Freud* (New York: The Modern Library, 1938), 183, 188–94, 208–09, 217–18.

in 1886 Freud opened his own practice to treat patients with nervous disorders. His clinical experience was the basis for his lifelong commitment to the scientific study of the human unconscious. He published The Interpretation of Dreams *in 1900. In it, he described dreams as windows into an individual's irrational desires and inner conflicts. Freud believed that by drawing out dreams' hidden meanings, he could expose the roots of his patients' psychological problems. Psychoanalysis was designed to do just that, thereby laying the foundation of modern psychology.*

In the following pages, I shall demonstrate that there is a psychological technique which makes it possible to interpret dreams, and that on the application of this technique, every dream will reveal itself as a psychological structure, full of significance, and one which may be assigned to a specific place in the psychic activities of the waking state. Further, I shall endeavor to elucidate the processes which underlie the strangeness and obscurity of dreams, and to deduce from these processes the nature of the psychic forces whose conflict or co-operation is responsible for our dreams. . . .

I am proposing to show that dreams are capable of interpretation; and any contributions to the solution of the problem which have already been discussed will emerge only as possible by-products in the accomplishment of my special task. On the hypothesis that dreams are susceptible of interpretation, I at once find myself in disagreement with the prevailing doctrine of dreams . . . for "to interpret a dream" is to specify its "meaning," to replace it by something which takes its position in the concatenation of our psychic activities as a link of definite importance and value. But, as we have seen, the scientific theories of the dream leave no room for a problem of dream-interpretation; since, in the first place, according to these theories, dreaming is not a psychic activity at all, but a somatic process which makes itself known to the psychic apparatus by means of symbols. Lay opinion has always been opposed to these theories. It asserts its privilege of proceeding illogically, and although it admits that dreams are incomprehensible and absurd, it cannot summon up the courage to deny that dreams have any significance. Led by a dim intuition, it seems rather to assume that dreams have a meaning, albeit a hidden one; that they are intended as a substitute for some other thought-process, and that we have only to disclose this substitute correctly in order to discover the hidden meaning of the dream.

The unscientific world, therefore, has always endeavored to "interpret" dreams, and by applying one or the other of two essentially different methods. The first of these methods envisages the dream-content as a whole, and seeks to replace it by another content, which is intelligible and in certain respects analogous. This is symbolic dream-interpretation; and of course it goes to pieces at the very outset in the case of those dreams which are not only unintelligible but confused. The construction which the biblical Joseph placed upon the dream of Pharaoh furnishes an example of this method. The seven fat kine, after which came seven lean ones that devoured the former, were a symbolic substitute for seven years of famine in the land of Egypt, which according to the prediction were to consume all the surplus that seven fruitful years had produced. Most of the artificial dreams contrived by the poets are intended for some such symbolic interpretation, for they reproduce the thought conceived by the poet in a guise not unlike the disguise which we are wont to find in our dreams.

The idea that the dream concerns itself chiefly with the future, whose form it surmises in advance—a relic of the prophetic significance with which dreams were once invested—now becomes the motive for translating into the future the meaning of the dream which has been found by means of symbolic interpretation.

A demonstration of the manner in which one arrives at such a symbolic interpretation cannot, of course, be given. Success remains a matter of ingenious conjecture, of direct intuition, and for this reason dream-interpretation has naturally been elevated into an art which seems to depend upon extraordinary gifts. The second of the two popular methods of dream-interpretation entirely abandons such claims. It might be described as the "cipher method," since it treats the dream as a kind of secret code in which every sign is translated into another sign of known meaning, according to an established key. For example, I have dreamt of a letter and also of a funeral or the like; I consult a "dream-book," and I find that "letter" is to be translated by "vexation" and "funeral" by "engagement." It now remains to establish a connection, which I am again to assume as pertaining to the future, by means of the rigmarole which I have deciphered. . . .

The worthlessness of both these popular methods of interpretation does not admit of discussion. As regards the scientific treatment of the subject, the symbolic method is limited in its application, and is not susceptible of a general exposition. In the cipher method everything depends upon whether the "key," the dream-book, is reliable, and for that all guarantees are lacking. So that one might be tempted to grant the contention of the philosophers and psychiatrists, and to dismiss the problem of dream-interpretation as altogether fanciful.

I have, however, come to think differently. I have been forced to perceive that here, once more, we have one of those not infrequent cases where an ancient and stubbornly retained popular belief seems to have come nearer to the truth of the matter than the opinion of modern science. I must insist that the dream actually does possess a meaning, and that a scientific method of dream-interpretation is possible. I arrived at my knowledge of this method in the following manner:

For years I have been occupied with the solution of certain psychopathological structures—hysterical phobias, obsessional ideas, and the like—with therapeutic intentions. . . . In the course of these psychoanalytic studies, I happened upon the question of dream-interpretation. My patients, after I had pledged them to inform me of all the ideas and thoughts which occurred to them in connection with a given theme, related their dreams, and thus taught me that a dream may be interpolated in the psychic concatenation, which may be followed backwards from a pathological idea into the patient's memory. The next step was to treat the dream itself as a symptom, and to apply to it the method of interpretation which had been worked out for such symptoms.

For this a certain psychic preparation on the part of the patient is necessary. A twofold effort is made to stimulate his attentiveness in respect of his psychic perceptions, and to eliminate the critical spirit in which he is ordinarily in the habit of viewing such thoughts as come to the surface. For the purpose of self-observation with concentrated attention it is advantageous that the patient should take up a restful position and close his eyes; he must be explicitly instructed to renounce all criticism of the thought-formations which he may perceive. He must also be told that the success of the psychoanalysis depends upon his noting and communicating everything that passes through his mind, and that he must not allow himself to suppress one idea because it seems to him unimportant or irrelevant to the subject, or another because it seems nonsensical. He must preserve an absolute impartiality in respect to his ideas; for if he is unsuccessful in finding the desired solution of the dream, the obsessional idea, or the like, it will be because he permits himself to be critical of them. . . .

As will be seen, the point is to induce a psychic state which is in some degree analogous, as regards the distribution of psychic energy (mobile attention), to the state of the mind before falling asleep—and also, of course, to the hypnotic state. On falling asleep the "undesired ideas" emerge, owing to the slackening of a certain arbitrary (and, of course, also critical) action, which is allowed to influence the trends of our ideas; we are accustomed to speak of fatigue as the reason of this slackening; the emerging undesired ideas are changed into visual and auditory images. In the condition which it utilized for the analysis of dreams and pathological ideas, this activity is purposely and deliberately renounced, and the psychic energy thus saved (or some part of it) is employed in attentively tracking the undesired thoughts which now come to the surface—thoughts which retain their identity as ideas (in which the condition differs from the state of falling asleep). *"Undesired ideas" are thus changed into "desired" ones.* . . .

The first step in the application of this procedure teaches us that one cannot make the dream as a whole the object of one's attention, but only the individual components of its content. If I ask a patient who is as yet unpractised: "What occurs to you in connection with this dream?" he is unable, as a rule, to fix upon anything in his psychic field of vision. I must first dissect the dream for him; then, in connection with each fragment, he gives me a number of ideas which may be described as the "thoughts behind" this part of the dream. In this first and important condition, then, the method of dream-interpretation which I employ diverges from the popular, historical and legendary method of interpretation by symbolism and approaches more nearly to the second or "cipher method." Like this, it is an interpretation in detail, not *en masse;* like this, it conceives the dream, from the outset, as something built up, as a conglomerate of psychic formations. . . .

When, after passing through a narrow defile, one suddenly reaches a height beyond which the ways part and a rich prospect lies outspread in different directions, it is well to stop for a moment and consider whither one shall turn next. We are in somewhat the same position after we have mastered this first interpretation of a dream. We find ourselves standing in the light of a sudden discovery. The dream is not comparable to the irregular sounds of a musical instrument, which, instead of being played by the hand of a musician, is struck by some external force; the dream is not meaningless, not absurd, does not presuppose that one part of our store of ideas is dormant while another part begins to awake. It is a perfectly valid psychic phenomenon, actually a wish-fulfilment; it may be enrolled in the continuity of the intelligible psychic activities of the waking state; it is built up by a highly complicated intellectual activity. . . .

It is easy to show that the wish-fulfilment in dreams is often undisguised and easy to recognize, so that one may wonder why the language of dreams has not long since been understood. There is, for example, a dream which I can evoke as often as I please, experimentally, as it were. If, in the evening, I eat anchovies, olives, or other strongly salted foods, I am thirsty at night, and therefore I wake. The waking, however, is preceded by a dream, which has always the same content, namely, that I am drinking. I am drinking long draughts of water; it tastes as delicious as only a cool drink can taste when one's throat is parched; and then I wake, and find that I have an actual desire to drink. The cause of this dream is thirst, which I perceive when I wake. From this sensation arises the wish to drink and the dream shows me this wish as fulfilled. It thereby serves a function, the nature of which I soon surmise. I sleep well, and am not accustomed to being waked by a bodily need. If I succeed in appeasing my thirst by means of the dream that I am drinking, I need not wake up in order to satisfy my thirst. It is thus a *dream of convenience.* The dream takes the place of action, as elsewhere in life. . . .

DISTORTION IN DREAMS

If I now declare that wish-fulfilment is the meaning of *every* dream, so that there cannot be any dreams other than wish-dreams, I know beforehand that I shall meet with the most emphatic contradiction. . . .

Nevertheless, it is not difficult to parry these apparently invincible objections. It is merely necessary to observe that our doctrine is not based upon the estimates of the obvious dream-content but relates to the thought-content, which, in the course of interpretation, is found to lie behind the dream. Let us compare and contrast the *manifest* and the *latent dream-content.* It is true that there are dreams the manifest content of which is of the most painful nature. But has anyone ever tried to interpret these dreams—to discover their latent thought-content? If not, the two objections to our doctrine are no longer valid; for there is always the possibility that even our painful and terrifying dreams may, upon interpretation, prove to be wish-fulfilment. . . .

■ **Discussion Questions**

1. How did Freud's theory of dream interpretation reject contemporary views about dreams on the one hand and accept them on the other?
2. What does Freud mean when he describes dreams as "wish-fulfilments"?
3. According to Freud, what is the relationship between a person's dreams and his or her waking state?

63. Emmeline Pankhurst, *Speech from the Dock*   (1908)

By granting working-class men the vote in 1884, the British government hoped to make politics more unified and orderly. Yet the realization of such hopes proved elusive, in part because a new political foe had appeared on the scene: the women's suffrage movement. The founder of the Women's Social and Political Union, Emmeline Pankhurst (1858–1928), was among the most influential voices of the movement. Although women in Britain had long been fighting for rights, the expansion of the male electorate further accentuated their political exclusion. In the following speech before a police court judge, Pankhurst defends the WSPU's tactics, which had become increasingly militant since its inception in 1903. She had been arrested for distributing a leaflet encouraging her supporters "to rush the House of Commons" and, along with two colleagues, faced a prison sentence for refusing to "bind themselves over"—in other words, to promise to behave properly. Her speech reflects her belief that the WSPU's struggle was more than a quest for the vote; it was a war against a patriarchical society.

Ever since my girlhood, a period of about 30 years, I have belonged to organisations to secure for women that political power which I have felt was essential to bringing about those reforms which women need. I have tried constitutional methods. I have been womanly. When you spoke to some of my colleagues the day before yesterday about their being unwomanly, I felt that bitterness which I know every one of them felt in their hearts. We have tried to be womanly, we have tried to use feminine influence, and we have seen that it is of no use. Men who have been impatient have invariably got reforms for their impatience. And they have not our excuse for being impatient. . . .

Now, while I share in the feeling of indignation which has been expressed to you by my daughter, I have lived longer in the world than she has. Perhaps I can look round the whole question better than she can, but I want to say here, deliberately, to you, that we are here to-day because we are driven here. We have taken this action, because as women—and I want you to understand it is as women we have taken this action—it is because we realise that the condition of our sex is so deplorable that it is our duty even to break the law in order to call attention to the reasons why we do so.

I do not want to say anything which may seem disrespectful to you, or in any way give you offence, but I do want to say that I wish, sir, that you could put yourself into the place of women for a moment before you decide upon this case. My daughter referred to the way in which women are huddled into and out of these police-courts without a fair trial. I want you to realise what a poor hunted creature, without the advantages we have had, must feel.

I have been in prison. I was in Holloway Gaol for five weeks. I was in various parts of the prison. I was in the hospital, and in the ordinary part of the prison, and I tell you, sir, with as

Emmeline Pankhurst, "Speech from the Dock [Police Court]," in *Votes for Women*, October 29, 1908, 1.

much sense of responsibility as if I had taken the oath, that there were women there who have broken no law, who are there because they have been able to make no adequate statement.

You know that women have tried to do something to come to the aid of their own sex. Women are brought up for certain crimes, crimes which men do not understand—I am thinking especially of infanticide—they are brought before a man judge, before a jury of men, who are called upon to decide whether some poor, hunted woman is guilty of murder or not. I put it to you, sir, when we see in the papers, as we often do, a case similar to that of Daisy Lord, for whom a great petition was got up in this country, I want you to realise how we women feel, because we are women, because we are not men, we need some legitimate influence to bear upon our law-makers.

Now, we have tried every way. We have presented larger petitions than were ever presented for any other reform; we have succeeded in holding greater public meetings than men have ever had for any reform, in spite of the difficulty which women have in throwing off their natural diffidence, that desire to escape publicity which we have inherited from generations of our foremothers; we have broken through that. We have faced hostile mobs at street corners, because we were told that we could not have that representation for our taxes which men have won unless we converted the whole of the country to our side. Because we have done this, we have been misrepresented, we have been ridiculed, we have had contempt poured upon us. The ignorant mob at the street corner has been incited to offer us violence, which we have faced unarmed and unprotected by the safeguards which Cabinet Ministers have. We know that we need the protection of the vote even more than men have needed it.

I am here to take upon myself now, sir, as I wish the prosecution had put upon me, the full responsibility for this agitation in its present phase. I want to address you as a woman who has performed the duties of a woman, and, in addition, has performed the duties which ordinary men have had to perform, by earning a living for her children, and educating them. In addition to that, I have been a public officer. I enjoyed for 10 years an official post under the Registrar, and I performed those duties to the satisfaction of the head of the department. After my duty of taking the census was over, I was one of the few Registrars who qualified for a special bonus, and was specially praised for the way in which the work was conducted. Well, sir, I stand before you, having resigned that office when I was told that I must either do that or give up working for this movement.

I want to make you realise that it is a point of honour that if you decide—as I hope you will not decide—to bind us over, that we shall not sign any undertaking, as the Member of Parliament did who was before you yesterday. Perhaps his reason for signing that undertaking may have been that the Prime Minister had given some assurance to the people he claimed to represent that something should be done for them. We have no such assurance. Mr. Birrell told the women who questioned him the other day that he could not say that anything would be done to give an assurance to the women that their claims should be conceded. So, sir, if you decide against us to-day, to prison we must go, because we feel that we should be going back to the hopeless condition this movement was in three years ago if we consented to be bound over to keep the peace which we have never broken, and so, sir, if you decide to bind us over, whether it is for three or six months, we shall submit to the treatment, the degrading treatment, that we have submitted to before.

Although the Government admitted that we are political offenders, and, therefore, ought to be treated as political offenders are invariably treated, we shall be treated as pickpockets and drunkards; we shall be searched. I want you, if you can, as a man, to realise what it means to women like us. We are driven to do this, we are determined to go on with agitation, because we feel in honour bound. Just as it was the duty of your forefathers, it is our duty to make this world a better place for women than it is to-day. . . .

This is the only way we can get that power which every citizen should have of deciding how the taxes she contributes to should be spent, and how the laws she has to obey should be made, and until we get that power we shall be here—we are here to-day, and we shall come here over and over again. You must realise how futile it is to settle this question by binding us over to keep the peace. You have tried it; it has failed. Others have tried to do it, and have failed. If you had power to send us to prison, not for six months, but for six years, for 16 years, or for the whole of our lives, the Government must not think that they can stop this agitation. It will go on.

I want to draw your attention to the self-restraint which was shown by our followers on the night of the 13th, after we had been arrested. It only shows that our influence over them is very great, because I think that if they had yielded to their natural impulses, there might have been a breach of the peace on the evening of the 13th. They were very indignant, but our words have always been, "be patient, exercise self-restraint, show our so-called superiors that the criticism of women being hysterical is not true; use no violence, offer yourselves to the violence of others." We are going to win. Our women have taken that advice; if we are in prison they will continue to take that advice.

Well, sir, that is all I have to say to you. We are here not because we are law-breakers; we are here in our efforts to become law-makers.

■ Discussion Questions

1. In what ways did the WSPU's tactics challenge conventional notions of proper behavior for women at the time?
2. According to Pankhurst, why was the WSPU forced to adopt such tactics?
3. Why did Pankhurst think that women had both a right to and a need for political enfranchisement?

CHAPTER 20

War, Revolution, and Reconstruction, 1914–1929

Contemporaries dubbed World War I the "Great War" with good reason. Over the course of four years, millions died in battle—victims of advanced military technologies, outdated tactics, wretched leadership, and a desire for total victory. The first document allows us to see these horrors through two soldiers' eyes. The second document reveals that civilians contributed to the staggering death toll, for it was they who manufactured the grenades, rifles, and other weapons used on the front with such devastating effects. Yet the war's legacy did not stop there, as the third document attests. Civilian protests against the war unleashed the Russian Revolution, which transformed the world's political landscape. To the west, governments faced their own challenges as they struggled under the weight of postwar reconstruction and popular discontent. Among the people who capitalized on these troubled times was the founder of Italian fascism, Benito Mussolini, who ushered in a new age of violent dictatorship in Europe.

64. Fritz Franke and Siegfried Sassoon, *Two Soldiers' Views of the Horrors of War* (1914–1918)

When the war broke out in August 1914, no one foresaw the years of massive destruction and bloodshed that lay ahead. By late autumn, the two sides were entrenched along a line that extended from France into Belgium, and so the western front was born. Here millions of soldiers like Fritz Franke and Siegfried Sassoon faced unspeakable horrors. In a letter written in the war's first months, Franke, a medical student from Berlin, describes trench warfare as a living hell of shells and corpses. His description also reveals what already had become and would remain the war's defining feature in the west: immobility and stalemate. Franke paid the ultimate price for both: he was killed in May 1915. By contrast, Sassoon, a British officer, survived and became famous for poems like the one following Franke's letter, "Counter-Attack," which describes the war's misery and futility.

FRITZ FRANKE

Louve, November 5th, 1914

Yesterday we didn't feel sure that a single one of us would come through alive. You can't possibly picture to yourselves what such a battle-field looks like. It is impossible to describe it, and even now, when it is a day behind us, I myself can hardly believe that such bestial barbarity and unspeakable suffering are possible. Every foot of ground contested; every hundred yards another trench; and everywhere bodies—rows of them! All the trees shot to pieces; the whole ground

---

A. F. Wedd, trans., *German Students' War Letters* (New York: E. P. Dutton, 1929), 123–25.

churned up a yard deep by the heaviest shells; dead animals; houses and churches so utterly destroyed by shell-fire that they can never be of the least use again. And every troop that advances in support must pass through a mile of this chaos, through this gigantic burial-ground and the reek of corpses.

In this way we advanced on Tuesday, marching for three hours, a silent column, in the moonlight, towards the Front and into a trench as Reserve, two to three hundred yards from the English, close behind our own infantry.

There we lay the whole day, a yard and a half to two yards below the level of the ground, crouching in the narrow trench on a thin layer of straw, in an overpowering din which never ceased all day or the greater part of the night—the whole ground trembling and shaking! There is every variety of sound—whistling, whining, ringing, crashing, rolling . . . the beastly things pitch right above one and burst and the fragments buzz in all directions, and the only question one asks is: "Why doesn't one get me?" Often the things land within a hand's breadth and one just looks on. One gets so hardened to it that at the most one ducks one's head a little if a great, big naval-gun shell comes a bit too near and its grey-green stink is a bit too thick. Otherwise one soon just lies there and thinks of other things. And then one pulls out the Field Regulations or an old letter from home, and all at once one has fallen asleep in spite of the row.

Then suddenly comes the order: "Back to the horses. You are relieved!" And one runs for a mile or so, mounts, and is a gay trooper once more; hola, away, through night and mist, in gallop and in trot!

One just lives from one hour to the next. For instance, if one starts to prepare some food, one never knows if one mayn't have to leave it behind within an hour. If you lie down to sleep, you must always be "in Alarm Order." On the road, you have just to ride behind the man in front of you without knowing where you are going, or at the most only the direction for half a day.

All the same, there is a lot that is pleasant in it all. We often go careering through lovely country in beautiful weather. And above all one acquires a knowledge of human nature! We all live so naturally and unconventionally here, every one according to his own instincts. That brings much that is good and much that is ugly to the surface, but in every one there is a large amount of truth, and above all strength—strength developed almost to a mania!

SIEGFRIED SASSOON

Counter-Attack

We'd gained our first objective hours before
While dawn broke like a face with blinking eyes,
Pallid, unshaved and thirsty, blind with smoke.
Things seemed all right at first. We held their line,
With bombers posted, Lewis guns well placed,
And clink of shovels deepening the shallow trench.
  The place was rotten with dead; green clumsy legs
  High-booted, sprawled and grovelled along the saps
  And trunks, face downward, in the sucking mud,
  Wallowed like trodden sand-bags loosely filled;
  And naked sodden buttocks, mats of hair,
  Bulged, clotted heads slept in the plastering slime.
  And then the rain began—the jolly old rain!

Siegfried Sassoon, *Collected Poems* (New York: Viking Press, 1949), 68–69.

A yawning soldier knelt against the bank,
Staring across the morning blear with fog;
He wondered when the Allemands would get busy;
And then, of course, they started with five-nines
Traversing, sure as fate, and never a dud.
Mute in the clamour of shells he watched them burst
Spouting dark earth and wire with gusts from hell,
While posturing giants dissolved in drifts of smoke.
He crouched and flinched, dizzy with galloping fear,
Sick for escape—loathing the strangled horror
And butchered, frantic gestures of the dead.

An officer came blundering down the trench:
"Stand-to and man the fire-step!" On he went . . .
Gasping and bawling, "Fire-step . . . counter-attack!"
        Then the haze lifted. Bombing on the right
        Down the old sap: machine-guns on the left;
        And stumbling figures looming out in front.
        "O Christ, they're coming at us!" Bullets spat,
And he remembered his rifle . . . rapid fire . . .
And started blazing wildly . . . then a bang
Crumpled and spun him sideways, knocked him out
To grunt and wriggle: none heeded him; he choked
And fought the flapping veils of smothering gloom,
Lost in a blurred confusion of yells and groans . . .
Down, and down, and down, he sank and drowned,
Bleeding to death. The counter-attack had failed.

■ Discussion Questions

1. Although they fought on opposite sides, what attributes did Franke and Sassoon share?
2. Given Franke's and Sassoon's descriptions of the battlefront, what physical and psychological effects did trench warfare have on soldiers?
3. How does Franke's letter challenge the Allies' propaganda in which German soldiers were depicted as being devoid of humanity?

65. L. Doriat, *Women on the Home Front* (1917)

Trench warfare was not the only distinctive feature of World War I. The massive mobilization of the home front also made the war like no other fought to date. Across Europe, thousands of civilians poured into factories to manufacture supplies for the troops. With casualties mounting and more and more men leaving to replenish the armed forces, women became particularly vital to sustaining the wartime labor force. Consequently, new employment opportunities arose for them, especially in traditionally masculine domains such as munitions. The following interview of a French factory worker in the city of Saint-Nazaire in Brittany by journalist L. Doriat puts a human face on this aspect of the war's impact beyond the battlefield. In it, the worker, whom Doriat never identifies, reveals her

Margaret R. Higonnet, ed., *Lines of Fire: Women Writers of World War I* (New York: Plume, 1999), 129–31.

sense of patriotic duty mingled with her determination not to lose her femininity amid the din and dirt of her job.

The dwelling I enter is tidy, sun lights up the main room and makes the household objects shine; everything speaks of an orderly woman who likes her home. A few flowers in a vase on the table near which she is working prove to me that I was right about the woman I've come to see. The factory has not destroyed her feminine sense of delicacy. Without a hat she seems to me younger; she is surprised to see me, she confesses, because she doubted I would come. Convalescent, she hasn't worked for a whole month, which is why I am lucky enough to find her.

"The very day after my arrival, I found work, thanks to the foreman of a factory of shells who knew my husband," she hastens to tell me. "There is no comparison between this extremely hard and much more precise work and the little toy-like petards that I was making. Here it's not sheets of white metal but big 120 shells. You must also pay much more attention, a defect is serious. The factory never stops, day and night shifts of eight alternate. It's intensive production; no mawkishness here, we are not women by the arms of the machine. Scarcely any apprenticeship, one or two days and you're set.

"I am in a workshop for tempering the steel, or rather I was—will they give me back my place and my machine when I return to the workshop? At the moment of my accident, which I'll tell you about, I was doing the shop-trial of the steel for the shell, testing or inspecting the casing, of course. Right after the tempering bath, when the steel is still hot and black, the other workers and I had to tap it with a buffing wheel in order to polish the steel on a small surface of the bottom and the ogive of the shell. Doing this we handle at least a thousand shells a day, and as I told you, they are big, very heavy to manipulate. Other workers take these same pieces and make a light mark on the polished area, which must not etch the steel further than a certain depth, in a kind of test; they are equipped with a graduated sheet of metal that lets them evaluate the etched lines. If the mark is too deep, the steel is too soft; if it's too shallow, it is too hard; in either case it can't be used and goes back to be recast. The inspection requires great attentiveness. A final verification is made by a controller and as we are always required to put our number on the pieces that pass through our hands, the imperfections, the errors can be traced to their authors.

"There too you don't talk, you don't even think of it. The deafening noise of the machines, the enormous heat of the ovens near which you work, the swiftness of the movements make this precision work into painful labor. When we do it at night, the glare together with the temperature of the furnace exhausts your strength and burns your eyes. In the morning when you get home, you throw yourself on your bed without even the strength to eat a bite. There are also the lathe workshops, I've never been there; many workers learn quickly to turn a shell without needing to calibrate it; some turners do piece work; they are always the ones who hurt themselves. At the job you become very imprudent, as I told you.

"However, you see, I hurt myself too. Forgetting that my buffing machine does an incalculable number of turns a second, I brushed against it with my arm. Clothing and flesh were all taken off before I even noticed. They had to scrape the bone, bandage me every day, I was afraid of an amputation, which luckily was avoided. Only in the last few days have I been able to go without a sling and use my arm; next week I go back to the workshop. I don't want them to change my job, I'm used to my machine and a fresh apprenticeship would not please me at all. I assure you, the first day I was in this noise, near these enormous blast furnaces, opposite the huge machine at which I had to work for hours, I was afraid. We are all like that, all the more so that we are not given time to reflect. You have to understand and act quickly. Those who lose their heads don't accomplish anything, but they are rare. In general, one week suffices to turn a novice into a skilled worker.

"The foremen scold now and then, but they mustn't count it against us; doesn't everyone know that a man is an apprentice before he becomes a mechanic? But at present, however simplified, however divided up the tasks may be, you become a qualified mechanic right away.

"Yet among us there are women like myself who had never done anything; others who did not know how to sew or embroider; nothing discouraged us. As for me I don't complain, this strained activity pleases me. I can thus forget my loneliness—and not having any children, what else should I do with all my time?

"When the war is over, I will look for a job that corresponds better to my taste. I have enough education to become a cashier in a store. I will then be able to be neater than now, for you can't imagine what care it takes to stay more or less clean if you work in a metallurgy.

"A woman is always a woman; I suffered a lot from remaining for hours with my hands and face dirty with dust and smoke. Everything is a matter of habit; among us there are women who seem fragile and delicate—well! if you saw them at work, you would be stunned: it's a total transformation. As for me, I would never have thought I had so much stamina; when I remember that the least little errand wore me out before, I don't recognize myself. Certainly when the day or the night is over, you go home, the fatigue is great, but we are not more tired than the men are. True, we are more sober because we maintain better hygiene and as a result, our sources of energy are more rational and regular, we don't turn to alcohol for strength.

"Our sense of the present need, of the national peril, of hatred for the enemy, of the courage of our husbands and sons—all this pricks us on, we work with all our heart, with all our strength, with all our soul. It is not necessary to stimulate us, each one is conscious of the task assigned to her and in all simplicity she does it, convinced that she defends her country by forging the arms that will free it. We are very proud of being workers for the national defence."

On that proud phrase, I left this valiant woman, with a warm handshake to thank her and to express my admiration.

■ **Discussion Questions**

1. What does this account suggest about women's role in the war effort?
2. How do both interviewer and interviewee cast light on people's fears about the war's effects on traditional gender roles?
3. In what ways does this interview reflect the national consensus supporting the war, as fostered by government-directed propaganda campaigns?

66. Benito Mussolini, *The Doctrine of Fascism*   (1932)

Like millions of his fellow Italians, Benito Mussolini (1883–1945) bitterly resented the outcome of War World I. The Allies had reneged on many of their territorial promises, and Italy's economy was in shambles. Mussolini tapped into these waves of discontent when he founded the Fascist movement in 1919, comprised of former socialists, war veterans, and others who embraced the radical right as the new symbol of authority and strength. Blaming the parliamentary government for the country's ills, the Fascists marched on Rome in 1922 to take matters into their own hands. Upon the king's request, Mussolini became prime minister. This marked the beginning of Mussolini's rise to political power. This excerpt from an article by Mussolini, first published in the Enciclopedia Italiana *in 1932,*

Michael Oakeshott, ed. and trans., *The Social and Political Doctrines of Contemporary Europe* (Cambridge: Cambridge University Press, 1947), 164–79.

illuminates the basic ideological contours of fascism as they had developed during the first decade of his authoritarian rule.

FUNDAMENTAL IDEAS

7. Against individualism, the Fascist conception is for the State; and it is for the individual in so far as he coincides with the State, which is the conscience and universal will of man in his historical existence. It is opposed to classical Liberalism, which arose from the necessity of reacting against absolutism, and which brought its historical purpose to an end when the State was transformed into the conscience and will of the people. Liberalism denied the State in the interests of the particular individual; Fascism reaffirms the State as the true reality of the individual. And if liberty is to be the attribute of the real man, and not of that abstract puppet envisaged by individualistic Liberalism, Fascism is for liberty. And for the only liberty which can be a real thing, the liberty of the State and of the individual within the State. Therefore, for the Fascist, everything is in the State, and nothing human or spiritual exists, much less has value, outside the State. In this sense Fascism is totalitarian, and the Fascist State, the synthesis and unity of all values, interprets, develops and gives strength to the whole life of the people.

8. Outside the State there can be neither individuals nor groups (political parties, associations, syndicates, classes). Therefore Fascism is opposed to Socialism, which confines the movement of history within the class struggle and ignores the unity of classes established in one economic and moral reality in the State; and analogously it is opposed to class syndicalism. Fascism recognizes the real exigencies for which the socialist and syndicalist movement arose, but while recognizing them wishes to bring them under the control of the State and give them a purpose within the corporative system of interests reconciled within the unity of the State.

9. Individuals form classes according to the similarity of their interests, they form syndicates according to differentiated economic activities within these interests; but they form first, and above all, the State, which is not to be thought of numerically as the sum-total of individuals forming the majority of a nation. And consequently Fascism is opposed to Democracy, which equates the nation to the majority, lowering it to the level of that majority; nevertheless it is the purest form of democracy if the nation is conceived, as it should be, qualitatively and not quantitatively, as the most powerful idea (most powerful because most moral, most coherent, most true) which acts within the nation as the conscience and the will of a few, even of One, which ideal tends to become active within the conscience and the will of all—that is to say, of all those who rightly constitute a nation by reason of nature, history or race, and have set out upon the same line of development and spiritual formation as one conscience and one sole will. . . .

POLITICAL AND SOCIAL DOCTRINE

Fascism is to-day clearly defined not only as a regime but as a doctrine. And I mean by this that Fascism to-day, self-critical as well as critical of other movements, has an unequivocal point of view of its own, a criterion, and hence an aim, in face of all the material and intellectual problems which oppress the people of the world.

3. Above all, Fascism, in so far as it considers and observes the future and the development of humanity quite apart from the political considerations of the moment, believes neither in the possibility nor in the utility of perpetual peace. It thus repudiates the doctrine of Pacifism—born of a renunciation of the struggle and an act of cowardice in the face of sacrifice. War alone brings up to their highest tension all human energies and puts the stamp of nobility upon the peoples who have the courage to meet it. All other trials are substitutes, which never really put a man in front of himself in the alternative of life and death. A doctrine, therefore, which begins with a prejudice in favour of peace is foreign to Fascism; as are foreign to the spirit of Fascism. . . .

5. Such a conception of life makes Fascism the precise negation of that doctrine which formed the basis of the so-called Scientific or Marxian Socialism: the doctrine of historical Materialism, according to which the history of human civilizations can be explained only as the struggle of interest between the different social groups and as arising out of change in the means and instruments of production. That economic improvements—discoveries of raw materials, new methods of work, scientific inventions—should have an importance of their own, no one denies, but that they should suffice to explain human history to the exclusion of all other factors is absurd: Fascism believes, now and always, in holiness and in heroism, that is in acts in which no economic motive—remote or immediate—plays a part. With this negation of historical materialism, according to which men would be only by-products of history, who appear and disappear on the surface of the waves while in the depths the real directive forces are at work, there is also denied the immutable and irreparable "class struggle" which is the natural product of this economic conception of history, and above all it is denied that the class struggle can be the primary agent of social changes. . . .

6. After Socialism, Fascism attacks the whole complex of democratic ideologies and rejects them both in their theoretical premises and in their applications or practical manifestations. Fascism denies that the majority, through the mere fact of being a majority, can rule human societies; it denies that this majority can govern by means of a periodical consultation; it affirms the irremediable, fruitful and beneficent inequality of men, who cannot be levelled by such a mechanical and extrinsic fact as universal suffrage. By democratic regimes we mean those in which from time to time the people is given the illusion of being sovereign, while true effective sovereignty lies in other, perhaps irresponsible and secret, forces. Democracy is a regime without a king, but with very many kings, perhaps more exclusive, tyrannical and violent than one king even though a tyrant. . . .

8. In face of Liberal doctrines, Fascism takes up an attitude of absolute opposition both in the field of politics and in that of economics. It is not necessary to exaggerate—merely for the purpose of present controversies—the importance of Liberalism in the past century, and to make of that which was one of the numerous doctrines sketched in that century a religion of humanity for all times, present and future. . . . The "Liberal" century, after having accumulated an infinity of Gordian knots, tried to untie them by the hecatomb of the World War. Never before has any religion imposed such a cruel sacrifice. Were the gods of Liberalism thirsty for blood? Now Liberalism is about to close the doors of its deserted temples because the peoples feel that its agnosticism in economics, its indifferentism in politics and in morals, would lead, as they have led, the States to certain ruin. In this way one can understand why all the political experiences of the contemporary world are anti-Liberal, and it is supremely ridiculous to wish on that account to class them outside of history; as if history were a hunting ground reserved to Liberalism and its professors, as if Liberalism were the definitive and no longer surpassable message of civilization. . . .

If it is admitted that the nineteenth century has been the century of Socialism, Liberalism and Democracy, it does not follow that the twentieth must also be the century of Liberalism, Socialism and Democracy. Political doctrines pass; peoples remain. It is to be expected that this century may be that of authority, a century of the "Right," a Fascist century. If the nineteenth was the century of the individual (Liberalism means individualism) it may be expected that this one may be the century of "collectivism" and therefore the century of the State. . . .

10. The keystone of Fascist doctrine is the conception of the State, of its essence, of its tasks, of its ends. For Fascism the State is an absolute before which individuals and groups are relative. Individuals and groups are "thinkable" in so far as they are within the State. The Liberal State does not direct the interplay and the material and spiritual development of the groups, but limits itself to registering the results; the Fascist State has a consciousness of its own, a will of its own, on this account it is called an "ethical" State. In 1929, at the first quinquennial assembly of the regime, I said: "For Fascism, the State is not the night-watchman who is concerned only with the personal security of the citizens; nor is it an organization for purely material ends, such as

that of guaranteeing a certain degree of prosperity and a relatively peaceful social order, to achieve which a council of administration would be sufficient, nor is it a creation of mere politics with no contact with the material and complex reality of the lives of individuals and the life of peoples. The State, as conceived by Fascism and as it acts, is a spiritual and moral fact because it makes concrete the political, juridical, economic organization of the nation and such an organization is, in its origin and in its development, a manifestation of the spirit. The State is the guarantor of internal and external security, but it is also the guardian and the transmitter of the spirit of the people as it has been elaborated through the centuries in language, custom, faith. The State is not only present, it is also past, and above all future. It is the State which, transcending the brief limit of individual lives, represents the immanent conscience of the nation. The forms in which States express themselves change, but the necessity of the State remains. It is the State which educates citizens for civic virtue, makes them conscious of their mission, calls them to unity; harmonizes their interests in justice; hands on the achievements of thought in the sciences, the arts, in law, in human solidarity; it carries men from the elementary life of the tribe to the highest human expression of power which is Empire; it entrusts to the ages the names of those who died for its integrity or in obedience to its laws; it puts forward as an example and recommends to the generations that are to come the leaders who increased its territory and the men of genius who gave it glory. When the sense of the State declines and the disintegrating and centrifugal tendencies of individuals and groups prevail, national societies move to their decline."

11. From 1929 up to the present day these doctrinal positions have been strengthened by the whole economico-political evolution of the world. It is the State alone that grows in size, in power. It is the State alone that can solve the dramatic contradictions of capitalism. What is called the crisis cannot be overcome except by the State, within the State. . . . Fascism desires the State to be strong, organic and at the same time founded on a wide popular basis. The Fascist State has also claimed for itself the field of economics and, through the corporative, social and educational institutions which it has created, the meaning of the State reaches out to and includes the farthest off-shoots; and within the State, framed in their respective organizations, there revolve all the political, economic and spiritual forces of the nation. A State founded on millions of individuals who recognize it, feel it, are ready to serve it, is not the tyrannical State of the medieval lord. It has nothing in common with the absolutist States that existed either before or after 1789. In the Fascist State the individual is not suppressed, but rather multiplied, just as in a regiment a soldier is not weakened but multiplied by the number of his comrades. The Fascist State organizes the nation, but it leaves sufficient scope to individuals; it has limited useless or harmful liberties and has preserved those that are essential. It cannot be the individual who decides in this matter, but only the State. . . .

13. The Fascist State is a will to power and to government. In it the tradition of Rome is an idea that has force. In the doctrine of Fascism, Empire is not only a territorial, military or mercantile expression, but spiritual or moral. One can think of an empire, that is to say a nation that directly or indirectly leads other nations, without needing to conquer a single square kilometre of territory. For Fascism the tendency to Empire, that is to say, to the expansion of nations, is a manifestation of vitality; its opposite, staying at home, is a sign of decadence: peoples who rise or re-rise are imperialist, peoples who die are denunciatory. Fascism is the doctrine that is most fitted to represent the aims, the states of mind, of a people, like the Italian people, rising again after many centuries of abandonment or slavery to foreigners. But Empire calls for discipline, co-ordination of forces, duty and sacrifice; this explains many aspects of the practical working of the regime and the direction of many of the forces of the State and the necessary severity shown to those who would wish to oppose this spontaneous and destined impulse of the Italy of the twentieth century, to oppose it in the name of the superseded ideologies of the nineteenth, repudiated wherever great experiments of political and social transformation have been courageously attempted:

especially where, as now, peoples thirst for authority, for leadership, for order. If every age has its own doctrine, it is apparent from a thousand signs that the doctrine of the present age is Fascism. That it is a doctrine of life is shown by the fact that it has resuscitated a faith. That this faith has conquered minds is proved by the fact that Fascism has had its dead and its martyrs.

Fascism henceforward has in the world the universality of all those doctrines which, by fulfilling themselves, have significance in the history of the human spirit.

■ Discussion Questions

1. According to Mussolini, how is fascism opposed to liberalism, democracy, and socialism?
2. How is this opposition rooted in Mussolini's concept of the individual's role in the Fascist state?
3. What does Mussolini mean when he describes fascism as "totalitarian"?
4. As elaborated here, in what ways were Mussolini's principles rooted in the legacy of World War II?

CHAPTER 21

An Age of Catastrophes, 1929–1945

The Great Depression of the 1930s ushered in an age of unprecedented violence and suffering around the globe. Millions were out of work, hungry, and disillusioned. Authoritarian leaders capitalized on the downhearted, gaining widespread support with their promises to revive the economy and restore national glory. The head of the Nazi Party, Adolf Hitler, was among the most menacing of these political strongmen, as the first document vividly shows. Western democracies responded cautiously to the Nazi menace, hoping to contain Hitler's ambition through a policy of appeasement rather than military force. The second document illuminates this policy in action at a critical juncture in Hitler's march toward war. Once the war began, no one was truly prepared for its horrors. As the last two documents show, the combination of ideology and advanced technology fueling the war was especially cruel to the civilian population, setting a dangerous precedent for the future.

67. Joseph Goebbels, *Nazi Propaganda Pamphlet* (1930)

Probably no one better personifies the power of authoritarian rulers to manipulate the minds of millions in the 1930s than Adolf Hitler. Among the secrets of Hitler's success was his propaganda chief, Joseph Goebbels (1895–1945). A member of the National Socialist Party since 1922, Goebbels shared Hitler's belief that the masses were easily managed if the message directed to them was simple and repetitive. To this end, Goebbels wrote pamphlets such as the one that follows in support of the Nazi cause. In it, he reveals the virulent anti-Semitism that shaped the Nazis' political program and set them apart from other totalitarian regimes. Goebbels's tactics helped propel Hitler to national leadership in 1933.

WHY ARE WE NATIONALISTS?

We are NATIONALISTS because we see in the NATION the only possibility for the protection and the furtherance of our existence.

The NATION is the organic bond of a people for the protection and defense of their lives. He is nationally minded who understands this IN WORD AND IN DEED.

Today, in GERMANY, NATIONALISM has degenerated into BOURGEOIS PATRIOTISM, and its power exhausts itself in tilting at windmills. It says GERMANY and means MONARCHY. It proclaims FREEDOM and means BLACK-WHITE-RED.

Louis L. Snyder, ed., *Documents of German History* (New Brunswick, N.J.: Rutgers University Press, 1958), 414–16.

Young nationalism has its unconditional demands. BELIEF IN THE NATION is a matter of all the people, not for individuals of rank, a class, or an industrial clique. The eternal must be separated from the contemporary. The maintenance of a rotten industrial system has nothing to do with nationalism. I can love Germany and hate capitalism; not only CAN I do it, I also MUST do it. The germ of the rebirth of our people LIES ONLY IN THE DESTRUCTION OF THE SYS-TEM OF PLUNDERING THE HEALTHY POWER OF THE PEOPLE.

WE ARE NATIONALISTS BECAUSE WE, AS GERMANS, LOVE GERMANY. And because we love Germany, we demand the protection of its national spirit and we battle against its destroyers.

WHY ARE WE SOCIALISTS?

We are SOCIALISTS because we see in SOCIALISM the only possibility for maintaining our racial existence and through it the reconquest of our political freedom and the rebirth of the German state. SOCIALISM has its peculiar form first of all through its comradeship in arms with the forward-driving energy of a newly awakened nationalism. Without nationalism it is nothing, a phantom, a theory, a vision of air, a book. With it, it is everything, THE FUTURE, FREEDOM, FATHERLAND!

It was a sin of the liberal bourgeoisie to overlook THE STATE-BUILDING POWER OF SOCIALISM. It was the sin of MARXISM to degrade SOCIALISM to a system of MONEY AND STOMACH.

We are SOCIALISTS because for us THE SOCIAL QUESTION IS A MATTER OF NECES-SITY AND JUSTICE, and even beyond that A MATTER FOR THE VERY EXISTENCE OF OUR PEOPLE.

SOCIALISM IS POSSIBLE ONLY IN A STATE WHICH IS FREE INSIDE AND OUTSIDE.

DOWN WITH POLITICAL BOURGEOIS SENTIMENT: FOR REAL NATIONALISM!

DOWN WITH MARXISM: FOR TRUE SOCIALISM!

UP WITH THE STAMP OF THE FIRST GERMAN NATIONAL SOCIALIST STATE!

AT THE FRONT THE NATIONAL SOCIALIST GERMAN WORKERS PARTY! . . .

WHY DO WE OPPOSE THE JEWS?

We are ENEMIES OF THE JEWS, because we are fighters for the freedom of the German people. THE JEW IS THE CAUSE AND THE BENEFICIARY OF OUR MISERY. He has used the social difficulties of the broad masses of our people to deepen the unholy split between Right and Left among our people. He has made two halves of Germany. He is the real cause for our loss of the Great War.

The Jew has no interest in the solution of Germany's fateful problems. He CANNOT have any. FOR HE LIVES ON THE FACT THAT THERE HAS BEEN NO SOLUTION. If we would make the German people a unified community and give them freedom before the world, then the Jew can have no place among us. He has the best trumps in his hands when a people lives in inner and outer slavery. THE JEW IS RESPONSIBLE FOR OUR MISERY AND HE LIVES ON IT.

That is the reason why we, AS NATIONALISTS and AS SOCIALISTS, oppose the Jew. HE HAS CORRUPTED OUR RACE, FOULED OUR MORALS, UNDERMINED OUR CUSTOMS, AND BROKEN OUR POWER.

THE JEW IS THE PLASTIC DEMON OF THE DECLINE OF MANKIND.

THE JEW IS UNCREATIVE. He produces nothing. HE ONLY HANDLES PRODUCTS. As long as he struggles against the state, HE IS A REVOLUTIONARY; as soon as he has power, he preaches QUIET AND ORDER, so that he can consume his plunder at his convenience.

ANTI-SEMITISM IS UN-CHRISTIAN. That means, then, that he is a Christian who looks on while the Jew sews straps around our necks. TO BE A CHRISTIAN MEANS: LOVE THY NEIGHBOR AS THYSELF! MY NEIGHBOR IS ONE WHO IS TIED TO ME BY HIS BLOOD. IF I LOVE HIM, THEN I MUST HATE HIS ENEMIES. HE WHO THINKS GERMAN MUST DESPISE THE JEWS. The one thing makes the other necessary.

WE ARE ENEMIES OF THE JEWS BECAUSE WE BELONG TO THE GERMAN PEOPLE. THE JEW IS OUR GREATEST MISFORTUNE.

It is not true that we eat a Jew every morning at breakfast.

It is true, however, that he SLOWLY BUT SURELY ROBS US OF EVERYTHING WE OWN. THAT WILL STOP, AS SURELY AS WE ARE GERMANS.

■ Discussion Questions

1. According to this pamphlet, what do the terms *nationalist* and *socialist* mean within the context of the Nazi party?
2. Why does the pamphlet target Jews as enemies of the German people?
3. What does the pamphlet suggest about the link between the Nazis' racial views and their goals for Germany's future?

68. Neville Chamberlain, *Speech on the Munich Crisis*   (1938)

During the troubled 1930s, a deep longing for peace clouded many Europeans' ability to see the true nature of the Nazi threat. The British politician Neville Chamberlain (1869–1940) was no exception. He became prime minister in 1937 when Hitler's preparations for war were well under way. Upon annexing Austria in March 1938, Hitler turned to his next target, Czechoslovakia. Chamberlain, Benito Mussolini (1883–1945), and French premier Edouard Daladier (1884–1970) met with Hitler in Munich in September 1938 to defuse the situation; their meeting resulted in an agreement that accepted Germany's territorial claims. In his closing speech, delivered during a debate on the agreement in the House of Commons, Chamberlain defended his policy of appeasement toward Hitler as the key to peace. Tragically, it was instead a prelude to war.

War today—this has been said before, and I say it again—is a different thing not only in degree, but in kind from what it used to be. We no longer think of war as it was in the days of Marlborough [John Churchill, first duke of Marlborough, a famed seventeenth-century military commander] or the days of Napoleon or even in the days of 1914. When war starts today, in the very first hour, before any professional soldier, sailor or airman has been touched, it will strike the workman, the clerk, the man-in-the-street or in the bus, and his wife and children in their homes. As I listened I could not help being moved, as I am sure everybody was who heard the hon. Member for Bridgeton (Mr. Maxton) when he began to paint the picture which he himself had seen and realised what it would mean in war—people burrowing underground, trying to escape from poison gas, knowing that at any hour of the day or night death or mutilation was ready to come upon them. Remembering that the dread of what might happen to them or to those dear to them might remain with fathers and mothers for year after year—when you think of these things you cannot ask people to accept a prospect of that kind; you cannot force them into a position that they have got to accept it; unless you feel yourself, and can make them feel, that the cause for which they are going to fight is a vital cause—a cause that transcends all the human values, a cause to which you can point, if some day you win the victory, and say, "That cause is safe."

Since I first went to Berchtesgaden [a town in southeast Germany and the site of Hitler's wartime villa, where Chamberlain traveled to meet with the Nazi leader] more than 20,000 letters and telegrams have come to No. 10, Downing Street. Of course, I have only been able to look

Parliamentary Debates. Fifth Series. Volume 339. House of Commons Official Report (London, 1938), 544–52.

at a tiny fraction of them, but I have seen enough to know that the people who wrote did not feel that they had such a cause for which to fight, if they were asked to go to war in order that the Sudeten Germans might not join the Reich. That is how they are feeling. That is my answer to those who say that we should have told Germany weeks ago that, if her army crossed the border of Czechoslovakia, we should be at war with her. We had no treaty obligations and no legal obligations to Czechoslovakia and if we had said that, we feel that we should have received no support from the people of this country. . . .

As regards future policy, it seems to me that there are really only two possible alternatives. One of them is to base yourself upon the view that any sort of friendly relations, or possible relations, shall I say, with totalitarian States are impossible, that the assurances which have been given to me personally are worthless, that they have sinister designs and that they are bent upon the domination of Europe and the gradual destruction of democracies. Of course, on that hypothesis, war has got to come, and that is the view—a perfectly intelligible view—of a certain number of hon. and right hon. Gentlemen in this House. I am not sure that it is not the view of some Members of the party opposite. [An HON. MEMBER: "Yes."] Not all of them. They certainly have never put it in so many words, but it is illustrated by the observations of the hon. Member for Derby (Mr. Noel-Baker), who spoke this afternoon, and who had examined the Agreement signed by the German Chancellor and myself, which he described as a pact designed by Herr Hitler to induce us to relinquish our present obligations. That shows how far prejudice can carry a man. The Agreement, as anyone can see, is not a pact at all. So far as the question of "never going to war again" is concerned, it is not even an expression of the opinion of the two who signed the paper, except that it is their opinion of the desire of their respective peoples. I do not know whether the hon. Member will believe me or attribute to me also sinister designs when I tell him that it was a document not drawn up by Herr Hitler but by the humble individual who now addresses this House.

If the view which I have been describing is the one to be taken, I think we must inevitably proceed to the next stage—that war is coming, broadly speaking the democracies against the totalitarian States—that certainly we must arm ourselves to the teeth, that clearly we must make military alliances with any other Powers whom we can get to work with us, and that we must hope that we shall be allowed to start the war at the moment that suits us and not at the moment that suits the other side. That is what some right hon. and hon. Gentlemen call collective security. Some hon. Members opposite will walk into any trap if it is only baited with a familiar catchword and they do it when this system is called collective security. But that is not the collective security we are thinking of or did think of when talking about the system of the League of Nations. That was a sort of universal collective security in which all nations were to take their part. This plan may give you security; it certainly is not collective in any sense. It appears to me to contain all the things which the party opposite used to denounce before the War—entangling alliances, balance of power and power politics. If I reject it, as I do, it is not because I give it a label; it is because, to my mind, it is a policy of utter despair.

If that is hon. Members' conviction, there is no future hope for civilisation or for any of the things that make life worth living. Does the experience of the Great War and of the years that followed it give us reasonable hope that if some new war started that would end war any more than the last one did? No. I do not believe that war is inevitable. . . . It seems to me that the strongest argument against the inevitability of war is to be found in something that everyone has recognised or that has been recognised in every part of the House. That is the universal aversion from war of the people, their hatred of the notion of starting to kill one another again. . . .

What is the alternative to this bleak and barren policy of the inevitability of war? In my view it is that we should seek by all means in our power to avoid war, by analysing possible causes, by trying to remove them, by discussion in a spirit of collaboration and good will. I cannot believe that such a programme would be rejected by the people of this country, even if it does mean the establishment of personal contact with dictators, and of talks man to man on the basis that each, while maintaining his own ideas of the internal government of his country, is willing to allow that other systems may suit better other peoples. The party opposite surely have the same idea in mind even if they put it in a different way. They want a world conference. Well, I have had some experience of conferences, and one thing I do feel certain of is that it is better to have no conference at all than a conference which is a failure. The corollary to that is that before you enter a conference you must have laid out very clearly the lines on which you are going to proceed, if you are at least to have in front of you a reasonable prospect that you may obtain success. I am not saying that a conference would not have its place in due course. But I say it is no use to call a conference of the world, including these totalitarian Powers, until you are sure that they are going to attend, and not only that they are going to attend, but that they are going to attend with the intention of aiding you in the policy on which you have set your heart.

I am told that the policy which I have tried to describe is inconsistent with the continuance, and much more inconsistent with the acceleration of our present programme of arms. I am asked how I can reconcile an appeal to the country to support the continuance of this programme with the words which I used when I came back from Munich the other day and spoke of my belief that we might have peace for our time. I hope hon. Members will not be disposed to read into words used in a moment of some emotion, after a long and exhausting day, after I had driven through miles of excited, enthusiastic, cheering people—I hope they will not read into those words more than they were intended to convey. I do indeed believe that we may yet secure peace for our time, but I never meant to suggest that we should do that by disarmament, until we can induce others to disarm too. Our past experience has shown us only too clearly that weakness in armed strength means weakness in diplomacy, and if we want to secure a lasting peace, I realise that diplomacy cannot be effective unless the consciousness exists, not here alone, but elsewhere, that behind the diplomacy is the strength to give effect to it.

One good thing, at any rate, has come out of this emergency through which we have passed. It has thrown a vivid light upon our preparations for defence, on their strength and on their weakness. I should not think we were doing our duty if we had not already ordered that a prompt and thorough inquiry should be made to cover the whole of our preparations, military and civil, in order to see, in the light of what has happened during these hectic days, what further steps may be necessary to make good our deficiencies in the shortest possible time. There have been references in the course of the Debate to other measures which hon. Members have suggested should be taken. I would not like to commit myself now, until I have had a little time for reflection, as to what further it may seem good to ask the nation to do, but I think nobody could fail to have been impressed by the fact that the emergency brought out that the whole of the people of this country, whatever their class, whatever their station, were ready to do their duty, however disagreeable, however hard, however dangerous it may have been.

I cannot help feeling that if, after all, war had come upon us, the people of this country would have lost their spiritual faith altogether. As it turned out the other way, I think we have all seen something like a new spiritual revival, and I know that everywhere there is a strong desire among the people to record their readiness to serve their country, wherever or however their services could be most useful. I would like to take advantage of that strong feeling if it is possible, and although I must frankly say that at this moment I do not myself clearly see my way to any particular scheme, yet I want also to say that I am ready to consider any suggestions that may be made to me, in a very sympathetic spirit.

Finally, I would like to repeat what my right hon. Friend the Chancellor of the Exchequer said yesterday in his great speech. Our policy of appeasement does not mean that we are going to seek new friends at the expense of old ones, or, indeed, at the expense of any other nations at all. I do not think that at any time there has been a more complete identity of views between the French Government and ourselves than there is at the present time. Their objective is the same as ours—to obtain the collaboration of all nations, not excluding the totalitarian States, in building up a lasting peace for Europe. . . .

■ **Discussion Questions**

1. How did Chamberlain justify his policy of appeasement?
2. According to Chamberlain, why did some people oppose this policy?
3. What does Chamberlain's defense indicate about popular attitudes toward war and peace?

69. Sam Bankhalter and Hinda Kibort, *Memories of the Holocaust* (1938–1945)

When Neville Chamberlain detailed the horrors that modern warfare would inflict on civilians, not even he knew how true his words would prove to be. Once the war erupted, one segment of the civilian population in particular was the target of Hitler's fury: Jews. The result was the Final Solution, a technologically and bureaucratically sophisticated system of camps for incarcerating or exterminating European Jews that the Germans put into place between 1941 and 1942. Either inmates were killed on their arrival or were spared to endure a different kind of death: from starvation, abuse, and overwork. The two interviews that follow allow us to see the Holocaust through the eyes of its victims. The first is that of Sam Bankhalter. At fourteen, he was captured by the Nazis in his native Poland and sent to Auschwitz. The second voice is that of Hinda Kibort, a Lithuanian who was nineteen when the Nazis began their assault on the local Jewish population. In 1944, she was deported to Stutthof, a labor camp in northern Poland.

SAM BANKHALTER

Lodz, Poland
There was always anti-Semitism in Poland. The slogan even before Hitler was "Jew, get out of here and go to Palestine." As Hitler came to power, there was not a day at school I was not spit on or beaten up.

I was at camp when the Germans invaded Poland. The camp directors told us to find our own way home. We walked many miles with airplanes over our heads, dead people on the streets. At home there were blackouts. I was just a kid, tickled to death when I was issued a flashlight and gas mask. The Polish army was equipped with buggies and horses, the Germans were all on trucks and tanks. The war was over in ten days.

The Ghetto   The German occupation was humiliation from day 1. If Jewish people were wearing the beard and sidecurls, the Germans were cutting the beard, cutting the sidecurls, laughing at you, beating you up a little bit. Then the Germans took part of Lodz and put on barbed wire, and all the Jews had to assemble in this ghetto area. You had to leave in five or ten minutes or half an hour, so you couldn't take much stuff with you. . . .

Auschwitz   We were the first ones in Auschwitz. We built it. What you got for clothing was striped pants and the striped jacket, no underwear, no socks. In wintertime you put paper in your shoes, and we used to take empty cement sacks and put a string in the top, put two together, one in back and one in front, to keep warm.

If they told you to do something, you went to do it. There was no yes or no, no choices. I worked in the crematorium for about eleven months. I saw Dr. Mengele's experiments on chil-

Rhoda G. Lewin, *Witnesses to the Holocaust: An Oral History* (Boston: Twayne Publishers, 1990), 5–8, 50–55.

dren, I knew the kids that became vegetables. Later in Buchenwald I saw Ilse Koch with a hose and regulator, trying to get pressure to make a hole in a woman's stomach. I saw them cutting Greek people in pieces. I was in Flossenburg for two weeks, and they shot 25,000 Russian soldiers, and we put them down on wooden logs and burned them. Every day the killing, the hanging, the shooting, the crematorium smell, the ovens, and the smoke going out.

I knew everybody, knew every trick to survive. I was one of the youngest in Auschwitz, and I was like "adopted" by a lot of the older people, especially the fathers. Whole families came into Auschwitz together, and you got to Dr. Mengele, who was saying "right, left, left, right," and you knew, right there, who is going to the gas chamber and who is not. Most of the men broke down when they knew their wives and their kids—three-, five-, nine-year-olds—went into the gas chambers. In fact, one of my brothers committed suicide in Auschwitz because he couldn't live with knowing his wife and children are dead.

I was able to see my family when they came into Auschwitz in 1944. I had a sister, she had a little boy a year old. Everybody that carried a child went automatically to the gas chamber, so my mother took the child. My sister survived, but she still suffers, feels she was a part of killing my mother. . . .

Looking Back   Once you start fighting for your life, all the ethics are gone. You live by circumstances. There is no pity. You physically draw down to the point where you cannot think any more, where the only thing is survival, and maybe a little hope that if I survive, I'm gonna be with my grandchildren and tell them the story.

In the camps, death actually became a luxury. We used to say, "Look at how lucky he is. He doesn't have to suffer any more."

I was a lucky guy. I survived, and I felt pretty good about it. But then you feel guilty living! My children—our friends are their "aunts" and "uncles." They don't know what is a grandfather, a grandmother, a cousin, a holiday sitting as a family.

As you grow older, you think about it, certain faces come back to you. You remember your home, your brothers, children that went to the crematorium. You wonder, how did your mother and father feel when they were in the gas chamber? Many nights I hear voices screaming in those first few minutes in the gas chamber, and I don't sleep.

I talk to a lot of people, born Americans, and they don't relate. They can't understand, and I don't blame them. Sometimes it's hard even for me to understand the truth of this whole thing. Did it really happen? But I saw it.

The majority of the people here live fairly good. I don't think there's a country in the world that can offer as much freedom as this country can offer. But the Nazi party exists here, now. This country is supplying anti-Semitic material to the whole world, printing it here and shipping it all over, and our leaders are silent, just as the world was silent when the Jews were being taken to the camps. How quick we forget.

When I sit in a plane, I see 65 percent of the people will pick up the sports page of the newspaper. They don't care what is on the front page! And this is where the danger lies. All you need is the economy to turn a little sour and have one person give out the propaganda. With 65 percent of the population the propaganda works, and then the other 35 percent is powerless to do anything about it.

HINDA KIBORT

Kovno, Lithuania

When the Germans marched in in July 1941, school had let out for the summer, so our whole family was together, including my brother who was in the university and my little sister who was in tenth grade. We tried to leave the city, but it was just like you see in the documentaries—

people with their little suitcases walking along highways and jumping into ditches because German planes were strafing, coming down very low, and people killed, and all this terror. German tanks overtook us, and we returned home.

The Occupation   We did not have time like the German Jews did, from '33 until the war broke out in '39, for step-by-step adjustments. For us, one day we were human, the next day we're subhuman. We had to wear yellow stars. Everybody could command us to do whatever they wanted. They would make you hop around in the middle of the street, or they made you lie down and stepped on you, or spit on you, or they tore at beards of devout Jews. And there was always an audience around to laugh. . . .

The Ghetto   In September all the Jews were enclosed in a ghetto. We lived together in little huts, sometimes two families to a room. There were no schools, no newspapers, no concerts, no theater. Officially, we didn't have any radios or books, but people brought in many books and they circulated. We also had a couple of radios and we could hear the BBC, so we were very much aware of what was going on with the war.

As long as we were strong and useful, we would survive. Everybody had to go to work except children under twelve and the elderly. There were workshops in the ghetto where they made earmuffs for the army, for instance, but mostly people went out to work in groups, with guards. A few tried to escape, but were caught.

We did not know yet about concentration camps.

In 1943 the war turned, and we could feel a terrible tension from the guards and from Germans we worked with on the outside. We could exchange clothing or jewelry for food, but this was extremely dangerous because every time a column came back from work, we were all searched. A baker, they found some bread and a few cigarettes in his pocket. He was hanged publicly, on a Sunday. There was a little orchard in the ghetto, a public place, and we Jews had to build a gallows there and a Jew had to hang him. We were all driven out by the guards and had to stand and watch this man being hanged.

November 5, 1943, was the day all the children were taken away. They brought in Romanian and Ukrainian S.S. to do it. All five of us in our family were employed in a factory adjacent to the ghetto, so we could see through the window what was happening. They took everybody out who stayed in the ghetto—all the children, all the elderly. When we came back after work we were a totally childless society! You can imagine parents coming home to—nothing. Everybody was absolutely shattered.

People were looking for answers, for omens. They turned to seances or to heaven to look for signs. And this was the day when we heard for the first time the word *Auschwitz*. There was a rumor that the children were taken there, but we didn't know the name so we translated it as *Der Schweiz*—Switzerland. We hoped that the trains were going to Switzerland, that the children would be hostages there.

The Transport   On July 16, 1944, the rest of the ghetto were put on cattle trains, with only what we could carry. We had no bathrooms. There was a pail on one side that very soon was full. We were very crowded. The stench and the lack of water and the fear, the whole experience, is just beyond explanation.

At one time, when we were in open country, a guard opened the door and we sat on the side and let our feet down and got some fresh air. We even tried to sing. But then they closed it up, and we were all inside again.

Labor Camp   When we arrived at Stutthof our family was separated—the men to one side of the camp, women to the other. My mother and sister and I had to undress. There were S.S. guards around, men and women. In the middle of the room was a table and an S.S. man in a white coat. We came in in batches, totally naked.

I cannot describe how you feel in a situation like this. We were searched, totally, for jewelry, gold, even family pictures. We had to stand spread-eagle and spread out our fingers. They looked through the hair, they looked into the mouth, they looked in the ears, and then we had to lie down. They looked into every orifice of the body, right in front of everybody. We were in total shock.

From this room we were rushed through a room that said above the door "shower room." There were little openings in the ceiling and water was trickling through. In the next room were piles of clothing, rags, on the floor. You had to grab a skirt, a blouse, a dress, and exchange among yourselves to find what fit. The same thing with shoes. Some women got big men's shoes. I ended up with brown suede pumps with high heels and used a rock to break off the heels, so I could march and stand in line on roll calls.

After this we went into registration and they took down your profession, scholastic background, everything. We got black numbers on a white piece of cloth that had to be sewn on the sleeve. My mother and sister and I had numbers in the 54,000s. People from all over Europe—Hungarian women and Germans, Czechoslovakia, Belgium, you name it—they were there. Children, of course, were not there. When families came with children, the children were taken right away.

As prisoners of Stutthof we were taken to outside work camps. A thousand of us women were taken to dig antitank ditches, a very deep V-shaped ditch that went for miles and miles. The Germans had the idea that Russian tanks would fall into those ditches and not be able to come up again!

When we were done, 400 of us were taken by train deeper into Germany. We ended up in tents, fifty women to a tent. We had no water for washing and not even a latrine. If at night you wanted to go, you had to call a guard who would escort you to this little field, stand there watching while you were crouching down, and then escort you back.

We were covered with lice, and we became very sick and weak. But Frau Schmidt taught us to survive. She was a chemist, and she taught us what roots or grasses we could eat that weren't poisonous. She also said that to survive we have to keep our minds occupied and not think about the hunger and cold. She made us study every day! . . .

By the middle of December we had to stop working because the snow was very deep and everything was frozen. January 20, 1945, they made a selection. The strong women that could still work would be marched out, and the sick, those who couldn't walk or who had bent backs, or who were just skeletons and too weak to work, would be left behind. My mother was selected and my sister and I decided to stay behind with her.

We were left without food, with two armed guards. We thought the guards will burn the tents, with us in them. Then we heard there was a factory where they boiled people's bodies to manufacture soap. But the next day the guards put us in formation and marched us down the highway until we came to a small town.

We were put in the jail there. There we were, ninety-six women standing in a small jail cell, with no bathroom, pressed so close together we couldn't sit down, couldn't bend down. Pretty soon everybody was hysterical, screaming. Then slowly we quieted down.

In the morning when they opened the doors, we really spilled outside! They had recruited a bunch of Polish guards and they surrounded us totally, as if in a box. So there we were, ninety-six weak, emaciated women, marching down the highway with all these guards with rifles.

Then the German guards told us to run into the woods. The snow was so deep, up to our knees, and most of us were barefoot, frozen, our feet were blistered. We couldn't really run, but we spread out in a long line, with my mother and sister and I at the very end. I was near one guard, and all of a sudden I heard the sound of his rifle going "click." I still remember the feeling in the back of my spine, very strange and very scary. Then the guards began to shoot.

There was a terrible panic, screams. People went really crazy. The three of us always hand-held with my mother in the middle, but now she let go of us and ran toward the guards, scream-ing not to shoot her children. They shot her, and my sister and I grabbed each other by the hand and ran into the woods.

We could hear screaming and shooting, and then it got very quiet. We were afraid to move. The guards wore those awesome-looking black uniforms with the skull and crossbones insignia, and every tree looked like another guard! A few women came out from behind the trees, and eventually, ten of us made it out to the highway.

With our last strength, we made it to a small Polish village about a mile away. We knocked on doors, but they didn't let us in, and they started to throw things at us. We went to the church, and the priest said he couldn't help us because the Germans were in charge.

We were so weak we just sat there on the church steps, and late in the evening the priest came with a man who told us to go hide in a barn that was empty. We did not get any other help, whatsoever, from that whole Polish village—not medical help, not a rag to cover ourselves, not even water. Nothing.

Liberation   The next morning there was a terrible battle right in front of the barn. We were so afraid. Then it got very quiet. We opened the door, and we saw Russian tanks. We were free!

The Russians put us into an empty farmhouse. They gave us Vaseline and some rags, all they had, to cover our wounds. Then they put us on trucks and took us to a town where we found a freight train and just jumped on it.

At the border Russian police took us off the train. They grilled us. "How did you survive? You must have cooperated with the Germans." It was terrible. But finally we got identity cards— in Russia, you are nobody without some kind of I.D.—and my sister and I decided to go to the small town where we had lived. We thought somebody might have survived. . . .

Looking Back   I was a prisoner from age nineteen to twenty-three. I lost my mother and twenty-eight aunts, uncles and cousins—all killed. To be a survivor has meant to me to be a witness be-cause being quiet would not be fair to the ones that did not survive.

There are people writing and saying the Holocaust never happened, it's a hoax, it's Jew-ish propaganda. We should keep talking about it, so the next generation won't grow up not knowing how a human being can turn into a beast, not knowing the danger in keeping quiet when you see something brewing. The onlooker, the bystander, is as much at fault as the per-petrator because he lets it happen. That is why I have this fear of what is called the "silent majority."

So when a non-Jewish friend or a student asks, "What can I do?" I say, when you see something anti-Semitic happen, get up and say, "This is wrong" or "I protest." Send a letter to the newspaper saying, "This should not happen in my community," and sign your name. Then maybe somebody else will be brave enough to come forward and say that he protests, too.

■ Discussion Questions

1. What role did the ghettos play in the Final Solution?
2. What was the principal difference between camps like Auschwitz and those like Stutthof?
3. What do these accounts reveal about conditions in the camps and the inmates' strategies for survival?
4. According to these survivors, what lessons does the Holocaust hold for the future?

CHAPTER 22

The Atomic Age, c. 1945–1960

Despite widespread feelings of relief and joy when World War II at last came to an end, an uncertain path lay ahead for the world. With Europe in shambles, two new superpowers emerged from the rubble: the United States and the Soviet Union. Their rivalry, known as the cold war, shaped international affairs for decades to come. The first document illuminates the ideological and political roots of U.S. and Soviet cold war policies. The bipolarization of world politics was not the only sign of Europe's diminished international identity, as the second document shows. War-weary and bitter, colonial peoples from Asia to Africa successfully battled for independence from European rule. The third document points to another campaign for freedom waiting in the wings. As societal and governmental pressures reasserted traditional boundaries between men and women that had been blurred by the war, some women called for change, setting the stage for the women's liberation movement in the 1960s.

70. National Security Council, *Paper Number 68*   (1950)

Although he had helped to end World War II, U.S. president Harry S. Truman (1945–1953) had little time to celebrate. Daunting challenges still lay ahead as the fragile wartime alliance between the United States and the Soviet Union collapsed. By 1949, the Soviet bloc in eastern Europe was firmly in place, and the threat of international communism loomed large with the triumph of Mao Zedong in China. In response, Truman set out to devise a coherent strategy for combating the expansion of Soviet power. To this end, he commissioned the State and Defense Departments to compile a report on the subject, which they completed in 1950, on the eve of the outbreak of the Korean War. The classified report, excerpted here, elucidates not only the basis of U.S. cold war tactics but also the fears and perceptions underlying them.

Within the past thirty-five years the world has experienced two global wars of tremendous violence. . . . During the span of one generation, the international distribution of power has been fundamentally altered. For several centuries it had proved impossible for any one nation to gain such preponderant strength that a coalition of other nations could not in time face it with greater strength. The international scene was marked by recurring periods of violence and war, but a system of sovereign and independent states was maintained, over which no state was able to achieve hegemony.

National Security Council, Paper Number 68, *Foreign Relations of the United States* (Washington, D.C.: Government Printing Office, 1977), 235–92.

Two complex sets of factors have now basically altered this historical distribution of power. First, the defeat of Germany and Japan and the decline of the British and French Empires have interacted with the development of the United States and the Soviet Union in such a way that power has increasingly gravitated to these two centers. Second, the Soviet Union, unlike previous aspirants to hegemony, is animated by a new fanatic faith, antithetical to our own, and seeks to impose its absolute authority over the rest of the world. Conflict has, therefore, become endemic and is waged, on the part of the Soviet Union, by violent or non-violent methods in accordance with the dictates of expediency. . . .

On the one hand, the people of the world yearn for relief from the anxiety arising from the risk of atomic war. On the other hand, any substantial further extension of the area under the domination of the Kremlin would raise the possibility that no coalition adequate to confront the Kremlin with greater strength could be assembled. It is in this context that this Republic and its citizens in the ascendancy of their strength stand in their deepest peril.

The issues that face us are momentous, involving the fulfillment or destruction not only of this Republic but of civilization itself. They are issues which will not await our deliberations. With conscience and resolution this Government and the people it represents must now take new and fateful decisions. . . .

Our overall policy at the present time may be described as one designed to foster a world environment in which the American system can survive and flourish. It therefore rejects the concept of isolation and affirms the necessity of our positive participation in the world community.

This broad intention embraces two subsidiary policies. One is a policy which we would probably pursue even if there were no Soviet threat. It is a policy of attempting to develop a healthy international community. The other is the policy of "containing" the Soviet system. . . .

As for the policy of "containment," it is one which seeks by all means short of war to (1) block further expansion of Soviet power, (2) expose the falsities of Soviet pretensions, (3) induce a retraction of the Kremlin's control and influence, and (4) in general, so foster the seeds of destruction within the Soviet system that the Kremlin is brought at least to the point of modifying its behavior to conform to generally accepted international standards.

It was and continues to be cardinal in this policy that we possess superior overall power in ourselves or in dependable combination with other like-minded nations. One of the most important ingredients of power is military strength. In the concept of "containment," the maintenance of a strong military posture is deemed to be essential for two reasons: (1) as an ultimate guarantee of our national security and (2) as an indispensable backdrop to the conduct of the policy of "containment." . . .

At the same time, it is essential to the successful conduct of a policy of "containment" that we always leave open the possibility of negotiation with the U.S.S.R. A diplomatic freeze—and we are in one now—tends to defeat the very purposes of "containment" because it raises tensions at the same time that it makes Soviet retractions and adjustments in the direction of moderated behavior more difficult. It also tends to inhibit our initiative and deprives us of opportunities for maintaining a moral ascendancy in our struggle with the Soviet system. . . .

It is quite clear from Soviet theory and practice that the Kremlin seeks to bring the free world under its dominion by the methods of the cold war. The preferred technique is to subvert by infiltration and intimidation. Every institution of our society is an instrument which it is sought to stultify and turn against our purposes. Those that touch most closely our material and moral strength are obviously the prime targets, labor unions, civil enterprises, schools, churches, and all media for influencing opinion. The effort is not so much to make them serve obvious Soviet ends as to prevent them from serving our ends, and thus to make them sources of confusion in our economy, our culture, and our body politic. The doubts and diversities that in terms of our values are part of the merit of a free system, the weaknesses and the problems that are peculiar to it, the rights and privileges that free men enjoy, and the disorganization and destruction left in the wake of the last attack in our freedoms, all are but opportunities for the Kremlin to do its evil work. Every advantage is taken of the fact that our means of prevention and retaliation are limited by those principles and scruples which are precisely the ones that give our freedom and democracy its meaning for us. None of our scruples deter those whose only code is, "morality is that which serves the revolution."

At the same time the Soviet Union is seeking to create overwhelming military force, in order to back up infiltration with intimidation. In the only terms in which it understands strength, it is seeking to demonstrate to the free world that force and the will to use it are on the side of the Kremlin, that those who lack it are decadent and doomed. In local incidents it threatens and encroaches both for the sake of local gains and to increase anxiety and defeatism in all the free world. . . .

Our position as the center of power in the free world places a heavy responsibility upon the United States for leadership. We must organize and enlist the energies and resources of the free world in a positive program for peace which will frustrate the Kremlin design for world domination by creating a situation in the free world to which the Kremlin will be compelled to adjust. Without such a cooperative effort, led by the United States, we will have to make gradual withdrawals under pressure until we discover one day that we have sacrificed positions of vital interest. . . .

In summary, we must, by means of a rapid and sustained build-up of the political, economic, and military strength of the free world, and by means of an affirmative program intended to wrest the initiative from the Soviet Union, confront it with convincing evidence of the determination and ability of the free world to frustrate the Kremlin design of a world dominated by its will [*sic*]. Such evidence is the only means short of war which eventually may force the Kremlin to abandon its present course of action and to negotiate acceptable agreements on issues of major importance.

The whole success of the proposed program hangs ultimately on recognition by this Government, the American people, and all free peoples, that the cold war is in fact a real war in which the survival of the free world is at stake. Essential prerequisites to success are consultations with Congressional leaders designed to make the program the object of nonpartisan legislative support, and a presentation to the public of a full explanation of the facts and implications of the present international situation. The prosecution of the program will require of us all the ingenuity, sacrifice, and unity demanded by the vital importance of the issue and the tenacity to persevere until our national objectives have been attained.

■ Discussion Questions

1. As described here, how did World War II transform the international distribution of power?
2. According to the report, in what ways did the Soviet Union pose a danger to Americans and all "free peoples"?
3. What solutions does the document set forth to counter this danger?
4. Why does the report describe the cold war as a "real" war?

71. Ho Chi Minh, *Declaration of Independence of the Republic of Vietnam*   (1945)

The devastation wrought by World War II encompassed more than the countless bombed buildings and millions of dead. The war also fatally weakened the European powers' grip on their empires, as colonial peoples around the globe rose up against imperialist rule. French Indochina was no exception.

Allan B. Cole, ed., *Conflict in Indo-China and International Repercussions: A Documentary History, 1945–1955* (Ithaca, N.Y.: Cornell University Press, 1956), 20–21.

In 1939, a small nationalist organization, Viet Minh, had formed, which achieved new prominence in the wake of World War II when the French sought to reassert their control in the region. Less than a month after Japan's surrender, the Viet Minh declared Vietnam's independence from France, reprinted in the following document. It was signed by "President Ho Chi Minh," one of the organization's original leaders who had lived in Paris, Moscow, and China. The document explicitly draws on the language of the French Enlightenment to further the Viet Minh's cause and condemn that of France.

"All men are created equal. They are endowed by their Creator with certain unalienable rights, among these are Life, Liberty and the pursuit of happiness."

This immortal statement was made in the Declaration of Independence of the United States of America in 1776. Now if we enlarge the sphere of our thoughts, this statement conveys another meaning: All the peoples on the earth are equal from birth, all the peoples have a right to live, be happy and free.

The Declaration of the Rights of Man and of the Citizen of the French Revolution in 1791 also states: "All men are born free and with equal rights, and must always be free and have equal rights."

BEFORE THE OUTBREAK OF WAR

Those are undeniable truths.

Nevertheless, for more than 80 years, the French imperialists deceitfully raising the standard of Liberty, Equality and Fraternity, have violated our Fatherland and oppressed our fellow-citizens. They have acted contrarily to the ideals of humanity and justice.

In the province of politics, they have deprived our people of every liberty.

They have enforced inhuman laws; to ruin our unity and national consciousness, they have carried out three different policies in the North, the Center and the South of Vietnam.

They have founded more prisons than schools. They have mercilessly slain our patriots; they have deluged our revolutionary areas with innocent blood. They have fettered public opinion; they have promoted illiteracy.

To weaken our race they have forced us to use their manufactured opium and alcohol.

In the province of economics, they have stripped our fellow-citizens of everything they possessed, impoverishing the individual and devastating the land.

They have robbed us of our rice fields, our mines, our forests, our raw materials. They have monopolized the printing of bank-notes, the import and export trade; they have invented numbers of unlawful taxes, reducing our people, especially our countryfolk, to a state of extreme poverty.

They have stood in the way of our businessmen and stifled all their undertakings; they have extorted our working classes in a most savage way.

In the Autumn of the year 1940, when the Japanese fascists violated Indochina's territory to get one more foothold in their fight against the Allies, the French imperialists fell on their knees and surrendered, handing over our country to the Japanese, adding Japanese fetters to the French ones. From that day on the Vietnamese people suffered hardships yet unknown in the history of mankind. The result of this double oppression was terrific: from Quangtri to the Northern border two million people were starved to death in the early months of 1945.

On the 9th of March 1945 the French troops were disarmed by the Japanese. Once more the French either fled, or surrendered unconditionally, showing thus that not only they were incapable of "protecting" us, but that they twice sold us to the Japanese.

Yet, many times before the month of March, the Vietminh had urged the French to ally with them against the Japanese. The French colonists never answered. On the contrary they intensified their terrorizing policy. Before taking their flight they even killed a great number of our patriots who had been imprisoned at Yenbay and Caobang.

DEMOCRATIC REPUBLIC OF VIETNAM

Nevertheless, towards the French people our fellow-citizens have always manifested an attitude pervaded with toleration and humanity. Even after the Japanese putsch of March 1945 the Vietminh have helped many Frenchmen to reach the frontier, have delivered some of them from the Japanese jails, and never failed to protect their lives and properties.

The truth is that since the Autumn of 1940 our country had ceased to be a French colony and had become a Japanese outpost. After the Japanese had surrendered to the Allies our whole people rose to conquer political power and institute the Republic of Vietnam.

The truth is that we have wrested our independence from the Japanese and not from the French. The French have fled, the Japanese have capitulated, Emperor Bao Dai has abdicated, our people has broken the fetters which for over a century have tied us down; our people has at the same time overthrown the monarchic constitution that had reigned supreme for so many centuries and instead has established the present Republican Government.

For these reasons, we, members of the provisional Government, representing the whole population of Vietnam, have declared and renew here our declaration that we break off all relations with the French people and abolish all the special rights the French have unlawfully acquired on our Fatherland.

The whole population of Vietnam is united in a common allegiance to the Republican Government and is linked by a common will which is to annihilate the dark aims of the French imperialists.

We are convinced that the Allied nations which have acknowledged at Teheran and San Francisco the principles of self determination and equality of status will not refuse to acknowledge the independence of Vietnam.

A people that has courageously opposed French domination for more than 80 years, a people that has fought by the Allies' side these last years against the fascists, such a people must be free, such a people must be independent.

For these reasons we, members of the Provisional Government of Vietnam, declare to the world that Vietnam has the right to be free and independent, and has in fact become a free and independent country. We also declare that the Vietnamese people is determined to make the heaviest sacrifices to maintain its independence and its Liberty.

■ Discussion Questions

1. How does the document characterize the actions of the French in Vietnam? Why does it describe them as deceitful?
2. In what ways did World War II further the cause of the Viet Minh?
3. Why did the Viet Minh believe that the Vietnamese people had an undeniable right to independence?

72. Simone de Beauvoir, *The Second Sex* (1949)

Like Ho Chi Minh, Simone de Beauvoir (1908–1986) challenged traditional power structures in the postwar era. However, although she watched the growing independence movement in French Indochina with interest, her battle did not center on the plight of colonized peoples. Rather, she dedicated herself to examining the condition of modern women, which, she argued, was similarly marked by injustice and discrimination. She presented her views to the world in her book The

Simone de Beauvoir, *The Second Sex*, trans. and ed. H. M. Parshley (New York: Knopf, 1953), xvi–xx.

Second Sex, published in 1949. In this excerpt, Beauvoir outlines the fundamental premise of her work: throughout history, women's identities have been defined by men and thus subjugated to them. Only by taking charge of their own lives could women break free from their subservience. Her views would help galvanize the women's liberation movement in the United States and Europe in the 1960s.

A man would never get the notion of writing a book on the peculiar situation of the human male. But if I wish to define myself, I must first of all say: "I am a woman"; on this truth must be based all further discussion. A man never begins by presenting himself as an individual of a certain sex; it goes without saying that he is a man. The terms *masculine* and *feminine* are used symmetrically only as a matter of form, as on legal papers. In actuality the relation of the two sexes is not quite like that of two electrical poles, for man represents both the positive and the neutral, as is indicated by the common use of *man* to designate human beings in general; whereas woman represents only the negative, defined by limiting criteria, without reciprocity. In the midst of an abstract discussion it is vexing to hear a man say: "You think thus and so because you are a woman"; but I know that my only defense is to reply: "I think thus and so because it is true," thereby removing my subjective self from the argument. It would be out of the question to reply: "And you think the contrary because you are a man," for it is understood that the fact of being a man is no peculiarity. A man is in the right in being a man; it is the woman who is in the wrong. It amounts to this: just as for the ancients there was an absolute vertical with reference to which the oblique was defined, so there is an absolute human type, the masculine. Woman has ovaries, a uterus; these peculiarities imprison her in her subjectivity, circumscribe her within the limits of her own nature. It is often said that she thinks with her glands. Man superbly ignores the fact that his anatomy also includes glands, such as the testicles, and that they secrete hormones. He thinks of his body as a direct and normal connection with the world, which he believes he apprehends objectively, whereas he regards the body of woman as a hindrance, a prison, weighed down by everything peculiar to it. . . . And she is simply what man decrees; thus she is called "the sex," by which is meant that she appears essentially to the male as a sexual being. For him she is sex—absolute sex, no less. She is defined and differentiated with reference to man and not he with reference to her; she is the incidental, the inessential as opposed to the essential. He is the Subject, he is the Absolute—she is the Other. . . .

Thus it is that no group ever sets itself up as the One without at once setting up the Other over against itself. If three travelers chance to occupy the same compartment, that is enough to make vaguely hostile "others" out of all the rest of the passengers on the train. In small-town eyes all persons not belonging to the village are "strangers" and suspect; to the native of a country all who inhabit other countries are "foreigners"; Jews are "different" for the anti-Semite, Negroes are "inferior" for American racists, aborigines are "natives" for colonists, proletarians are the "lower class" for the privileged. . . .

No subject will readily volunteer to become the object, the inessential; it is not the Other who, in defining himself as the Other, establishes the One. The Other is posed as such by the One in defining himself as the One. But if the Other is not to regain the status of being the One, he must be submissive enough to accept this alien point of view. Whence comes this submission in the case of woman?

There are, to be sure, other cases in which a certain category has been able to dominate another completely for a time. Very often this privilege depends upon inequality of numbers—the majority imposes its rule upon the minority or persecutes it. But women are not a minority, like the American Negroes or the Jews; there are as many women as men on earth. Again, the two groups concerned have often been originally independent; they may have been formerly unaware of each other's existence, or perhaps they recognized each other's autonomy. But a historical event has resulted in the subjugation of the weaker by the stronger. The scattering of the Jews, the introduction of slavery into America, the conquests of imperialism are examples in point. In these cases the oppressed retained at least the memory of former days; they possessed in common a past, a tradition, sometimes a religion or a culture.

The parallel drawn . . . between women and the proletariat is valid in that neither ever formed a minority or a separate collective unit of mankind. And instead of a single historical event it is in both cases a historical development that explains their status as a class and accounts for the membership of *particular individuals* in that class. But proletarians have not always existed, whereas there have always been women. They are women in virtue of their anatomy and physiology. Throughout history they have always been subordinated to men, and hence their dependency is not the result of a historical event or a social change—it was not something that *occurred*. The reason why otherness in this case seems to be an absolute is in part that it lacks the contingent or incidental nature of historical facts. A condition brought about at a certain time can be abolished at some other time, as the Negroes of Haiti and others have proved; but it might seem that a natural condition is beyond the possibility of change. In truth, however, the nature of things is no more immutably given, once for all, than is historical reality. If woman seems to be the inessential which never becomes the essential, it is because she herself fails to bring about this change. Proletarians say "We"; Negroes also. Regarding themselves as subjects, they transform the bourgeois, the whites, into "others." But women do not say "We," except at some congress of feminists or similar formal demonstration; men say "women," and women use the same word in referring to themselves. They do not authentically assume a subjective attitude. The proletarians have accomplished the revolution in Russia, the Negroes in Haiti, the Indo-Chinese are battling for it in Indo-China; but the women's effort has never been anything more than a symbolic agitation. They have gained only what men have been willing to grant; they have taken nothing, they have only received.

The reason for this is that women lack concrete means for organizing themselves into a unit which can stand face to face with the correlative unit. They have no past, no history, no religion of their own; and they have no such solidarity of work and interest as that of the proletariat. They are not even promiscuously herded together in the way that creates community feeling among the American Negroes, the ghetto Jews, the workers of Saint-Denis, or the factory hands of Renault. They live dispersed among the males, attached through residence, housework, economic condition, and social standing to certain men—fathers or husbands—more firmly than they are to other women. If they belong to the bourgeoisie, they feel solidarity with men of that class, not with proletarian women; if they are white, their allegiance is to white men, not to Negro women. The proletariat can propose to massacre the ruling class, and a sufficiently fanatical Jew or Negro might dream of getting sole possession of the atomic bomb and making humanity wholly Jewish or black; but woman cannot even dream of exterminating the males. The bond that unites her to her oppressors is not comparable to any other. The division of the sexes is a biological fact, not an event in human history. . . . The couple is a fundamental unity with its two halves riveted together, and the cleavage of society along the line of sex is impossible. Here is to be found the basic trait of woman: she is the Other in a totality of which the two components are necessary to one another.

▪ Discussion Questions

1. What does Beauvoir mean when she describes women as the "Other"?
2. According to Beauvoir, how does women's status both resemble and differ from that of other oppressed groups, such as colonized peoples?
3. Why, unlike some of these groups, have women been unable to change their status?

CHAPTER 23

Challenges to the Postindustrial West, 1960–1980

The 1960s was a decade of turmoil fueled by both optimism and despair. Millions of people across Europe and the United States took to the streets to challenge cold war politics and society. At the same time, technological changes transformed everyday life. The first two documents illuminate the effects of the increasing importance of technology in the postindustrial world. On the one hand, technological advances improved people's lives and enhanced their knowledge of the world and the universe. On the other, technology offered new opportunities for mass destruction and seemed to undermine religious beliefs and values. As the third document shows, for many, nothing was sacred, whether in politics, as the student protesters of 1968 revealed, or in culture, as the popularity of rock music demonstrated.

73. The *New York Times* and Neil Armstrong and Edwin Aldrin, *The First Men Walk on the Moon* (1969)

Along with the rise of civic activism and youth culture, the expanding role of technology in postindustrial society changed people's worldview. Perhaps nothing captures technology's growing importance more dramatically than U.S. astronauts Neil Armstrong and Edwin ("Buzz") Aldrin's walk on the moon in July 1969. Spurred by the United States' desire to demonstrate its technological superiority over the Soviet Union, their moon walk was an unprecedented technological feat. So, too, was the fact that the event was broadcast on television to millions of viewers around the world. These two pieces capture the mood at the time of both the astronauts and their audience. The first is an editorial published in the New York Times *on July 20, the day Armstrong and Aldrin took their momentous steps. In the second, we hear Armstrong's and Aldrin's recollections of their historic lunar landing.*

To Walk on the Moon

In a world long given to marking off its historical progress in periods—the Age of Faith, the Renaissance, the Age of Reason, the Industrial Revolution—language seems too impoverished to encompass so neatly the era that begins with man's first walk on the moon. As a term, the Space Age is grossly inadequate, failing completely to convey the nature of the change that this event portends. For the lunar landing of the astronauts is more than a step in history; it is a step in evolution.

From "To Walk on the Moon," *New York Times* editorial, July 20, 1969. Copyright © 1969 by The New York Times Company. From *The First on the Moon: A Voyage with Neil Armstrong, Michael Collins, and Edwin E. Aldrin Jr.*, written with Gene Farmer and Dora Jane Hamblin (Boston: Little, Brown, 1970), 324, 350–51.

The journey of Neil Armstrong and his companions cannot be viewed in the same perspective as the voyage of Columbus or of any other traveler in recorded time—and the difference is not at all in degrees of courage or individual skill. In truth, Columbus's feat may well have taken more courage than Armstrong's because it was preceded by no unmanned probes and took him to regions unknown to the science of his day, in contrast to the photographed, spectographed and charted terrain of the moon.

What gives the astronauts' expedition a different dimension entirely, what removes it indeed from any venture in the whole history of the human race are two circumstances that stagger the mind: it is man's first step in adapting to an environment beyond this planet's and it is a *willed* step in the evolutionary process, one made deliberately and in the full consciousness of its import.

For the adaptation itself there are comparable precedents in nature, though for one as full of meaning for the future one might have to go back to the first fishy creature that emerged from the Devonian sea to make a feeble try at life on dry land.

For the conscious willing of an evolutionary act there is no precedent. Man has of course taught himself to ride over and under the waves and to fly through space, but what is contemplated now is no such passing accommodation but in time the transfer of human life to other sites in the universe—with ultimate consequences that almost surely must be evolutionary in nature.

It will take years, decades, perhaps centuries, for man to colonize even the moon, but that is the end inherent in Armstrong's first step on extraterrestrial soil. Serious and hard-headed scientists envision, even in the not remote future, lunar communities capable of growing into domed cities subsisting on hydroponically grown food, of developing the moon's resources, and eventually of acquiring a breathable atmosphere and a soil capable of being farmed. What with the dire threats of population explosion at best and nuclear explosion at worst, the human race, as Sir Bernard Lovell warns, may find itself sometime in the 21st century "having to consider how best to insure the survival of the species."

It is not possible to imagine that any such cosmic movement would leave the transported segment of mankind unchanged. Over the centuries and through countless transitions it would adapt biologically and psychologically, following Darwinian law, to existence in an environment differing as much from its earthly ancestors as that of the early mammals differed from the environment in the primeval seas.

Reflections on man's social shortcomings, speculation on what else he might have done instead of sending men to the moon—all this melts away in the moment of awe and wonder.

FIRST ON THE MOON

Neil Armstrong said . . . "The most dramatic recollections I had were the sights themselves. Of all the spectacular views we had, the most impressive to me was on the way to the moon, when we flew through its shadow. We were still thousands of miles away, but close enough so that the moon almost filled our circular window. It was eclipsing the sun, from our position, and the corona of the sun was visible around the limb of the moon as a gigantic lens-shaped or saucer-shaped light, stretching out to several lunar diameters. It was magnificent, but the moon was even more so. We were in its shadow, so there was no part of it illuminated by the sun. It was illuminated only by earthshine. It made the moon appear blue-gray, and the entire scene looked decidedly three-dimensional.

"I was really aware, visually aware, that the moon was in fact a sphere, not a disc. It seemed almost as if it were showing us its roundness, its similarity in shape to our earth, in a sort of welcome. I was sure that it would be a hospitable host. It had been awaiting its first visitors for a long time." . . .

[Buzz Aldrin:] "The moon was a very natural and very pleasant environment in which to work. It had many of the advantages of zero-gravity, but it was in a sense less *lonesome* than zero G, where you always have to pay attention to securing attachment points to give you some means of leverage. In one-sixth gravity, on the moon, you had a distinct feeling of being *somewhere*, and you had a constant, though at many times ill defined, sense of direction and force.

"One interesting thing was that the horizontal reference on the moon is not at all well defined. That is, it's difficult to know when you are leaning forward or backward and to what degree. This fact, coupled with the rather limited field of vision from our helmets, made local features of the moon appear to change slope, depending on which way you were looking and how you were standing. The weight of the backpack tends to pull you backward, and you must consciously lean forward just a little to compensate. I believe someone has described the posture as 'tired ape'—almost erect but slumped forward a little. It was difficult sometimes to know when you were standing erect. It felt as if you could lean farther in any direction, without losing your balance, than on earth. By far the easiest and most natural way to move on the surface of the moon is to put one foot in front of the other. The kangaroo hop did work, but it led to some instability; there was not so much control when you were moving around.

"As we deployed our experiments on the surface we had to jettison things like lanyards, retaining fasteners, etc., and some of these we tossed away. The objects would go away with a slow, lazy motion. If anyone tried to throw a baseball back and forth in that atmosphere he would have difficulty, at first, acclimatizing himself to that slow, lazy trajectory; but I believe he could adapt to it quite readily. . . .

"Odor is very subjective, but to me there was a distinct smell to the lunar material—pungent, like gunpowder or spent cap-pistol caps. We carted a fair amount of lunar dust back inside the vehicle with us, either on our suits and boots or on the conveyor system we used to get boxes and equipment back inside. We did notice the odor right away.

"It was a unique, almost mystical environment up there."

■ Discussion Questions

1. What does the editorial mean when it describes Armstrong and Aldrin's lunar landing as a step in human evolution?
2. How does the editorial link this event to contemporary concerns about the future of humankind?

74. Pope John XXIII, *Vatican II*   (1961)

As scientists raced to put a man on the moon and protesters took to the streets, the Catholic church devised its own response to the changes of the day. In 1961, Pope John XXIII (r. 1958–1963) announced his plans in this document to convene an ecumenical council to promote spiritual renewal and reevaluate the place of the church in the modern world. Almost one hundred years had passed since the last council of this type had met. A new council was urgently needed, the pope proclaimed, because the technological and economic advances of the twentieth century posed unprecedented challenges to the church and its faithful. The result was the largest Catholic council ever assembled, known as Vatican II, which met between 1962 and 1965. The decrees, constitutions, and declarations issued by the council established the blueprint for Catholic worship in the postindustrial world.

Walter M. Abbott, trans. and ed., *The Documents of Vatican II: All Sixteen Official Texts Promulgated by the Ecumenical Council* (New York: Herder and Herder, 1966), 703–07.

PAINFUL CONSIDERATIONS

Today the Church is witnessing a crisis under way within society. While humanity is on the edge of a new era, tasks of immense gravity and amplitude await the Church, as in the most tragic periods of its history. It is a question in fact of bringing the modern world into contact with the vivifying and perennial energies of the gospel, a world which exalts itself with its conquests in the technical and scientific fields, but which brings also the consequences of a temporal order which some have wished to reorganize excluding God. This is why modern society is earmarked by a great material progress to which there is not a corresponding advance in the moral field.

Hence there is a weakening in the aspiration toward the values of the spirit. Hence an urge for the almost exclusive search for earthly pleasures, which progressive technology places with such ease within the reach of all. And hence there is a completely new and disconcerting fact: the existence of a militant atheism which is active on a world level.

REASONS FOR CONFIDENCE

These painful considerations are a reminder of the duty to be vigilant and to keep the sense of responsibility awake. Distrustful souls see only darkness burdening the face of the earth. We, instead, like to reaffirm all our confidence in our Savior, who has not left the world which He redeemed.

Indeed, we make ours the recommendation of Jesus that one should know how to distinguish the "signs of the times" (Mt. 16:4), and we seem to see now, in the midst of so much darkness, a few indications which auger well for the fate of the Church and of humanity.

The bloody wars that have followed one on the other in our times, the spiritual ruins caused by many ideologies, and the fruits of so many bitter experiences have not been without useful teachings. Scientific progress itself, which gave man the possibility of creating catastrophic instruments for his destruction, has raised questions. It has obliged human beings to become thoughtful, more conscious of their own limitations, desirous of peace, and attentive to the importance of spiritual values. And it has accelerated that progress of closer collaboration and of mutual integration toward which, even though in the midst of a thousand uncertainties, the human family seems to be moving. And this facilitates, no doubt, the apostolate of the Church, since many people who did not realize the importance of its mission in the past are, taught by experience, today more disposed to welcome its warnings.

PRESENT VITALITY OF THE CHURCH

Then, if we turn our attention to the Church, we see that it has not remained a lifeless spectator in the face of these events but has followed step by step the evolution of peoples, scientific progress, and social revolution. It has opposed decisively the materialistic ideologies which deny faith. Lastly, it has witnessed the rise and growth of the immense energies of an apostolate of prayer, of action in all fields. It has seen the emergence of a clergy constantly better equipped in learning and virtue for its mission; and of a laity which has become ever more conscious of its responsibilities within the bosom of the Church, and, in a special way, of its duty to collaborate with the Church hierarchy.

To this should be added the immense suffering of entire Christian communities, through which a multitude of admirable bishops, priests, and laymen seal their adherence to the faith, bearing persecutions of all kinds and revealing forms of heroism which certainly equal those of the most glorious periods of the Church.

Thus, though the world may appear profoundly changed, the Christian community is also in great part transformed and renewed. It has therefore strengthened itself socially in unity; it has been reinvigorated intellectually; it has been interiorly purified and is thus ready for trial.

THE SECOND VATICAN ECUMENICAL COUNCIL

In the face of this twofold spectacle—a world which reveals a grave state of spiritual poverty and the Church of Christ, which is still so vibrant with vitality—we, from the time we ascended to the supreme pontificate, despite our unworthiness and by means of an impulse of Divine Providence, have felt immediately the urgency of the duty to call our sons together, to give the Church the possibility to contribute more efficaciously to the solution of the problems of the modern age.

For this reason, welcoming as from above the intimate voice of our spirit, we considered that the times now were right to offer to the Catholic Church and to the world the gift of a new Ecumenical Council, as an addition to, and continuation of, the series of the twenty great councils, which have been through the centuries a truly heavenly providence for the increase of grace and Christian progress. . . .

The forthcoming Council will meet therefore and at a moment in which the Church finds very alive the desire to fortify its faith, and to contemplate itself in its own awe-inspiring unity. In the same way, it feels more urgent the duty to give greater efficiency to its sound vitality and to promote the sanctification of its members, the diffusion of revealed truth, the consolidation of its agencies. . . .

And, finally, to a world, which is lost, confused, and anxious under the constant threat of new frightful conflicts, the forthcoming Council must offer a possibility for all men of good will to turn their thoughts and their intentions toward peace, a peace which can and must, above all, come from spiritual and supernatural realities, from human intelligence and conscience, enlightened and guided by God the Creator and Redeemer of humanity.

■ **Discussion Questions**

1. Why did Pope John XXIII think that modern society was in a state of crisis?
2. How did the pope link this crisis specifically to the effects of scientific and technological progress on everyday life?
3. How did the pope hope that Vatican II would counter these effects?

75. *Student Voices of Protest*   (1968)

College campuses were hotbeds of social activism in the 1960s, and students exploded into action with unprecedented force in the spring of 1968. The year was beset with tragedy, from the mounting number of casualties in the Vietnam War to the assassination of American civil rights leader Martin Luther King Jr. From New York to Paris to Berlin, students rose up in protest, particularly over racial and antiwar issues. They demonstrated, occupied buildings, shut down classes, and went on strike. These excerpts bring students to life in their own words, which convey not only frustration and despair but also a desire to bring about lasting change.

My most vivid memory of May '68? The new-found ability for everyone to *speak*—to speak of anything with anyone. In that month of talking during May you learnt more than in the whole of your five years of studying. It was really another world—a dream world perhaps—but that's what I'll always remember: the need and the right for everyone to speak.—*René Bourrigaud, student at the École Supérieure d'Agriculture, Angers, France*

Ronald Fraser et al., *1968: A Student Generation in Revolt* (New York: Pantheon Books, 1988), 9–12.

People were learning through doing things themselves, learning self-confidence. It was magic, there were all these kids from nice middle-class homes who'd never done or said anything and were now suddenly speaking. It was democracy of the public space in the market place, a discourse where nobody was privileged. If anything encapsulated what we were trying to do and why, it was that. . . . —*Pete Latarche, leader of the university occupation at Hull, England, 1968*

It's a moment I shall never forget. Suddenly, spontaneously, barricades were being thrown up in the streets. People were building up the cobblestones because they wanted—many of them for the first time—to throw themselves into a collective, spontaneous activity. People were releasing all their repressed feelings, expressing them in a festive spirit. Thousands felt the need to communicate with each other, to love one another. That night has forever made me optimistic about history. Having lived through it, I can't ever say, "It will never happen. . . ."—*Dany Cohn-Bendit, student leader at Nanterre University, on the night of the Paris barricades, 10/11 May 1968*

The unthinkable happened! Everything I had ever dreamt of since childhood, knowing that it would never happen, now began to become real. People were saying, fuck hierarchy, authority, this society with its cold rational elitist logic! Fuck all the petty bosses and the mandarins at the top! Fuck this immutable society that refuses to consider the misery, poverty, inequality and injustice it creates, that divides people according to their origins and skills! Suddenly, the French were showing they understood that they had to refuse the state's authority because it was malevolent, evil, just as I'd always thought as a child. Suddenly they realized that they had to find a new sort of solidarity. And it was happening in front of my eyes. That was what May '68 meant to me!—*Nelly Finkielsztejn, student at Nanterre University, Paris*

My world had been very staid, very traditional, very frightened, very middle-class and respectable. And here I was doing these things that six months before I would have thought were just horrible. But I was in the midst of an enormous tide of people. There was so much constant collective reaffirmation of it. The ecstasy was stepping out of time, out of traditional personal time. The usual rules of the game in capitalist society had been set aside. It was phenomenally liberating. . . . At the same time it was a political struggle. It wasn't just Columbia. There *was* a fucking war on in Vietnam, and the civil rights movement. These were profound forces that transcend that moment. 1968 just cracked the universe open for me. And the fact of getting involved meant that never again was I going to look at something outside with the kind of reflex condemnation or fear. Yes, it was the making of me—or the unmaking.—*Mike Wallace, occupation of Columbia University, New York, April 1968*

We'd been brought up to believe in our hearts that America fought on the side of justice. The Second World War was very much ingrained in us, my father had volunteered. So, along with the absolute horror of the war in Vietnam, there was also a feeling of personal betrayal. I remember crying by myself late at night in my room listening to the reports of the war, the first reports of the bombing. Vietnam was the catalyst. . . . —*John Levin, student leader at San Francisco State College*

I was outraged, what shocked me most was that a highly developed country, the super-modern American army, should fall on these Vietnamese peasants—fall on them like the conquistadores on South America, or the white settlers on the North American Indians. In my mind's eye, I always saw those bull-necked fat pigs—like in Georg Grosz's pictures—attacking the small, child-like Vietnamese.—*Michael von Engelhardt, German student*

The resistance of the Vietnamese people showed that it could be done—a fight back was possible. If poor peasants could do it well why not people in Western Europe? That was the importance of Vietnam, it destroyed the myth that we just had to hold on to what we had because the whole world could be blown up if the Americans were "provoked." The Vietnamese showed that if you were attacked you fought back, and then it depended on the internal balance of power whether you won or not.—*Tariq Ali, a British Vietnam Solidarity Campaign leader*

So we started to be political in a totally new way, making the connection between our student condition and the larger international issues. A low mark in mathematics could become the focal point of an occupation by students who linked the professor's arbitrary and authoritarian behaviour to the wider issues, like Vietnam. Acting on your immediate problems made you understand better the bigger issues. If it hadn't been for that, perhaps the latter would have remained alien, you'd have said "OK, but what can *I* do?"—*Agnese Gatti, student at Trento Institute of Social Sciences, Italy*

Creating a confrontation with the university administration you could significantly expose the interlocking network of imperialism as it was played out on the campuses. You could prove that they were working hand-in-hand with the military and the CIA, and that ultimately, when you pushed them, they would call upon all the oppressive apparatus to defend their position from their own students.—*Jeff Jones, Students for a Democratic Society (SDS), New York regional organizer*

Everybody was terribly young and didn't know what was going on. One had a sort of megalomaniac attitude that by sheer protest and revolt things would be changed. It was true of the music, of the hallucinogenics, of politics, it was true across the board—people threw themselves into activity without experience. The desire to do something became tremendously intense and the capacity to do it diminished by the very way one was rejecting the procedures by which things could be done. It led to all sorts of crazy ideas.—*Anthony Barnett, sociology student, Leicester University, England*

■ **Discussion Questions**

1. What were some of the students' principal targets for criticism, and why?
2. In what ways did the events of 1968 personally transform many of these students?
3. Some historians argue that the student protests of 1968 made governments less inviolable and sacred. What evidence can you find here to support this assertion?

CHAPTER 24

The New Globalism: Opportunities and Dilemmas, 1980 to the Present

After decades of conflict, the cold war virtually came to a halt in 1989 when the Soviet empire disintegrated. The end of superpower rivalries ushered in a new age of global challenges and opportunities. The first two documents pull back the curtain on the opening act of this drama, revealing that an explosive combination of government-sponsored reforms and grassroots political activism fueled communism's demise. The third document, from French president François Mitterrand, illuminates the collaborative efforts of European leaders to redefine Europe's place on the post–cold war stage, just as they had done after World War II. Yet, as Mitterrand's speech to the European parliament in 1995 reveals, the world was now a far different place, where peoples, cultures, and economies were increasingly bound together, as were the problems they faced.

76. *Glasnost and the Soviet Press* (1988)

When Mikhail Gorbachev (b. 1931) became general secretary of the Soviet Communist Party in 1985, the nation's economy was in ruins, and people struggled to meet even their most basic needs. Gorbachev implemented revolutionary policies of economic restructuring (perestroika) and "openness" (glasnost) to confront the crisis. The two articles excerpted here illuminate the crucial role of the Soviet press in this process as a forum for public debate. Never before had Soviet citizens experienced such freedom of speech and expression. Written by Nina Andreyeva, the first article appeared as a letter to the editor on the front page of the prestigious newspaper Sovetskaya Rossiya in March 1988. Politically conservative, Andreyeva attacked Gorbachev's reforms as a violation of socialist ideology. Gorbachev and his supporters countered her assault in an article of their own, published three weeks later in Pravda, defending glasnost and perestroika as the path to a better future.

POLEMICS: I CANNOT WAIVE PRINCIPLES

Nina Andreyeva
I decided to write this letter after lengthy deliberation. I am a chemist, and I lecture at Leningrad's Lensovet Technology Institute. Like many others, I also look after a student group. Students nowadays, following the period of social apathy and intellectual dependence, are gradually becoming charged with the energy of revolutionary changes. Naturally, discussions develop about the ways of restructuring and its economic and ideological aspects. *Glasnost*, openness, the disappearance

Isaac J. Tarasulo, ed., *Gorbachev and Glasnost: Viewpoints from the Soviet Press* (Wilmington, Del.: SR Books, 1989), 277–78, 281–85, 290–95, 299–302.

of zones where criticism is taboo, and the emotional heat of mass consciousness (especially among young people) often result in the raising of problems that are, to a greater or lesser extent, "prompted" either by Western radio voices or by those of our compatriots who are shaky in their conceptions of the essence of socialism. And what a variety of topics that are being discussed! A multi-party system, freedom of religious propaganda, emigration to live abroad, the right to broad discussion of sexual problems in the press, the need to decentralize the leadership of culture, abolition of compulsory military service. There are particularly numerous arguments among students about the country's past. . . .

In the numerous discussions now taking place on literally all questions of the social sciences, as a college lecturer I am primarily interested in the questions that have a direct effect on young people's ideological and political education, their moral health, and their social optimism. Conversing with students and deliberating with them on controversial problems, I cannot help concluding that our country has accumulated quite a few anomalies and one-sided interpretations that clearly need to be corrected. I would like to dwell on some of them in particular.

Take, for example, the question of Joseph Stalin's place in our country's history. The whole obsession with critical attacks is linked with his name, and in my opinion this obsession centers not so much on the historical individual himself as on the entire highly complex epoch of transition, an epoch linked with unprecedented feats by a whole generation of Soviet people who are today gradually withdrawing from active participation in political and social work. The industrialization, collectivization, and cultural revolution which brought our country to the ranks of the great world powers are being forcibly squeezed into the "personality cult" formula. All of this is being questioned. Matters have gone so far that persistent demands for "repentance" are being made of "Stalinists" (and this category can be taken to include anyone you like). There is rapturous praise for novels and movies that lynch the epoch of "storms and onslaught," which is presented as a "tragedy of the peoples." . . .

I support the party's call to uphold the honor and dignity of the trailblazers of socialism. I think that these are the party-class positions from which we must assess the historical role of all leaders of the party and the country, including Stalin. In this case, matters cannot be reduced to their "court" aspect or to abstract moralizing by persons far removed both from those stormy times and from the people who had to live and work in those times, and to work in such a fashion as to still be an inspiring example for us today. . . .

I think that, no matter how controversial and complex a figure in Soviet history Stalin may be, his genuine role in the building and defense of socialism will sooner or later be given an objective and unambiguous assessment. Of course, unambiguous does not mean an assessment that is one-sided, that whitewashes, or that eclectically sums up contradictory phenomena making it possible subjectively (albeit with slight reservations) "to forgive or not forgive," "to reject or retain." Unambiguous means primarily a specific historical assessment detached from short-term considerations which would demonstrate—according to historical results!—the dialectics of the correlation between the individual's actions and the basic laws governing society's development. In our country these laws were also linked with the answer to the question "Who will defeat whom?" in its domestic as well as international aspects. If we are to adhere to the Marxist-Leninist methodology of historical analysis then, in Mikhail Gorbachev's words, we must primarily and vividly show how the millions of people lived, how they worked, and what they believed in, as well as the coupling of victories and failures, discoveries and errors, the bright and the tragic, the revolutionary enthusiasm of the masses and the violations of socialist legality and even crimes at times. . . .

It seems to me that the question of the role and position of socialist ideology is extremely acute today. The authors of timeserving articles circulating under the guise of moral and spiritual "cleansing" erode the dividing lines and criteria of scientific ideology, manipulate *glasnost*, and foster nonsocialist pluralism, which applies the brakes on *perestroika* in the public conscience.

This has a particularly painful effect on young people which, I repeat, is clearly sensed by us, the college lecturers, schoolteachers, and all who have to deal with young people's problems. As Mikhail Gorbachev said at the CPSU Central Committee February *plenum*, "our actions in the spiritual sphere—and maybe primarily and precisely there—must be guided by our Marxist-Leninist principles. Principles, comrades, must not be compromised on any pretext whatever."

This is what we stand for now, and this is what we will continue to stand for. Principles were not given to us as a gift, we have fought for them at crucial turning points in the fatherland's history.

Principles of *Perestroika*: The Revolutionary Nature of Thinking and Acting

Pravda Editorial

The CPSU Central Committee February *plenum* solidified the party's new tasks in restructuring all spheres of life at the present stage. The *plenum* speech of Mikhail Gorbachev, general secretary of the CPSU Central Committee ("Revolutionary *Perestroika* Requires Ideology of Renewal") made a clear analysis of today's problems and set forth a program of ideological support for *perestroika*. People want to be better aware of the nature of the changes that have begun in society, to see the essence and significance of the proposed solutions, and to know what is meant by the new quality of society we want to achieve. The struggle for *perestroika* is being waged both in production and in the spiritual sphere. And even though this struggle does not take the form of class antagonisms, it is proceeding sharply. The emergence of something new always excites attitudes toward and judgments about the new thing.

The debate itself and its nature and thrust attest to the democratization of our society. The diversity of judgments, assessments, and positions is one of the most important signs of the times and attests to the socialist pluralism of opinions which really exists now.

But it is impossible not to notice one very specific dimension of this debate. It occasionally declares itself not in a desire to interpret what is happening and to investigate it nor in a wish to advance the cause but, on the contrary, in attempts to slow it down by shouting the usual incantations: "They are betraying ideals!" "Abandoning principles!" "Undermining foundations!" . . .

The long article "I Cannot Waive Principles" that appeared in the newspaper *Sovetskaya Rossiya* on March 13 was a reflection of such feelings. . . .

Whether the author wanted it or not, primarily the article artificially sets off certain categories of Soviet people against one another. And this at precisely the moment when the unity of creative forces, despite all the shades of opinion, is more necessary than ever and when such unity is the prime requirement of *perestroika* and an absolute necessity simply for normal life, work, and the constructive renewal of society. Herein resides the fundamental feature of *perestroika*, which is designed to unite the maximum number of like-minded people in the struggle against phenomena impeding our life. Precisely and principally against all of these phenomena, not only or simply against certain incorrigible proponents of bureaucracy, corruption, abuse, and so forth.

In addition, the article is unconstructive. In an extensive, pretentiously titled article essentially no space was found to work out a single problem of *perestroika*. Whatever it discussed—*glasnost*, openness, the disappearance of areas free from criticism, youth—these processes and *perestroika* itself were linked only with difficulties and adverse consequences. . . .

There are, in point of fact, two basic theses running throughout the article: Why all of this *perestroika*, and haven't we gone too far with democratization and *glasnost*? The article urges us to amend and adjust *perestroika*; otherwise, it is alleged, "people in authority" will have to rescue socialism.

It is evident that not everyone has realized clearly yet the dramatic nature of the situation the country found itself in by April 1985, a situation which today we rightfully describe as pre-crisis. It is evident that not everyone is fully aware yet that administrative edict methods are totally obsolete. It is time that anyone who still places hopes in these methods or in their modi-fication understands that all of this has already been tried, tried repeatedly, and it has failed to produce the desired results. Any ideas about the simplicity and effectiveness of these methods are nothing but illusions without any historical justification.

So, how is socialism to be "saved" today?

Should authoritarian methods, the practice of blind obedience, and the stifling of initiative be retained? Should we retain the system in which bureaucratism, lack of control, corruption, bribery, and petty bourgeois degeneration flourished lavishly?

Or should we revert to Leninist principles, whose essence is democratism, social justice, eco-nomic accountability, and respect for the individual's honor, life, and dignity? Do we have the right, in the face of the real difficulties and unsatisfied needs of the people, to adhere to the same old approaches that prevailed in the 1930s and 1940s? Has not the time come to clearly differ-entiate between the essence of socialism and the historically restricted forms of its implementa-tion? Has not the time come for a scientifically critical investigation of our history, primarily in order to change the world in which we live and to learn harsh lessons for the future?

Almost half of the article is devoted to an assessment of our distant and recent history. The last few years have provided graphic proof of the growing interest in the past shown by the broad-est strata of the population. The principles of scientific historicism and truth are increasingly the basis on which the people's historical awareness is taking shape. At the same time, there are in-stances of people playing on the idea of patriotism. Those who loudly scream about alleged "in-ternal threats" to socialism, those who join certain political extremists and look everywhere for internal enemies, "counterrevolutionary nations," and so on, those are not patriots. The patriots are those who act in the country's interests and for the people's benefit, without fearing any dif-ficulties. We do not need contemplative or verbal patriotism, we need creative patriotism. Not nostalgic and backward-looking patriotism, but the patriotism of socialist transformations. Patriotism based not only on love for the area of your birth, but also imbued with pride in the accomplishments of the great motherland of socialism.

Past experience is vitally necessary for the present, for solving the tasks of *perestroika*. Life's demand—"More socialism!"—makes it incumbent upon us to investigate what we did yesterday and how we did it, what has to be rejected and what has to be retained. Which principles and values ought to be considered really socialist? And if today we are taking a critical look at our history, we are doing so only because we want a better and more complete idea of our path into the future. . . .

The best teacher of *perestroika*—the one to whom we should constantly listen—is life, and life is dialectical. We should constantly remember the words of [Friedrich] Engels to the effect that nothing has been unconditionally established once and for all as sacrosanct. It is this con-tinual motion and the constant renewal of nature, society, and our thinking that is the point of departure for and the initial, most cardinal principle in our thinking.

Let us return to the question: What has been done already? How are the party's course and the decisions of the 27th Party Congress and Central Committee *plenums* being implemented? What positive changes are taking place in people's lives?

We have really got down to tackling the most pressing, highest priority problems: housing, food, and the supply of goods and services to the population. A turn toward accelerated devel-opment of the social sphere has begun. Concrete decisions about restructuring education and health care have been adopted. Radical economic reform, our main lever for implementing large-scale transformations, is being put into practice. "That is the main political result of the last three years," M. Gorbachev said at the 4th All-Union Congress of *kolkhoz* members.

The voice of the intelligentsia and of all the working people has begun to make itself heard powerfully and strongly in society's spiritual life. This is one of the first gains accomplished by *perestroika*. Democratism is impossible without freedom of thought and speech, without the open, broad clash of opinions, without keeping a critical eye on our life. . . .

There are no prohibited topics today. Journals, publishing houses, and studios decide for themselves what to publish. But the appearance of the article "I Cannot Waive Principles" is part of an attempt little by little to revise party decisions. It has been said repeatedly at meetings in the party Central Committee that the Soviet press is not a private concern, that Communists writing for the press and editors should have a sense of responsibility for articles and publications. In this case the newspaper *Sovetskaya Rossiya*, which, let us be frank, has done much for *perestroika*, departed from this principle.

Debates, discussions, and polemics are, of course, necessary. They lie in store for us in our future, too. There are also many pitfalls in store for us, traps laid by the past. We must all work together to clear these traps from our path. We need disputes that help to advance *perestroika* and lead to the consolidation of forces, to cohesion around *perestroika*, and not to disunity. . . .

More light. More initiative. More responsibility. A more rapid mastery of the full profundity of the Marxist-Leninist concept of *perestroika*, of the new political thinking. We can and must revive the Leninist practice of the socialist society—the most humane, the most just. We will firmly and steadily follow the revolutionary principles of *perestroika*: more *glasnost*, more democracy, more socialism.

■ Discussion Questions

1. Why is Andreyeva so critical of Gorbachev's reforms?
2. What arguments do Gorbachev's supporters use to counter Andreyeva's criticisms?
3. According to the *Pravda* article, what are the fundamental features of *glasnost* and *perestroika*?
4. In what ways do these two articles reflect different understandings of Soviet history and its role in shaping the country's future?

77. Cornelia Matzke, *Revolution in East Germany: An Activist's Perspective* (1989)

Gorbachev's reforms had a ripple effect throughout the Soviet bloc, sparking an explosion of political debate and civic activism. In the following interview, conducted in 1990, we hear the voice of a young East German activist, Cornelia Matzke, who was caught up in these currents of change. On the one hand, she was an ordinary citizen, leading her life as a physician-in-training in Leipzig, far removed from the activities of well-known dissenters. On the other, people like her were the backbone of the "year of miracles," 1989, which toppled Soviet communism. As she recounts, they were the ones who organized meetings, passed out pamphlets, and successfully urged others to challenge the status quo. Their efforts culminated on November 9, when the Berlin Wall came down.

So much has happened lately that I haven't thought about me and my development for a long time. . . .

I am a woman who has been interested in political issues as far back as I can remember. I always had a desire to have influence. Of course, one would have to reflect on the question as to what it means to "have influence," but it represented a basic motivation to become active politically; otherwise, I could have continued to live a normal life, like most others. . . .

During my training at the university I began to seek contact with grassroots groups here in Leipzig and with the ESG [Evangelical Student Community]. In November of 1985 I organized

Dirk Philipsen, *We Were the People: Voices from East Germany's Revolutionary Autumn of 1989* (Durham, N.C.: Duke University Press, 1993), 69–75, 248.

a presentation on the fortieth anniversary of the victory over fascism within the context of the Protestant Peace Decade that was held in Leipzig at the time. Before that, I had only had sporadic contacts with the church. . . .

My problem had always been to find a way to express myself politically, to find a context or people with whom I could work. . . .

Actually, I was trying to find the women's movement, except that I had not yet quite realized that at the time. . . .

You see, the church was the only possible alternative for any kind of political activism. There was absolutely nothing else. For a while I had considered joining one of the satellite parties, such as the LDPD [Liberal Democratic Party of Germany], but all of them were really the same as the SED [Socialist Unity Party]; they were completely controlled by the SED and followed in every respect the party line. Just the language these people were using was appalling to me. One cannot express oneself in these abstract party-line categories.

So trying to change something from within the party, perhaps with friends who thought along the same lines as you, was never an option for you?

Well, maybe if I had fallen in love with a party member or something like that, but short of that, no. I don't think this would have been possible at all. You see, I always perceived myself as someone from the left, and I had always been very angry about how this party was ruining and corrupting left-wing ideas. I just felt betrayed by this party which claimed to be the bearer of an ideology which they themselves did not live up to at all. But this never resulted in my giving up on left-wing ideas, on the idea of socialism, on a more democratic and egalitarian alternative to capitalism. And I still think that way. . . .

My experiences with working in environmental groups was, on the other hand, that men were always in charge of everything, and they knew they were. . . .

Were women's issues ever debated in any of those groups?

No, not really. It was simply not an issue, mostly because the women's movement was not an issue in the GDR. Women had no support for their grievances or their issues anywhere in the country. Which is, by the way, the main reason why I think women should organize their own groups: so that they can have a support network, a place where their issues and problems are taken seriously, and a forum through which to form some kind of political lobby. Because if women simply join male-dominated groups and parties—and I am not saying they should not do that as well—they will never get this kind of support; they will not be able to identify themselves as women. Women can only achieve some kind of identity by organizing as women, by having a network which allows them to realize that their problems are not individual problems, but rather that many other women have the same problems. . . .

How or when did you realize that you wanted to focus your political activities on women's issues?

The discussions with the men in the environmental group were just dreadful to me. In fact, that was true in all the groups I participated in. One of those was a so-called "discussion group." We met about once a month and talked about certain issues that had been decided upon earlier. Of course, we particularly focused on issues that one could not talk about in public anywhere else. What always bothered me a great deal was that if women came with their partners or husbands, they always ended up not saying anything. I was always drawn to these women in an emotional sense. I just wanted to find out how it would be to have such discussions only with women. . . .

There was an incredible atmosphere in the country during most of 1989, a sort of depression, a feeling of being severely oppressed, a sense that all the things we had put up with and we had suffered could not go on much longer. Everyone felt like that in one way or another.

We had organized a street music festival in June 1989, where I was arrested. I was totally depressed afterward. We simply could not believe that they could be that stupid, that they actually dared to arrest people at a street music festival. They simply went beyond their limits, or at least they did not seem to know anymore where those limits were. If they ever had, they certainly no longer understood where they had to allow some space in order then to be able to crack down on people when it *really* got dangerous for them. They were not even clever as holders of power. They certainly did not belong in the category of "intelligent dictators." In retrospect, it is amazing to see how many blatant mistakes they made from their point of view—in fact, it is astonishing how long they managed to hold on to power.

It was my understanding that this street music festival in 1989 was conceptualized not merely as a cultural event, but rather as a political statement as well. Is that correct?

Well, yes and no. It was not a political rally of any sort. But it was supposed to be a test as to whether the party would in fact react as if it were a political event. We had even tried to get an official permit for this festival, which we did not receive. But we decided to go ahead and invite bands and people anyway. Prior to this, the musicians were put under a lot of pressure from the officials who said that if the musicians participated in the festival, they would lose their licenses. Most of the musicians buckled under this pressure and did not show up. So we mostly had amateur musicians and bands from other cities.

At first, the festival did not really get started, because the Stasi had a lot of agents there who were talking to the musicians, trying to convince them not to play, putting pressure on them and such. A few friends and I walked up to one of those conversations between Stasi officials and musicians and just began to sing—which was difficult, because we didn't really have any songs everyone readily knew.

Well, in the end we found one, and this idea of just beginning to sing and play spread rapidly. So this is how the festival started. Everything was OK until about noon, when the police drove up with trucks and began to arrest people. First, they arrested the musicians, and then others who had played any active role in putting together this festival.

Later on, I got to know quite a few very interesting people in the detention cell, people who had organized the monitoring of the elections in May and who had made public the large-scale election fraud that had been revealed by those members of the grassroots groups who had organized this. It was a very interesting experience.

Why exactly did they arrest you?

Well, at the end they pretty much picked up people at random in front of the Thomas Church. Of course, they were particularly looking for people who they already knew were engaged in "subversive activities" and those who somehow looked conspicuously "alternative." I did not particularly look "alternative," and I could probably have avoided arrest. But first of all I thought that it was time for me to go through this experience as well, and second of all I figured it would be important for them also to arrest people once who did not fit into their preconceptions of who was and who was not opposed to the regime they were serving.

How long did they keep you in detention?

Until about 2:30 at night.

How did they treat you?

Not too badly. The guy who interrogated me was talking about "enemies of the state" and things like that, but that was normal. Surprisingly, I was also not scared at all. We knew, for example, that they were eavesdropping on us, but that did not matter to us at all; we talked to one another completely freely. There was a mood among us—the kind of mood that prevailed until October and, I think, that goes a long way in explaining the mass demonstrations of October—that it did not matter anymore. Things were so bad, it really no longer mattered. Something just *had* to happen, and people were increasingly willing to take risks in order to bring about change. . . .

Many things happened after, . . . the wave of emigration through Hungary and such. What also seemed important to me at the time was the fact that Honecker was sick, and that the entire party leadership simply came across as desolate. They seemed no longer capable of any real decisions. All of this, of course, left the impression that this "power"—this party and state leadership that we had come to know simply as "the power"—that this power had disintegrated so much primarily because Honecker was sick. It was somehow encouraging, because if that was true, it could not be all that great a "power" after all. I at least experienced it that way, and I believe many others did as well. It just signified that such power cannot be infinite.

I well remember a meeting we had in September among opposition activists and church members, and one person said "the whole system is so well organized, so stable, that it will certainly defend itself to the last man." Particularly older citizens, due to all their experiences, thought that this entire party apparatus could never be broken.

Many thought that inertia, or a kind of self-perpetuating dynamic would keep the apparatus in place indefinitely. How wrong everybody was. . . .

How did you experience the period between August and November of 1989?
I was kind of vacillating between doing more within the country and leaving it for good. All of my friends were in this position. We were simply not sure whether it could ever be more than hopeless martyrdom to get involved more openly and actively. It was a very difficult time. . . .

I think many of us would have left as well if nothing had happened until the end of the year. And, don't misunderstand me, not because we ever wanted to leave. Somehow we all felt responsible for this absolutely desolate country.

Let me ask you as someone who perceives herself to be "on the left": did you ever think that socialism in the GDR could be reformed, perhaps along the lines of what was happening in the Soviet Union, or at least that the opposition could be more decisive in determining the future political course, as perhaps it was the case in Czechoslovakia?
Yes, absolutely, that was our goal.

I am asking because you said earlier that you were thinking about emigrating because of how little, if anything, was possible in the GDR. So why did you think that it was more difficult to achieve reforms in the GDR than, for example, in the Soviet Union?
There were many reasons for that. But before I say something more, it is important to point out that what was going on in the Soviet Union was decisive for the entire movement; otherwise nothing would have ever happened here. So this was the basic event. And it was simply terrible how the GDR leadership responded to these openings and changes in the Soviet Union, high-ranking party functionaries like Kurt Hager saying, for example, "just because our neighbor changes his tapestry does not mean we have to do so as well."

■ **Discussion Questions**

1. What general factors fueled Matzke's political activism?
2. What does Matzke's description of the street festival and its aftermath reveal about the political atmosphere in East Germany in 1989?
3. How did Matzke's gender shape her political identity?

78. François Mitterrand, *Speech to the European Parliament* (1995)

Although the collapse of the Soviet empire brought the cold war to an end, another enemy loomed on the horizon: the economic clout of Asia. European leaders responded by campaigning for the further social, economic, and political integration of Europe. Their campaign bore fruit in 1994 with the creation of the European Union. These extracts from a speech given by French president François

Debates of the European Parliament, 1994–95, no. 4–456/45–51.

Mitterrand (president 1981–1995) to the European parliament in 1995 capture the mood at the time that a truly unified Europe could be achieved. His words reveal that the goals of the EU extended far beyond the concerns of the marketplace; they struck at the heart of Europe's ongoing quest to reshape its identity in the post–cold war age.

Besides the essential coordination of our policies, . . . we must also, in the longer term, build the foundations of a Europe in which renewed—and, I hope, strong, sound and lasting—economic growth can take place. This will be possible, if we prove capable of using three of our major assets to the full. What is the first of those assets? It is the size of our internal market. So far, we have essentially succeeded in removing the administrative, customs and regulatory barriers which partitioned this vast economic area. That is the task that was accomplished by means of the Single European Act. We now have to eliminate or reduce the remaining barriers—which are far from insignificant—including the physical barriers which still restrict the free movement of people, goods and ideas. . . .

Our second major asset is, of course, economic and monetary union, which is the natural and essential complement, in my view, to the single market, and without which the single market—which I and, of course, others were so anxious to achieve, and which was the object of so much hard work—would be a recipe for anarchy and the worst forms of unfair competition.

The monetary tensions which we have witnessed in the past—and which, at least as far as the last few weeks are concerned, we are witnessing today—make clear the need to advance as quickly as possible towards the introduction of a single currency. I know that this is still the subject of discussion, that not everyone has been convinced. In any event, I wish to convey to you my personal conviction—which, I believe, is shared by the majority of people in authority in France; the introduction of a single currency is the only means of ensuring that Europe remains a great economic and monetary power, and it is the best means of ensuring the sustained growth of our economies. . . .

Our third major asset is the European Union's technological excellence. Our research scientists have been responsible for countless innovations. Such capital cannot fail to yield a profit if we prove capable of utilising it properly, and on a European scale. I shall not dwell on this point, but I am sure that the extraordinary number of technological, scientific, inventive and innovative successes which Europe has achieved since the second half of the nineteenth century will come to mind—whilst not forgetting, of course, those elsewhere in the world who have contributed to the general progress. . . .

Let us make no mistake: markets are no more than instruments, no more than mechanisms which are all too often governed by the law of the strongest, mechanisms which can lead to injustice, exclusion and dependence, unless the necessary counterweight is provided by those who can assert their democratic legitimacy. Alongside the markets, there is room for economic and social activities based on the concepts of solidarity, cooperation, partnership, reciprocity and the common interest—in short, public services. So far, we have drawn the outline of a social Europe, but it has no content. And will it not be an exciting, exhilarating venture to provide that content? Will it not be the task of the coming months and years? At that point, I shall be observing the social progress made from the outside and I shall rejoice whenever I see all Europe's leaders coming together—leaving behind their natural divisions and differences of opinion—to ensure that the Europe which is being built does not simply resemble a mechanical or Meccano toy, but is the potent work of men and women who are capable of shaping their own destiny. At present, there are some difficulties, but I hope that in collaboration with the social partners, we shall succeed in taking initiatives in the areas of training, education, the organisation of labour, and the campaign against all forms of exclusion. Indeed, nothing will be possible unless the social partners take their rightful place in the process of European integration.

. . . Such a Europe, our Europe, must be embodied in something more than simply balance sheets and freight tonnages. I would go as far as to say, while not wishing to become too rhetorical, that it needs a soul, so that it can give expression—and let us use more modest language here—to its culture, its ways of thinking, the intellectual make-up of its peoples, the fruits of the centuries of civilisation of which we are the heirs. The expressions of Europe's many forms of genius are rich and diverse; and, as in the past, we must share with the whole world—while not seeking to impose them, somewhat differently from in the past—our ideas, our dreams and, to the extent that they are of the right kind, our passions. . . .

To strengthen our approach, let us rediscover those places and objects which represent our common past. I should like to see the devising and implementation of a vast project to develop the sites of our European heritage. At the same time, let us teach about Europe. Let us educate our children on the subject. Let our schools prepare them for citizenship. Let them develop the teaching of history, geography and culture. Let us encourage the twinning of schools and universities, exchanges of schoolchildren and students. Let us stress the importance of multilingualism. To this end, France will be submitting a draft intergovernmental convention on the teaching of at least two foreign languages. At the same time, let us step up our efforts to promote the translation of written works. I have long observed that the French, my fellow countrymen, frequently complain that their great authors are seldom translated in, for example, some of the countries of Central and Eastern Europe. And I have also observed that in fact, we, the French, do not translate their works either; we complain of a fault of which we ourselves are guilty—because the Europe of cultures is the whole of Europe. . . .

. . . I thank you for the patience and attention with which you have been kind enough to listen to me, and I should like to finish with a few remarks of a more personal nature. Fate would have it that I was born during the First World War and fought in the Second. I therefore spent my childhood in the surroundings of families torn apart, all of them mourning loved ones and feeling great bitterness, if not hatred towards the recent enemy, the traditional enemy. However, ladies and gentlemen, such enemies have changed from century to century, as traditions have always changed. I have had occasion to say to this House before that France has engaged in wars with every European country, with the exception, I believe, of Denmark. We have to wonder why. . . .

But my generation has almost completed its work; it is carrying out its last public acts, and this will be one of my last. It is therefore vital for us to pass on our experience. Many of you will remember the teaching of your parents, will have felt the suffering of your countries, will have experienced the grief, the pain of separation, the presence of death—all as a result of the mutual enmity of the peoples of Europe. It is vital to pass on not this hatred but, on the contrary, the opportunity which we have for reconciliation, thanks—it must be said—to those who, after 1944–1945, themselves blood-stained and with their personal lives destroyed, had the courage to envisage a more radiant future which would be based on peace and reconciliation. That is what we have done.

However, I did not acquire my own convictions in this way by chance. I did not acquire them in the German prisoner-of-war camps in which I was a captive, or in a country which itself was occupied—a situation which many of you will have experienced. I remember that even families who practiced the virtues of humanity, of kindness, spoke with animosity when they talked about the Germans. When I was an escaped prisoner of war—or rather, when I was in the process of escaping—I met some Germans, then I spent some time in a prison in Baden-Württemberg, and I used to talk to the people, Germans, there and I came to realise that the Germans liked the French more than the French liked the Germans.

I say this without wishing to denigrate my country, which is no more nationalistic than any other, far from it. I say this to make it clear that, at that time, everyone saw the world from his or her own viewpoint, and that those viewpoints were generally distorting. We must overcome such prejudices. What I am asking you to do is almost impossible, because it means overcoming our past. And yet, if we fail to overcome our past, let there be no mistake about what will follow: ladies and gentlemen, nationalism means war!

War is not only our past, it could also be our future! And it is us, it is you, ladies and gentlemen, the Members of the European Parliament, who will henceforth be the guardians of our peace, our security and our future!

■ **Discussion Questions**

1. According to Mitterrand, which assets must Europe use to ensure its economic growth?
2. What other factors does Mitterrand consider to be important to European unity?
3. How did Mitterrand's understanding of Europe's past shape his vision for its future?

Acknowledgments (continued)

Giovanni Pico della Mirandola. *Oration on the Dignity of Man* (1496). From *The Italian Renaissance Reader*, edited by Julia Conaway Bondanella and Mark Musa. Copyright © 1987 by Julia Conaway Bondanella and Mark Musa. Reprinted with the permission of Dutton Signet, a division of Penguin Putnam Inc.

Alessandra Strozzi. *Letters from a Widow and Matriarch of a Great Family* (1450–1465). From *University of Chicago Readings in Western Civilization, 5: The Renaissance*, edited by Eric Cochrane and Julius Kirshner. Copyright © 1986 by The University of Chicago. Reprinted with the permission of The University of Chicago Press.

Chapter 12

Argula von Grumbach and John Hooker. *Women's Actions in the Reformation* (1520s–30s). Excerpt from *The Dissolution of the Monasteries* by Joyce Youings. Copyright © 1971 by Joyce Youings. Reprinted with the permission of HarperCollins Publishers, Ltd.

Henry IV. *Edict of Nantes* (1598). From "The Great Pressures and Grievances of the Protestants in France," Edmund Everand. Saint Ignatius of Loyola. *A New Kind of Catholicism* (1546, 1549, 1553). From *St. Ignatius of Loyola: Personal Writings: Reminiscences, Spiritual Diary, Select Letters including the text of The Spiritual Exercises*, edited and translated by Joseph A. Munitiz and Philip Endean. Copyright © 1996 by Joseph A. Munitiz and Philip Endean. Reprinted with the permission of Penguin Books, Ltd.

Galileo, *Letter to the Grand Duchess Christina* (1615). *From Discoveries and Opinions of Galileo*, translated by Stillman Drake. Copyright © 1957 by Stillman Drake. Reprinted with the permission of Doubleday, a division of Random House, Inc.

Chapter 13

Louis de Rouvroy, Duke of Saint-Simon. *Memoirs* (1694–1723). From *The Memoirs of The Duke of Saint-Simon*, translated by Bayle St. John, Vol. II.

Ludwig Fabritius. *The Revolt of Stenka Razin* (1670). From *Russia Under Western Eyes 1517–1825*, edited by Anthony Glenn Cross. Copyright © 1971 by Anthony Glenn Cross. Reprinted with permission.

British Parliament. *The English Bill of Rights* (1689). From *The Statutes*: revised edition, 1871, vol. II.

Chapter 14

Olaudah Equiano. *The Interesting Narrative of the Life of Olaudah Equiano, Written by Himself* (1789). From *Equiano's Travels: His Autobiography*, edited by Paul Edwards. Published by Frederick A. Praeger, 1966.

Montesquieu. *Persian Letters: Letter 37* (1721). Translated by John Davidson, Vol. I.

Mary Astell. *Reflections upon Marriage* (1706). Excerpt from *The First English Feminist: Reflections Upon Marriage and Other Writings*, edited by Bridget Hill. Copyright © 1986 by Bridget Hill. Reprinted by permission.

Chapter 15

Marie-Therese Geoffrin and Monsieur d'Alembert. *The Salon of Madame Geoffrin* (1765). Reprinted in *Historical and Literary Memoirs and Anecdotes Selected from the Correspondence of Baron de Grimm and Diderot with the Duke of Saxe-Gotha, and Many Other Distinguished Persons between the Years of 1753–1790*, Second edition, vol. III (1815) and from *Memoir of d'Alembert*. Reprinted in *Connection with the Past: The D. C. Heath Document Sets for Western Civilization*, Vol. II.

Jacques-Louis Menetra. Excerpt from *Journal of My Life* (1764–1802). Translated by Arthur Goldhammer. Copyright © 1986 by Arthur Goldhammer. Reprinted with the permission of the publisher.

Frederick II. *Political Testament* (1752). Excerpt from "The Rise of Prussia" in *Europe in Review*, edited by George Lachmann Mosse, Rondo E. Cameron, Henry Bertram Hill, and Michael B. Petrovich. Published by Rand McNally & Company, 1957. Reprinted by permission.

Chapter 16

National Assembly. *The Declaration of the Rights of Man and of the Citizen* (1789). *Readings in European History: A Collection of Extracts from the Sources* by James Harvey Robinson. Published by Ginn and Company, 1906.

Francois Dominique Toussaint L'Ouverture. *Revolution in the Colonies* (1794–1795). Translated by Katharine J. Lualdi, from *Toussaint Louverture a travers sa correspondence* by Gerard M. Laurent, 1953. Reprinted with permission.

Abd al-Rahman al-Jabarti. *Napoleon in Egypt* (1798). From *Napoleon in Egypt: Al-Jabarti's Chronicle of the French Occupation*, 1798, translated by Shumel Moreh. Copyright © 1993 by Shumel Moreh. Reprinted with the permission of E. J. Brill Publishers, Leiden, The Netherlands.

Chapter 17

Factory Rules in Berlin (1844). From *Documents of European Economic History: The Process of Industrialization 1750–1870* by Sidney Pollard and C. Holmes, Vol. I. Copyright © 1968 by St. Martin's Press, Inc. Reprinted with permission of the publisher.

T. B. Macaulay. *Speeches on Parliamentary Reform* (1831). From *Miscellanies*, Vol. 1, by Lord Macaulay. Published by Houghton Mifflin and Company, 1901.

Friedrich Engels. *Draft of a Communist Confession of Faith* (1847). From *Collected Works*, vol. 6, by Karl Marx and Frederick Engels. Reprinted with the permission of International Publishers.

Victor Hugo. *Preface to Cromwell* (1827). From *The Dramatic Works of Victor Hugo*, vol. III. Published by The Athenaeum Society, 1909.

Chapter 18

Alexander II. *Address in the State Council* (1861). From *A Source Book for Russian History* by George Vernadsy, general editor, vol. II. Copyright © 1972 by Yale University. Reprinted with the permission of Yale University Press.

Krupa Sattianadan. *Saguna: A Story of Native Christian Life* (1887–1888). *From Women Were Writing in India 600 B.C. to the Present*, edited by Susie Tharu and K. Lalita, vol. I. Copyright © 1991 The Feminist Press at the City University of New York. Reprinted with the permission of the publisher.

Charles Darwin. *The Descent of Man* (1871). From *The Descent of Man and Selection in Reform to Sex*. Published by Appelton and Company, 1896.

Chapter 19

Jules Ferry. *Speech before the French National Assembly* (1883). From *Modern Imperialism, Western Overseas Expansion and Its Aftermath 1776–1965*, edited by Ralph Austen. Published by D. C. Heath and Company, 1969.

The I-ho-ch'uan (Boxers). *The Boxers Demand Death for All "Foreign Devils"* (1900). From *The Imperialism reader: Documents and Readings on Modern Expansionism*, edited by Louis L. Snyder. Published by D. Van Nostrand Company, Inc. 1962.

Chapter 20

L. Doriat. *Women on the Home Front* (1917). From *Lines of Fire: Women Writers of World War I* edited by Margaret R. Higonnet.

Benito Mussolini. *The Doctrine of Facism* (1932). From *The Social and Political Doctrines of Contemporary Europe*, edited and translated by Michael Oakeshott. Reprinted with the permission of Cambridge University Press.

Chapter 21

Joseph Goebbels. *Nazi Propaganda Pamphlet* (1930). From *Documents of German History*, edited and translated by Louis L. Snyder. Copyright © 1958 by Rutgers, The State University. Reprinted with the permission of Rutgers University Press.

Neville Chamberlain. *Speech on the Munich Crisis* (1938). From *Parliamentary Debates, Fifth Series*, Vol. 339, House of Commons Official Report.

Sam Bankhalter and Hinda Kibort. *Memories of the Holocaust* (1938–1945). From *Witnesses to the Holocaust: An Oral History*, edited by Rhoda G. Lewin. Copyright © 1980 by the Jewish Community Relations Council and Anti-Defamation League of Minnesota and the Dakotas. Reprinted with the permission of The Gale Group.

Chapter 22

National Security Council. *Paper Number 68* (1950). From *Foreign Relations of the United States*. National Security Council reports, Washington, D.C. 1977.

Ho Chi Minh. *Declaration of Independence of the Republic of Vietnam* (1945). From *Conflict in Indo-China and International Repercussions: A Documentary History 1945-1955,* edited by Allen B. Cole. Copyright © 1956 Cornell University Press. Reprinted with the permission of Cornell University Press.

Simone de Beauvoir. *The Second Sex* (1949). Translated and edited by H. M. Parshley. Copyright © 1952 and renewed 1980 by Alfred A. Knopf, Inc. Reprinted with the permission of Alfred A. Knopf, a division of Random House, Inc.

Chapter 23

The New York Times and Neil Armstrong and Edwin Aldrin. "To Walk on the Moon" editorial, July 20, 1969. Copyright © 1969 The New York Times Company. Reprinted with permission. Excerpt from *First Man on the Moon: A Voyage with Neil Armstrong, Michael Collins and Edwin E. Aldrin, Jr.* Copyright © 1970 by Neil Armstrong, Michael Collins, Edwin E. Aldrin, Jr., Gene Farmer and Dora Jane Hamblin. Reprinted with the permission of Little, Brown and Company, subsidiary of Time Warner Trade Publishing.

Pope John XXIII, Vatican II (1961). From *The Documents of Vatican II: All Sixteen Official Texts Promulgated by the Ecumenical Council* published by Herder & Herder, 1966.

Student Voices of Protest (1968). From *Takin' it to the streets': A Sixties Reader,* edited by Alexander Bloom and Wini Brienes. Copyright © 1955 by Alexander Bloom and Wini Brienes. Reprinted with the permission of Oxford University Press, Inc. *A Student Generation in Revolt* by Ronald Fraser. Copyright © 1968 by Ronald Fraser. Reprinted with the permission of Pantheon Books, a division of Random House, Inc.

Chapter 24

Glasnost and the Soviet Press (1988). From *Gorbachev and Glasnost: Viewpoints from the Soviet Press,* edited by Isaac J. Tarasulo. Published by SR Books, 1989.

Cornelia Matzke. *Revolution in East Germany: An Activist's Perspective* (1989). From *We Were the People: Voices from East Germany's Revolutionary Autumn of 1989,* edited by Dirk Philipsen. Copyright © 1993 by Duke University Press. Reprinted with the permission of the publisher. All rights reserved.

François Mitterrand. *Speech to the European Parliament* (1995). From *Debates of the European Parliament 1994/95.* No. 4-456/45-51.